Eccentric Laughter

RECENT TITLES

Hannah Holtzman, *Through a Nuclear Lens*
Matthew Cipa, *Is Harpo Free?*
Seth Barry Watter, *The Human Figure on Film*
Daniel Varndell, *Torturous Etiquettes*
Jonah Corne and Monika Vrečar, *Yiddish Cinema*
Jason Jacobs, *Reluctant Sleuths, True Detectives*
Lucy J. Miller, *Distancing Representations in Transgender Film*
Tomoyuki Sasaki, *Cinema of Discontent*
Mary Ann McDonald Carolan, *Orienting Italy*
Matthew Rukgaber, *Nietzsche in Hollywood*
David Venditto, *Whiteness at the End of the World*
Fareed Ben-Youssef, *No Jurisdiction*
Tony Tracy, *White Cottage, White House*
Tom Conley, *Action, Action, Action*
Lindsay Coleman and Roberto Schaefer, editors, *The Cinematographer's Voice*
Nolwenn Mingant, *Hollywood Films in North Africa and the Middle East*
Charles Warren, edited by William Rothman and Joshua Schulze, *Writ on Water*
Jason Sperb, *The Hard Sell of Paradise*
William Rothman, *The Holiday in His Eye*
Brendan Hennessey, *Luchino Visconti and the Alchemy of Adaptation*

A complete listing of books in this series can be found online at www.sunypress.edu.

Eccentric Laughter

Queer Possibilities in
Postwar British Film Comedy

Benedict Morrison

SUNY PRESS

Cover credit: *The Lavender Hill Mob* (Charles Crichton, 1951) courtesy of Photofest.

Frame grabs from *The Belles of St Trinian's, The Green Man, Hue and Cry, Kind Hearts and Coronets, Laughter in Paradise, The Lavender Hill Mob, The Man in the White Suit, Passport to Pimlico, The Stranger Left No Card, Alive and Kicking, It's Never Too Late*, and *Young Wives' Tale* courtesy of STUDIOCANAL.

Published by State University of New York Press, Albany

© 2024 State University of New York

All rights reserved

Printed in the United States of America

No part of this book may be used or reproduced in any manner whatsoever without written permission. No part of this book may be stored in a retrieval system or transmitted in any form or by any means including electronic, electrostatic, magnetic tape, mechanical, photocopying, recording, or otherwise without the prior permission in writing of the publisher.

Links to third-party websites are provided as a convenience and for informational purposes only. They do not constitute an endorsement or an approval of any of the products, services, or opinions of the organization, companies, or individuals. SUNY Press bears no responsibility for the accuracy, legality, or content of a URL, the external website, or for that of subsequent websites.

For information, contact State University of New York Press, Albany, NY
www.sunypress.edu

Library of Congress Cataloging-in-Publication Data

Name: Morrison, Benedict, author.
Title: Eccentric laughter : queer possibilities in postwar British film comedy / Benedict Morrison.
Description: Albany : State University of New York Press, [2024]. | Series: SUNY series, horizons of cinema | Includes bibliographical references and index.
Identifiers: LCCN 2024012386 | ISBN 9798855800036 (hardcover : alk. paper) | ISBN 9798855800043 (ebook)
Subjects: LCSH: Comedy films—Great Britain—History—20th century. | Homosexuality in motion pictures. | Gay people in motion pictures. | Motion pictures—Great Britain—History—20th century. | LCGFT: Film criticism.
Classification: LCC PN1995.9.C55 M645 2024 | DDC 791.43/617—dc23/eng/20230523
LC record available at https://lccn.loc.gov/2024012386

For Andrzej
who laughs eccentrically and seizes queer possibilities everywhere

Contents

List of Illustrations — ix

Acknowledgments — xi

Introduction: Unstraightening Postwar British Comedy — 1

Part 1: Coming to Terms

1 Exploding Ex-Centricity — 37

2 Doing the Domestic Drag — 71

3 Laughing at Nothing — 105

Part 2: Going over the Top

4 Ruining Everything — 141

5 Being Beside Yourself — 175

6 Going Wild — 201

Conclusion: Concluding Nothing — 231

Notes — 239

Filmography	259
Bibliography	263
Index	273

Illustrations

I.1	*The Belles of St. Trinian's* (Frank Launder, 1954)	2
I.2	*The Man in the White Suit* (Alexander Mackendrick, 1951)	6
I.3	*The Man in the White Suit* (Alexander Mackendrick, 1951)	8
1.1	*Passport to Pimlico* (Henry Cornelius, 1949)	38
1.2	*The Stranger Left No Card* (Wendy Toye, 1952)	55
1.3 & 1.4	*Passport to Pimlico* (Henry Cornelius, 1949)	62
1.5	*Passport to Pimlico* (Henry Cornelius, 1949)	67
2.1	*Young Wives' Tale* (Henry Cass, 1951)	83
2.2	*Sailor Beware!* (Gordon Parry, 1956)	93
2.3	*Sailor Beware!* (Gordon Parry, 1956)	95
2.4	*Simon and Laura* (Muriel Box, 1955)	103
3.1	*The Lavender Hill Mob* (Charles Crichton, 1951)	106
3.2	*The Lavender Hill Mob* (Charles Crichton, 1951)	121
3.3	*It's Never Too Late* (Michael McCarthy, 1956)	130
3.4	*Laughter in Paradise* (Mario Zampi, 1951)	135
4.1	*Hue and Cry* (Charles Crichton, 1947)	150
4.2	*Hue and Cry* (Charles Crichton, 1947)	154

4.3	*Genevieve* (Henry Cornelius, 1953)	164
4.4	*The Green Man* (Robert Day, 1956)	170
5.1	*The Belles of St. Trinian's* (Frank Launder, 1954)	177
5.2	*The Belles of St. Trinian's* (Frank Launder, 1954)	178
5.3	*Kind Hearts and Coronets* (Robert Hamer, 1949)	182
5.4	*The Square Peg* (John Paddy Carstairs, 1959)	195
6.1	*An Alligator Named Daisy* (J. Lee Thompson, 1955)	215
6.2	*An Alligator Named Daisy* (J. Lee Thompson, 1955)	217
6.3	*Alive and Kicking* (Cyril Frankel, 1958)	223
6.4	*Alive and Kicking* (Cyril Frankel, 1958)	227

Acknowledgments

This is a book that has, in one way or another, been in the works since I first encountered postwar British comedies as a child. Dozens of gleeful Saturday afternoons spent in the company of the resplendent Alastair Sim and Margaret Rutherford haunt its pages. For encouraging the ideas about the films that fill the chapters that follow, I must thank my family: my father, who introduced me to explosively eccentric cinema; my sister Emily who has always shared and encouraged my love of the eccentrics; and my mother whose rejection of domestic convention first opened my eyes to domestic drag and the nonsense of heterocentric myths.

I offer thanks and love to my brilliant and ever-encouraging friends Marco Alessi, Roy Joseph Butler, Hannah Croft, Miranda Pountney, and Anna Wetherell in whose electric company I laugh eccentrically, often at nothing, and who always sharpen and queer my ideas. I count myself fortunate to know such magnificent scholars as Peter Riley, Ranita Chatterjee, and Debra Ramsay who, even when I found myself lost among what seemed like the ruins of my arguments, inspired and galvanized me to build back differently. The students with whom I have been lucky enough to work at the University of Exeter have been a constant source of delight, merrily ex-centering what I think I know about almost everything and wonderfully sharing my passion for Ealing comedies; Sabina Messent, in particular, has inspired me with their playfully scintillating research into the performances of Alec Guinness. I am grateful for the time that I spent beside myself with delight in the company of Diana Rigg, who generously shared her memories of and passions for the great actors and directors whose names course through this book. I thank Stephan

Dahl and my friends at the Quinta Project for teaching me to go a little wilder and to celebrate queernesses beyond the human. And, with love and solidarity, I thank Princess and Jordy who continue to teach me so much.

Massimo Moretti and everyone at StudioCanal have gone out of their way to encourage my research and to support the publication of this book; I offer them my gratitude for their permissions to use many of the images that illuminate my arguments. I am also very grateful to James Peltz and everyone at SUNY Press for their support and guidance. They have made this the most enjoyable publishing experience imaginable. I give special thanks to Murray Pomerance, editor of the Horizons of Cinema series. It was his entirely unexpected enthusiasm for my ideas that saw them ballooning into the book you now hold. He is, alongside being one of the most exciting writers on film, an extraordinary friend and ally, and without him this book would simply not exist. He is also precisely the kind of iconoclastic thinker whom I admire and celebrate in this study of explosive and exquisite eccentricity.

The biggest thanks of all go to Andrzej, my boyfriend and greatest inspiration. With tireless enthusiasm and love, he has advised, suggested, supported, motivated, bribed, cajoled, reassured, and emboldened. He transforms every idea he encounters into something subtler and wittier. I dedicate this book to him with love.

Introduction

Unstraightening Postwar British Comedy

I REMEMBER THE DELIGHT OF watching, as a child, *The Belles of St. Trinian's* (Frank Launder, 1954). In it, Alastair Sim—who made art out of a kind of spectacularly lugubrious discomfort—plays headmistress Millicent Fritton. The performance pleasurably disorientated me. The eager, anarchic destructiveness of the schoolgirls seemed dull by contrast with the unsettling oddnesses of Sim's performance: the bobbing walk, seemingly more committed to rise and fall than to forward motion; the constant pawing at the beads around his neck, transforming his body into a space of constant agitation without repose; the delirious two-fingered whistle used to attract the attention of Flash Harry (George Cole), with which Sim suggests that Millicent is discovering both her fingers and her mouth—and certainly their ecstatic combination—for the first time (see fig. I.1); and the elongated derangement of the word "afford" in the line "I can no longer afford to have continual arson about in my school," where other actors might have emphasized, with wearying predictability, the puerile pun on *arsin' about*. These gestures, only four among many, and each fleeting, made me howl with laughter all those years ago, and still leave me helpless today. They also destabilize—*make strange*—authority, gender, and the body. As a child, I had no word for the particularity of either this hilarity or this strangeness. My father described it as *eccentric*. Later, I would come to call it *queer*.

The terms *eccentric* and *queer*—companions, despite many differences in their histories and significances—skip through this book

Figure I.1. Eccentric performance in *The Belles of St. Trinian's* (Frank Launder, 1954). *Source:* London Films/Courtesy of STUDIOCANAL.

hand in hand. They are joined in a ménage à trois by a third term: *comic*. All three, under the crushing weight of familiarity, risk becoming critically mundane and ceasing to register as *strange* and *estranging*. My hope is that by setting them to work together on a series of films, the terms can regain a valuable transgressive critical edge. The comedies looked at in detail in this book were all produced in Britain in the fifteen years that followed the Second World War and the term *eccentricity* has run through criticism of this moment in film history like a refrain. Some comedies from this period (especially those made at Ealing Studios) have attracted the serious and affectionate attention of critics as "universally loved exercises in national eccentricity."[1] Others have been dismissed as "routine whimsical comedies which celebrated British eccentricity."[2] Raymond Durgnat, in *A Mirror for England*, his seminal work on postwar British cinema, argues that films in this period were "forced back into a narrower range of subjects and stereotypes . . . [before they could] extend their range" as the fifties closed and *Room at the Top* (Jack Clayton, 1959) ushered in the New Wave; Durgnat associates this period of narrowness and stereotype with the image of the "typical British eccentric."³ Oxymoron notwithstanding—what, after all, is a *typical eccentric* when eccentricity implies atypicality?—the term *eccentric* haunts Durgnat's work without any real sense of *what it signifies*. It is pinned to certain examples as though its sense is self-evident. And so it has haunted British film criticism generally. Unqualified and unexplored, the word has often been yoked uncomfortably to other terms, including *whimsical* and *cozy*, to imply the unthreatening dottiness of lovable, upper- and upper-middle-class oddballs.

I find this a waste of a word whose etymology gestures toward a more transgressive potential. The sheer ubiquity of the term blurs its root suggestions of strangeness, difference, and disorderliness. Durgnat cites postwar cinema's "veneration for the eccentrics, and their much-touted sense of humour" as a means of challenging "the grinding effect of puritanical submission to the system," but only as "essential safety-valves."⁴ There is, however, nothing safe about eccentricity as I see it (and as I explore at more length in chapter 1). It threatens every structure through which society organizes itself into hegemonic systems of knowledge. In postwar British comedy, it is outrageousness hidden in plain sight. It is a mechanism through which the frame is given over to the unusual, the bizarre, the usually-excluded. It shows up the limits of convention and performs alternatives. It is not just outside the center; it shakes the authority of the idea of a center. It queries expectations of glamor and desire. Eccentricity's lack of convention disrupts the blessed order of the home and the family business and the community. This disruption is both destructive and affirmative; the agents of eccentricity who stride and strut and stumble through these films, both *funny-peculiar* and *funny-ha-ha*, challenge habitual ways of seeing the world. The peculiarities of these characters cannot be fixed with *identity labels* and display themselves through their disruptive and contagious *effects*. Ian Christie suggests that the political force of eccentricity lies in its capacity to defamiliarize "what has become unnoticed or invisible through routine" in "a fine display of eccentrist 'turning the conventional inside out.'"⁵ This is near to the sense in which I use the term, but Christie applies it specifically to a canon of experimental work. I find eccentric effects also working indiscriminately in mainstream, cheap, and popular films, where they *ex-center* structures of meaning and identity, shaking assumptions about what is normal, natural, and obvious.[6]

This emphasis on the challenges posed by the *funny-peculiar* situates the idea of *eccentricity* adjacent to *queerness* as I use the term (and which I discuss further in chapter 2). I am interested in the many strategies used to ex-center identity, including sexual identity. My decision to consider only films made before 1960 is guided by the fact that in 1961 *Victim* (Basil Dearden) changed British screen sexuality with its explicit representation of a gay man—and a sympathetically respectable middle-class gay man at that. Stephen Bourne argues that the release of *Victim* "had an enormous impact on the lives of gay men who, for the first time, saw credible representations of themselves and their situations in a commercial British film."[7] Although *Victim* was not part of the movement, its release coincided with "the emergence of the British New Wave in the late 1950s, with its overt commitment to sexual frankness and emotional realism."[8] Andy Medhurst identifies a watershed between what he calls "pre-gay" British films and those made after "*Victim*, that battered old landmark wherein one queer at last got to say 'I wanted him' about another one, and as such made it possible, eventually, for homosexual lives to occupy the centre of certain films."[9] Medhurst describes post-*Victim* openness in centrist terms; the aspiration, as he sets it out, is to rearrange cultural structures so that their normative center can accommodate homosexuality. While this strategy for tackling the problem of homophobia has produced important results (including the partial decriminalization of sex between men in England and Wales in 1967) it nevertheless preserves the fundamental operation of a hierarchical structure, ultimately offering assimilation for some and continued exclusion for others. Given that the eccentric queerness that I am most interested in is not assimilationist but rather varied and capaciously inclusive, post-*Victim* centricity offers only a partial reward.

Queerness, as I understand it, is not an identity as such, but rather a play of and with possibilities, always deconstructing the conventional scripts through which a culture understands and articulates desire. It refers to any challenge to prevailing *heterocentric* structures. Such challenges in predecriminalization cinema are not only represented by what Medhurst describes as "the nebulous nancies who hover in the background of heterosexual narratives."[10] My readings will not generally focus on finding suggestions of gay relationships or sex as Richard Hornsey does in *The Lavender Hill Mob* (Charles Crichton, 1951): "If gold in the . . . diegesis is replaced with sperm—a conceptual substitution with an established history within modern Western culture—then the mob's crime becomes emphatically that of queer male sex."[11] While these approaches to pre-*Victim* films are both enlightening and entertaining, their understanding of *queerness* is tethered to defined homosexual identities. I am more interested in how the eccentric comedies of postwar Britain—with their glimpses of unruly lives lived behind closed doors that threaten the insistent logics that have dominated British social and sexual life—offer images of *heterocentric failure*. Erupting mirthfully from a moment in which Britain was reimagining itself after the cataclysm of war, when improvisation was the order of the day and questions of gender, sexuality, and family were being debated with unprecedented regularity, these films make a joke out of domesticated heterocentricity.

Heterocentrically structured British culture has historically coerced social practice and political policy into orbit around the fixed and privileged centers of monogamous mixed-sex marriage, the gendered arrangement of roles within a nuclear family, the unique legitimacy of biological reproduction, the ambition for financial and cultural inheritance, and the responsibility of community to defer to and uphold these values. The queer, as I describe it, is not simply the *opposite* or *absence* of heterocentricity. To argue that would require an admission that heterocentric cultural structures are solid. I argue, instead, that the queer exposes the fact that heterocentricity is precariously built on a series of *myths*, that its privileged centers are unstable and, in crucial ways, never really exist. The instability of such myths can be seen at work in *The Man in the White Suit* (Alexander Mackendrick, 1951), in which the forces of capital and labor go into crisis over the development of a new suit that threatens to recenter the social structures on which they rely to underpin their sense of status and identity. The suit, created by maverick research chemist Sidney Stratton (Alec Guinness), is made from a fabric so durable—and therefore so *superior*—that it renders all other forms of fabric unendurable. But before capital and labor have a chance to destroy it, the suit unravels itself (see fig. I.2). The suit does not become queer by substituting an alternative norm, by restructuring the status quo, but by revealing the contingency of all structures, including its own and those of the status quo. These structural flaws gesture to the structural

Figure I.2. Myths unravel in *The Man in the White Suit* (Alexander Mackendrick, 1951). *Source:* Ealing Studios/Courtesy of STUDIOCANAL.

flaws in a capitalist social system that can be so easily shaken. As this capitalist system shakes, it reveals also the shaky foundations of family and marriage; mill owner Birnley (Cecil Parker) tries to offer his daughter (Joan Greenwood) to Sidney in return for the formula. The sense of solidity that underpins notions of self-evident superiority and status is unraveled and shown to be a myth.

In Roland Barthes's words, myth "abolishes the complexity of human acts, gives them the simplicity of essences, . . . [creating] a world which is open and wallowing in the evident, it establishes a blissful clarity."[12] Heterocentricity is the network of mythic statements that, between them, construct and constrain the conditions in which sexuality, sex, and gender are experienced and expressed within British culture. It purports to *describe* preexisting conditions—namely the naturalness of certain forms of sexual and romantic behavior—but actually *produces* the reality of that behavior's hegemony. It is not identical with heterosexuality; it is the *reprocentric, biocentric, genocentric* myths that insist that the center (in the form of the origin, the function, the purpose, the destiny) of human nature or culture is heterosexual(ity). This mythology inculcates belief in conventions that lend "blissful clarity" by allowing no sexual contradiction. It is tethered to certain endorsed identities (the monogamously married, the childbearing and child-rearing, the biologically and culturally inheriting) that assume the privileged position in a concentric structure, while others are relegated to satellite positions, to marginalized orbits in the structure's outer circles, both excluded and constrained by the dominant and mythic center.

The queer, as it appears in this book, is not simply a marker of one of those identities relegated to the outer rings of a heterocentric structure; it is the tug on a thread that sets the whole structure unraveling. If "queer" were a stable identity, it could be located within an artificial and damaging cultural hierarchy, a structure that might learn to embrace the "queer" while still excluding and decentering the unmarried, the promiscuous, the polyamorous, the sex-professional, the gender nonconforming, the nonreproductive, the sexually unorthodox. The queer that giggles playfully through the comedies in this book rejects the concentric, binary *either/or* logics of identity that insist that a subject is *either* culturally centric—with its claims of being especially natural, normal, good, legitimate, inevitable, and valuable—*or* not. Instead, it delights in *both/and* paradoxes, in which the center becomes porous and mobile and abandons any claims to exceptionalism or superiority. This queer does not wallow in the evident but in the indeterminate; it does not abolish the complexity of human acts but indulges in all sorts of complex acts with cheeky permissiveness. In some historical moments, it has exposed itself through full-frontal confrontation, as with the post-Stonewall cinematic provocations of Derek Jarman. In the very different chuckling world of postwar comedy, its effects are glimpsable in the mischievous performance of the *absurdity* of conventional domestic life. What interests me in the films explored in this book is, therefore, not primarily the representation of same-sex desire or sex but the comic scenarios in which, like Stratton's suit, heterocentricity, despite all its avowed and shining durability, unravels before my eyes. As Sidney stands in the street, wearing nothing but his underwear, surrounded by a laughing mob, he represents for me those fleeting, queering moments in which heterocentric logic is caught with its trousers down, failing to be the organizing and dependable center that it claims to be (see fig. I.3). The queer, as I see it in these films, is the merrily affirmative performance of heteronormativity's weaknesses, its contingencies and interruptions, its proliferating Achilles' heels, its illogicality, its constant flirtation with its own ruination. It laughs concentricity into eccentricity; the stability of *normal* sexual desire and the *normal* family becomes the contingency of *just-one-way-of-desiring-among-many* and *just-one-type-of-kinship-among-many*.

In order to demonstrate this queerness at work onscreen, I draw on an eccentric canon. Andrew Higson warns against any cultural history that "identifies a select series of relatively self-contained quality film movements to carry forward the banner of national cinema," notably "Ealing Studios and the quality film movement of

Figure I.3. Heterocentricity caught with its trousers down in *The Man in the White Suit* (Alexander Mackendrick, 1951). *Source:* Ealing Studios/Courtesy of STUDIOCANAL.

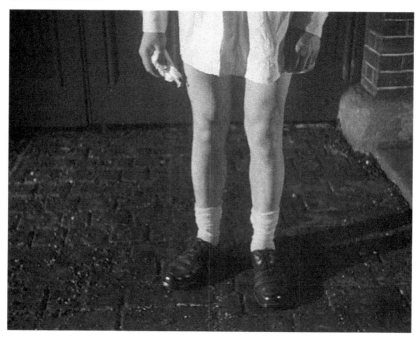

the mid-1940s."[13] Although Ealing is well represented in these pages, it rubs shoulders with sex comedies and farces as part of an inelegantly capacious canon that welcomes all images that make laughter out of the leaky limits of heterocentric structures. No film is tiresomely pegged on such problematic binaries as highbrow–lowbrow, elite–popular, or art–entertainment. Sue Harper and Vincent Porter's defense of 1950s cinema that it "was not a dull period in which only war or comedy films were made" implies that criticism should move beyond the familiar comedies (and war films) of the period in order to find anything of interest.[14] Queering, however, precisely invites the return to a reimagined familiar in order to identify and unsettle the limits of heterocentric mythology. Challenges to these limits of domestic and sexual convention are often critically associated with the familiar comic figure of the eccentric. This figure represents alterity, and throws conventional expectations about matrimony, reproduction, biological and material legacy, authority, and domestic arrangements into disarray. The often riotous and almost indescribable social and sexual idiosyncrasies of Margaret Rutherford, Alastair Sim, Irene Handl, Esma Cannon, Terry-Thomas, Stanley Holloway, Miles Malleson, Charles Hawtrey, Joan Greenwood, Alec Guinness, Joyce Grenfell, Edie Martin, and scores of others queer the screen. They are shameless and unassimilable, resisting any attempt to boil them down to a clear identity. They do not act as though they are in a concentric position around centered normality; they act as though there is no center at all. On behalf of the marginalized, these eccentrics stoke laughter at the fractures in the structures of convention.

My interest in textual effects is generally indifferent to the conditions of production; useful histories exist elsewhere as part of a different kind of intellectual and political project and give details of how the postwar film "industry was a battleground in which different factions—in finance, in class politics, in gender representation, in technology—struggled for dominance."[15] While such histories are valuable in rescuing the obscured lives of personnel, they also risk drawing the eye away from textual complexities and suggesting that meaning in British popular films is straightforward. If meaning is too firmly centered on production and personnel, certain readings become more difficult. I am not concerned with whether a particular director or producer is politically or sexually radical but, rather, with how films themselves resist the totalizing attempts by their makers or their critics to regiment them into the neat concentric patterns of a canon.

Making Myths

Despite what I see as the queer sensibility of postwar cinematic eccentricity, this period of film history retains, to some extent, a reputation for reproducing heterocentric structures. This is the result of a national mythologization of those years, predicated on ideas of consensus and traditional values. I was born sixteen months into Margaret Thatcher's first term of office as British prime minister. Her government reproduced heterocentric mythology so aggressively that it became a difficult period to be gay in the UK. In 1988, Section 28 of the Local Government Act prohibited the promotion of homosexuality by any local authority across Britain, effectively resulting in a ban on schools' "teaching of the acceptability of homosexuality as a pretended family relationship."[16] This drew a silencing veil over the openness of a sexual minority increasingly emboldened since the decriminalization of some sexual behavior between men in England and Wales in 1967 and in need of support during the AIDS crisis. A rhetoric that insisted that nonheterosexual, nonbiological kinships could only ever aspire to the status of "pretended family" represented a fundamental assault on the slow progress achieved by LGBT+ individuals in the previous two decades.

Thatcher generally pitched this assertion of traditional sexual morality in nostalgic terms; Raphael Samuel describes how "Mrs Thatcher annexed 'Victorian values' to her Party's platform and turned them into a talisman for lost stabilities"; these lost stabilities included heterocentric sexual and gender identity.[17] According to this conservatism, moral relativism was a cultural weakness; heterocentric marriage and the biological family were to be protected at all costs as obvious goods and anything that threatened their hegemony was to be repressed through the application of dogmatic legislation and moral authority. But the image of the past on which this project was built was a manufactured mirage, occupying "an allegorical rather than a temporal space" according to Samuel; it was a piece of political hocus-pocus whose force derived from its dishonest simplicity, answering "to one of the most universal myths . . . that once upon a time things were simpler and the people were at one with themselves."[18] Abandoning complexity, this "hegemonic management of the historical" was mythopoeic and invented an impossible and exclusive utopia against which contemporary society could be found wanting.[19]

The postwar years were key to this nostalgic mythopoeia. An interview between Thatcher and David English, published in the *Daily Mail* in April 1988, hails "an old-fashioned Britain, structured and courteous. A Britain which was clean and orderly. People were safe and secure whether in their homes or on the streets. A faintly shabby but decidedly nice country" not yet disturbed by the 1960s, when "permissiveness, selfish and uncaring, proliferated under the guise of the new sexual freedom."[20] English describes Thatcher's "crusade to restore the social environment to what it was before the Sixties polluted it."[21] Pulsing to a dogmatic beat, the interview references *ad delirium* the moral "rules" that defined the prepermissive years, apparently dismissed as "old-fashioned" by intellectuals since "Britain lost its way."[22] The Neverland of this imagined postwar golden age continues to haunt aspects of contemporary British life. For some, it marks a time before the loss of empire and the humiliating cozying up to what would become the European Union; Brexit, with its rallying cries of "*Sovereignty!*" and "*British values!*," has attempted (and failed) to reset that clock. Current illiberal concerns about a snowflake generation that insists on sharing narratives of personal experience reference a mythologized simplicity before the riot of 1960s permissiveness: sex as a biologically determined binary, gender as corresponding uncomplicatedly to sex, and sexuality as resolutely straight. British postwar cinema is conscripted as a set of seemingly totemic artifacts in the campaign to reinforce these myths of national and sexual identity, endlessly reassuring because endlessly clear. The films, and especially the comic films, of the era apparently serve as a reminder of a morally comfortable period in which, as Durgnat frames it, "a happier and shallower mood prevails."[23] They are made to look like the products of a conservative—and, perhaps, a Conservative—cinema whose people are at one with themselves, whose marriages are made in heaven, whose sex is only hinted at and definitely heterosexual, whose families are spirited but secure, whose children represent a hopeful future, and whose communities consist of good and largely unobtrusive neighbors. They seem to hold a mirror up to the twenty-first-century world and to show how much decency it lacks.

From a progressive perspective, it is tempting, given this conservative reputation, to dismiss postwar Britain as "the most settled, deferential, smug, un-dynamic society in the advanced world . . . [with] Crown, Parliament and the Civil Service at the centre."[24] From such a vantage point, postwar cinema seems to be a dull interlude before the New Wave broke just in time for the 1960s. Jeffrey Richards argues that "the 1960s witnessed a revitalisation of British cinema and the emergence of a flourishing and diverse film culture after what was perceived to be the 'doldrums era' of the 1950s."[25] Harper and Porter describe this postwar era's undistinguished reputation for being "a dull period—an interregnum sandwiched between the inventive 1940s and the exciting 1960s. Critics and film-makers as influential as Lindsay Anderson have berated it as dull and uninventive—'a "hack" period . . . a long period of marking time' . . . and the editorial board of *Movie* regarded it as simply 'dead.'"[26] Andrew Spicer describes the reputation of "a period conventionally considered in the historiography of British cinema as the doldrums era with its cast of dull and boring 'tweed men.'"[27] Half-engaged with this charge, Durgnat describes the "affluence cycle" of films, moribundly congealing in "lower-upper-middle-class cosiness," never extending beyond an "air of gay, youthful, relatively modest contentment and sauciness."[28] And Melanie Bell describes how "for a long time British cinema's output from this decade was written off as moribund and dull; an endless parade of war films and trite comedies."[29] Each of these critics goes on to complicate the period's reputation, but nevertheless the comedies of these years are popularly imagined to lack political edge, to be nice but dull. Such an account of postwar cinema makes the films look suspiciously like Thatcher's dreams of moral simplicity committed to celluloid.

The Thatcherite and counter-Thatcherite readings of the films, as decent or dull respectively, are both exercises in mythmaking and find common ground in agreeing that this era is emphatically prepermissive. Popular British cinema of the late 1940s and 1950s has too often been constrained by this critical binary that sees it either as the champion of blissful heterosexual marriage and a class system still clinging to deference, the last bastion of Victorian values, or a trivial, tired, and sometimes tedious litany of social and aesthetic clichés crying out to be replaced by something more *authentic*. Depending on a critic's affiliation, the reimagined realisms of the 1960s (overseen by such directors as Karel Reisz, Lindsay Anderson, and Tony Richardson) represent either the corruption of a cinematic Eden or a much-needed shot in the arm for a flagging national art form.

But this binary approach does not square with my viewing of postwar comedy film. I do *not* see a reinforcement of traditional values and I *do* see inventiveness and mischief. Thatcher argues in the *Daily Mail* that "young people were bewitched" by the doctrines of the 1960s, which "did a whole generation a great disservice."[30] But when I was young, it was the antics of the marvelous figures from postwar cinema that queerly bewitched me; it was a merry band of playmates in a celluloid landscape of collapsing conventions that did me the "disservice" of exposing the nonsense of orthodoxy. Some may find my responses to the films idiosyncratic, but idiosyncrasy is the beginning of a rebuttal of the disciplining pressures of mythologizing normalization. If I were to accept that postwar cinema unquestioningly embraces the heterocentric values of Thatcher's moral "rules of a civilised society," it would initiate a crisis in pleasure.[31] Charles Barr, in his celebrated study of *Ealing Studios*, argues that *Passport to Pimlico* (Henry Cornelius, 1949—see chapter 1), typically for postwar cinema, "plays down or leaves out . . . desire of all kinds."[32] I wonder what desires Barr includes in "all kinds." Does he restrict the prohibition on desire to the characters? Or the filmmakers? I cannot agree with his analysis when it comes to the question of *my* desires. My desires *do* circulate through *Passport to Pimlico*—and many other comedies of the era—including the desire to mock heterocentric logics.

Rather than accepting a conservative reading of these films, I trace the way in which they openly *laugh at* any attempt to construct mythopoeic fantasies about a simpler time and reveal, instead, a disorderly complexity in which the securities valued by Thatcher—of *sexual propriety, family values, social niceties*—are exploded and give way to something queerer. The ambition of this book is to argue that the filmic work of unsettling sexual pieties began in popular comedy long before *Victim* offered the first big-screen utterance of the word *homosexual*. I not only argue that there was same-sex desire and unconventional gender expression onscreen in the late 1940s and 1950s, but also that, more importantly, it was a decade and a half in which British culture queered and destabilized conventional heterocentric attitudes about sex, family, marriage, and reproduction. In absolute rejection of Thatcher's claims about the period, I see a queer vein running disruptively through its cinema. Alan Sinfield presents this as the moment when a "vivid phase of cultural and political challenge began, and 'old-fashioned Britain' generated its own supersession."[33] I argue that part of this challenge came in the—perhaps unlikely—shape of comedy films. My hope with this book is to rescue postwar comedy cinema from a rhetoric that has tried to make it the prop of a cultural imaginary that dreams nostalgically of a repressive moral consensus.

It is easy enough to reject the uncomfortable critical binaries that see this decade of British cinema as either secure or stuffy, cozy or charmless, tidy or tedious—but what should replace them? It is not as simple as arguing that these binaries encourage dishonest or inaccurate statements about the films and that what could and should replace them would permit the honest assessment of the films' achievements. Such an assertion would reinscribe precisely the same totalizing critical mechanisms as the model it replaces. The ambition of this book is to register the indeterminacies and instabilities of the films; it is not to reduce them to watertight interpretative conclusions; it is to avoid reading them as neatly packaged products for consumption and to view them, instead, as processes of disturbance, outmaneuvering critical attempts to settle them into clear meaning. This book tries to escape mythmaking's monolithic meanings and run, instead, toward capaciousness. I argue that it is precisely the prepermissive logic of the era—emboldened by the Second World War's shifting of social norms but still conscious of a sense of the unsayable—that invites capacious readings. "Eccentricity" is one name for this capaciousness, and the principal work of this book will be to rejuvenate it as a productive critical term. Always open and inviting, capacious eccentricity resists closure, and only acts of critical coercion will tame it into something that poses as definitive meaning. The stability of a critical binary—which finds either moral reassurance or political dullness in the films—is upset by such eccentricity. Ultimately, any prescriptive interpretation that tries to reduce the eccentric play of these films into neat conclusions—into fixed structures—is destined to unravel as comprehensively as Sidney's white suit.

Making Histories

Alongside conservative mythopoeic projects, reductive social and political histories are also resisted by the unruliness of these comedies. The fifteen years after the end of the war witnessed shifts in government, economic performance, and social attitudes in the United Kingdom. A Labour government under Clement Atlee oversaw periods of both idealism and despondency as an optimistic program of rebuilding was at times eclipsed by economic hardship, continued rationing, and terrible weather. The Conservatives were reelected to government in 1951, the year of the Festival of Britain, overseeing an age of renewed affluence and optimism, although Anthony Eden, succeeding Churchill, had to resign over the Suez Crisis, which effectively marked the end of empire and Britain's status as a superpower. Despite these shifts and complexities, the postwar British moment, and how it materializes on screens, is frequently distilled into the term *consensus*. This idea of consensus describes a perceived agreement on how Britain should be rebuilt according to the economic theories of John Maynard Keynes, a mixed economy of nationalized and privatized industries, the creation of a welfare state and the National Health Service (NHS), and a general sense of shared national purpose. Hornsey details how plans for postwar rebuilding, including the literal rebuilding of bomb-devastated urban areas, relied on "soothing images of peaceful consensus."[34] To support this soothing imagery, domestic metaphors were called on to bind Britain's disparate groups; Britain saw itself "as a united, organic society, an extended family standing on layer upon layer of history and tradition."[35] These traditions were resolutely heterocentric, predicated not only on pageantry and ritual but also on logics of inheritance and birthright. Family values were etched deeply into the consensual plans for the postwar New Jerusalem.

This postwar cultural dedication to family-centric history and tradition can give an impression of impeded progress. Paul Addison argues that "the economic and social structure of Britain was much the same as it had been in the 1920s and 1930s and the same was true of moral and cultural attitudes."[36] He suggests that "the People's War . . . had resulted in a People's Peace . . . [and] the People, for the most part, had been moral and cultural conservatives, and . . . the war had also deepened that conservatism by vindicating British institutions."[37] The films explored in this book, at least as I view them, do not tell so consensual a story. Dramatic narrative, with its investment in the particular and the individual, complicates the homogenizing idea of the *People*, and this is especially the case when the dramatic individuals in question are *eccentric*. It is difficult to dragoon images of Rutherford, or Sim, or Handl, or Malleson, or Grenfell into bearing the burden of representation for this putative *People*. These images of idiosyncratic and untamed figures, as I read them, become a comic variation on the theme of domestic unrest that Jeffrey Weeks suggests was emerging in British society:

> The 1950s has been looked back to with nostalgia by cultural conservatives as the last period of stable family life. . . . The companionate relationship was reaffirmed as the privileged site of intimate life. Marriage rates were high, divorce rates were low, and marriage remained the gateway to respectable adulthood. The sexual division of labour was modernised, though not in such a way as to challenge traditional roles. . . . Yet under the surface a clear sense of unease was growing. . . . This was accompanied by a sharper divide between heterosexuality and homosexuality than ever before in public discourse. Heterosexuality seemed more self confident than ever, while homosexuality became the explicit Other, whose shameful existence confirmed and reinforced the accepted norms in public discourse. Yet even here change was happening.[38]

This is not a portrait of consensus but of strain. As Weeks makes clear, it is not the case that the war had wiped away the institutions—political, cultural, educational, religious, moral—that existed before. However, many of these institutions had been shaken. Nostalgic for lost certainties, the conservative philosopher Roger Scruton describes a general "derision, in which some of the most intelligent voices of English post-war culture took part" that saw "English culture . . . ransacked for its myths and hypocrisies, and the old English virtues made to look like worn-out theatrical costumes."[39] By the late 1940s, gone was the "quasi-propaganda" of wartime film comedy *Tawny Pipit* (Bernard Miles and Charles Saunders, 1944) in which "the landscape and the human life contained in it are portrayed as symbols of political stability and of unhurried order—antidotes to the tumult of war, and places to which we come home in imagination, as we hope to come home in fact."[40] As Britain's former certainties about its place in the world were at risk of unraveling—tugged at by the strain of continued rationing and privation, economic hardship in the wake of war, a collapsing empire, an uncertain Cold War, and a fading sense of the country's international role and status—cinema screens in Britain became canvases for discussions of uncertainty and fantasies of *possibility*.

Shifts in behavior during the years of conflict changed ideas about what was possible: the intense experience of homosociality in wartime left its mark and "male homosexuality became increasingly visible, through the writings of medical and psychoanalytical experts, official enquiries, high-profile court cases and the moral panics promoted by the tabloid press"; women's social position shifted because "the Second World War gave rise to a crisis in gender roles with women increasingly replacing men in the workforce"; and the empire, symbol of the heterocentric ideal of the British birthright of power over a family of nations, failed, contributing "over the next few years to the growth of a national inferiority complex."[41] The war had not straightforwardly changed the country's moral framework on the family and sex and status, but "the moorings . . . were coming loose from their bearings in a midcentury England forever changing."[42] Divergence from heterocentric convention—in the various forms of homosexuals, divorced couples, working mothers, active-at-home fathers, and so on—could not be overlooked or dismissed and was increasingly the subject of newspaper coverage, published personal testimony, parliamentary debate, and, in the case of homosexuality, police surveillance. Disapproval remained rife, but there was no way to put the genies of sexual and domestic freedom back in their bottles once they had become part of the culture's discourse. It was in this mood of possibility that the Wolfenden Report—written by a committee set up by the Conservative government in 1954 because of mounting pressure to review the legal status of homosexuals and sex workers—ultimately supported the partial decriminalization of sex between men in Britain. While some newspapers dismissed the report (with the *Sunday Express* referring to it as a "Pansies' Charter"), others welcomed it. Even the Archbishop of Canterbury, in a gesture unimaginable before the war, supported decriminalization.[43] This "postwar British identity crisis" was reflected on in 1952 by Aneurin Bevan, architect of the NHS:

> It is a dangerous period in the lifetime of a nation when the convictions, beliefs, and values of one epoch are seen to be losing their vitality, and those of the new have not

> yet won universal acceptance. . . . Those whose habits and possessions are bound up with the vanishing social order are filled with pessimism. A future which threatens with destruction all that they had come to regard as fixed and eternal, that sacrilegiously laughs at assumptions which they always believed to lie in the foundations of life, that projects itself into the present in strange words and even stranger thoughts; such a future does not seem to them to be worth struggling for.[44]

The postwar years in the victorious-but-diminished UK were a moment of political and social contingency, in which revised structures had yet to be set in stone after the old structures had received a battering during the conflict. It is in this mood of dangerous instability, in which the prevailing myths of sexual and social identity were shifting amid often acrimonious debates, that British film comedies sacrilegiously laughed at heterocentric assumptions.

My argument is that the comedies explored in this book—and many others besides—contribute to this mythoclastic moment not by debating sexual nonconformity *as an issue* but by presenting heterocentric values *as a joke*. But this joke fails to land if the films are insistently mistaken for simple exercises in consensus politics. Pam Cook defines consensus films as "those on which an uneasy alliance of opinion between producers and critics (mainly from the quality press) and official bodies . . . conferred the status of quality British cinema. Generally, these were films set in contemporary British locales, addressing specifically national issues and adopting an aesthetic of restrained realism."[45] Such films as *Passport to Pimlico* may seem to offer images of consensus. I am, however, indifferent to the shared opinions—uneasy or otherwise—of producers, critics, and official bodies; they should not limit the films' possible significances. As I encounter them, the films chucklingly distort, derange, and dissemble, so playfully chockablock with unstable symbolism, irony, and connotation—quite possibly against the avowed intent of their makers—that they become sites of *dissensus*. Harper suggests that cinema's "most important function is to provide a site for the restatement and the questioning of notions of the sacred and the profane, the pure and the dangerous."[46] The queer energy in the films, as I have already suggested, unravels such hierarchical and concentric binaries. The stability of such conventional icons as the sacred mother or the innocent child are exploded in comedies of domestic profanity and danger that question cultural values in a queerly conditional mood; they are often more interested in *what if* than *what is*, in possibility than in certainty.

This interest in possibility, speculation, and play makes the films slippery—they slip through the fingers of anyone attempting to pin them down as indicative *statements* on their historical moment. One response to this slipperiness has been to engage in what Nikki Sullivan describes as "spot the queer," aiming "to dis-cover the (repressed) homosexual or homoerotic elements (the 'dirty secrets') contained in mainstream cinematic texts."[47] Such games contribute to the writing of what Laura Doan describes as "a critical history of the homosexual and homosexuality . . . a historical narrative that, in the popular realm in modern Britain, starts about the middle of the twentieth century."[48] If Doan's timings are right—and timing is everything in both history and comedy—then the postwar period is a crucial moment in the birth of modern homosexuality. However, while games of spot-the-queer can be valuable, they risk stifling capacious instability with the imposition of *structure* and *order*, translating the queerly conditional mood of *what if* into the concentric binaries of the indicative, in which things (and specifically people's sexual identities) either are or are not. My hope is, instead, to locate cinematic expressions of a more nebulous queerness peculiar to the postwar moment, in which resistance takes the form of a cultural dynamic that behaves badly, moves irregularly, and engages antisocially. This dynamic is not about individuals who identify as queer but about an ex-centering queerness that offers a parade of alternative possibilities for a postwar country reimagining itself. In this analysis, eccentricity is not merely the locatable characteristic of an individual, but a diffuse indeterminacy in a text and its wider culture, "a dialogue with difference, discontinuity, alterity, and rupture . . . [in which] the discovery of fixed and stable identities cannot be an investigatory end point."[49] This eccentricity, this queerness, animates images into a dance that deforms and deranges the very stabilities that Thatcher sought to locate in the postwar period, replacing them with unruly comedy.

Measuring the political impact of such unruliness is difficult. I am not hoping to prove—or even whisperingly to suggest—that *The Man in the White Suit* provoked increased unionization or entrepreneurship, or that *Passport to Pimlico* inspired regional campaigns for devolution, or that *Genevieve* (Henry Cornelius, 1953—see chapter 4) prompted outbreaks of road rage, or that *The Green Man* (Robert Day, 1956—see chapter 4) encouraged a generation of political assassins or vacuum-cleaner salesmen. I am mindful of Durgnat's indictment of a frustratingly apolitical national cinema that "regularly perpetrated distortions and omissions which proved extremely galling to this writer's critical generation."[50] But it is these distortions and omissions that I find both funny and eccentrically political. They may omit serious discussion of the issues of homosexuality or unmarried mothers or mixed-heritage marriage, but by *looking* trivial—that is, by showing the artifice and absurdity of heterocentric structures—they trivialize outmoded sureties around sex, gender, family, and reproduction while giving glimpses of otherness. Bruce Babington may consider that *The Belles of St. Trinian's* offers only "harmlessly comic versions of the female sex out of control" but, to the child I was when I watched with my father and to the adult I now am, the spectacle of girls and women "susceptible neither to the traditional disciplines of religion and morality nor education" remains political.[51] To those—including the sexual nonconformists—who have been poorly served by such disciplines, the film gives glimpses of the answer to the scandalous question: *What if* education, and friendship, and relationships with authority, and all other aspects of life were experienced according to a logic of *shameless fun* rather than of discipline? What flights of both fantasy and achievement would that liberate? When Scruton, in his elegy for the England lost after 1945, panegyrizes "sexual puritanism [as] an attempt to safeguard possessions more valuable than pleasure" and argues that British people's "repression prevented them from carelessly throwing away those things—chastity, marriage and the family—which slip so easily from the grasp" he is making no allowance for the girls of St. Trinian's—or this writer—for whom the value of such possessions is not a foregone conclusion.[52] The films that I see when I watch postwar British comedy bear the rib-tickling contingency of a historical moment when these things begin slipping from the nation's grasp, offering glimpses of a more inclusive disorder.

Making Futures, Laughing Forward

Despite this interest in the historical moment in which these films were made, this book is not intended primarily as a history of either

British cinema or queer culture between 1945 and 1960.[53] I am less interested in the past as a defined object for study and more interested in how historical artifacts might indicate certain possibilities to the present. To clarify my stance, it is useful to contrast it with the starting point for many film historians. Barr is clear that "the films at least project their makers' picture of Britain and the British character."[54] Building on this argument, Harper and Porter suggest that the job of the film historian is "to recreate the consciousness of those who made the films, and to explain the structures of feeling which reside within film texts. . . . Films are popular because they set up a 'parish of belief' between the filmmaker and film-goer—a set of shared assumptions, a safe place in which dangers can be explored and neutralized, and confidence restored."[55] The job of the queer history presented in this book is neither to recreate the consciousness of anyone nor to explain what resides inside a text. To resurrect a filmmaker, with all the theological connotations of such an act, is to generate a fictional authority that can be used to justify particular interpretative conclusions and exclude others. The argument that a producer (say, Michael Balcon) and a director (say, Henry Cornelius) would not have recognized a film (say, *Passport to Pimlico*) as queer can only be an act of imaginative reconstruction. It offers evidence of nothing and risks constraining a film's meanings around a centering figure. At one level, it may be true that films are popular because they establish "parishes of belief," but their importance lies in being able to hop across parish boundaries and reach different audiences elsewhere. For some parishes, there is more comfort in seeing dangers amplified than neutralized; unruly postwar British comedy often leaves dangers to the structure of heterocentric institutions in play, unresolved and assuredly unneutralized.

The postwar history that I am interested in making, then, is not first and foremost reconstitutive. It is less concerned with indicative statements of *what was*—of the "way of seeing and feeling, that is specific to a given historical period"—and more interested in exploring how the myriad possibilities played out onscreen in the years after the war still perform as possibilities in the twenty-first century.[56] Postwar eccentrics do not only—and, perhaps, primarily—offer insights into their own period. Performances by Rutherford and Sim and Handl may happen among specific icons of postwar British life—ruins and ration books, bomb sites and bubble cars, pencil skirts and suburban semis—but the performers are too extraordinary just to offer a representative glimpse of life in the 1940s or 1950s. Instead, in their shameless and unassimilable queerness they open up possible futures that never came to be but that I still consider to be valuable. Much of this eccentric postwar play makes visible a kind of unsettled queer possibility that has been submerged in the decades since 1960 by an identity-based system of knowledge predicated on assimilation and a redefinition of the normative. Doan, in her account of female sexuality in the twentieth century, has advised stepping "outside the logic of identity history because its knowledge apparatus seemed to bring sexuality into the light at the expense of casting other knowledge regimes into the dark."[57] It is these other knowledge regimes—and sometimes gleeful ignorance regimes—that this book locates in postwar comedy: unnamed and unnameable, eccentric and unassimilable, a danger to the solid structures of home and gender and identity by privileging, instead, the fluid play of desire. Doan suggests that queer history "forces us to raise our tolerance for conceptual messiness as we engage in the pleasures of conjecturing about what may in the end prove unknowable and irresolvable."[58] Postwar comedy, it seems to me, is the celebration of mess over knowledge, of openness over resolution, and of laughter over order.

What I envisage is a *pre-post*-erous history in which the past is (re)placed *after* the present. Christian Hite, referencing the works of Jacques Derrida, defines the preposterous as "meaning literally 'with hindsight in front'" and "rendering undecidable the straightforward positionalities of 'before' and 'after,' 'front' and 'behind.'"[59] Hite describes a temporal sequence in which "the 'future'—what lies ahead—is already 'behind' (*derrière*)."[60] Such a future becomes a "'*catastrophic* future,' precisely in the etymological sense of an 'overturning.'"[61] Such a preposterous catastrophe, according to Lee Edelman, works with the "(il)logic that structures the moebius loop, the (il)logic that dislocates such spatio-temporal 'situations' as 'pre' and 'post,' or before and behind."[62] Edelman goes on to queer such eccentric temporalities by linking them with the eccentric spatialities of same-sex sex in which "what is behind can also, and properly, come before," meaning that the preposterous is always "precisely—and 'in principle'—sodomitical."[63] A preposterous history, then, in its queerly sodomitical logic, is one that confuses those models of sequence, position, hierarchy, and structure that have passed as natural and have insisted on a uniform legitimate order of things. Instead, preposterous history acknowledges that the past can still remain ahead of the present, *before* it in both the sense of *previous to* and *in front of*. Such a history is indifferent to linear models of *progress* and *regress* and does not repeat the claims that modern British history is the straightforward teleological movement from pre-1960s sexual conservatism and prejudice to a contemporary sexual freedom. Such claims carry some truth and are important in structuring politically and emotionally coherent movements. Every history that focuses its gaze on *progress*, however, risks overlooking the tapestry of possible futures that were not—but still could be—lived. Many of these untried possibilities would, no doubt, be outrageous, ruinous, and violent if put into practice. Others, however, might be compassionate and constructive.

Such preposterous speculation may be dismissed by some as a pointless intellectual pursuit, fun for the armchair historian but unworthy of serious attention. For some marginalized groups and individuals, however, the traces of those speculative pasts represent significant opportunities. Queer history, as I understand it, consists of traces in the present of still-future possibilities discoverable in past artifacts. In the chapters that follow, I outline (that is, I will outline and have already outlined) some of the glimpses for queer futures that I detect in postwar British comedy. That queer future is neither singular nor clearly defined. Its shifting features include capaciousness, mirth, and a rejection of assimilationist logic. It resists the conventional terms with which the twenty-first century may patronizingly try to speak about postwar sexual primitivism. Michel Foucault, advocating a critical genealogical approach to the past, argues that "history serves to show how that-which-is has not always been; i.e., that the things which seem most evident to us are always formed in the confluence of encounters and chances, during the course of a precarious and fragile history."[64] The comedy films discussed in this book form an archive of the encounters and chances of a precarious and fragile society that, in a moment of contingency that followed conflict, was reimagining its own moral, sexual, and domestic attitudes. Before Britain's contemporary understandings of sexuality, gender, family, nation, and sex (sodomitical and otherwise) settled in the closing decades of the twentieth century and replaced the outmoded heterocentric structures inherited from the prewar world with new more permissive structures, there was a catastrophic (in Hite's sense of an overturning) moment of screen *eccentricity* that defies categorization and presents deconstruction more than reconstruction.

Part of the effectiveness of this deconstruction lies in the films' *funniness*. My desire to write about these films stems from how they—or at least moments in them—make me roar with laughter. Their often preposterous comedy (one that is absurd, built on the unconventional repositioning of incongruous elements and the rearrangement of expectation) is related to the temporal preposterousness of their past images giving glimpses of possible futures to the present in which the films are being watched; I refer to that relationship throughout this book with the phrase *laughing forward*. Queer theory has discussed both the opportunities and the risks of a turn to the past. Heather Love asks "is it better to move on toward a brighter future or to hang back and cling to the past? Such divided allegiances result in contradictory feelings: pride and shame, anticipation and regret, hope and despair. Contemporary queers find ourselves in the odd situation of 'looking forward' while we are 'feeling backward.'"[65] This feeling backward offers "an account of the corporeal and psychic costs of homophobia . . . [which stimulates] feelings such as nostalgia, regret, shame, despair, *ressentiment*, passivity, escapism, self-hatred, withdrawal, bitterness, defeatism, and loneliness . . . tied to the experience of social exclusion and to the historical 'impossibility' of same-sex desire."[66]

It is certainly possible to read these postwar films in these terms, and it is important not to forget the horrors of criminalization and coercion, the ways in which sexually nonconformist lives were beset by hesitancies, humiliations, and harassments in the 1940s and 1950s. I take Medhurst very seriously when he remarks, "I wouldn't be able to write this chapter, and you wouldn't be able to read this book, if we were all still Michael Wards," that is, repressed homosexuals living in fear of social exclusion and arrest.[67] Nevertheless, my looking backward does not only reveal "an image repertoire of queer modernist melancholia," as Love's does, but also a shock of queer laughter that echoes into the future.[68] In the bursts of this laughter are revealed glimpses of radical possibilities of same-sex desire as well as gender nonconformity, family reinvention, and domestic unorthodoxy. Love writes, movingly and compellingly, that "queers are intimately familiar with the *costs* of being queer—that, as much as anything, makes us queer."[69] Postwar British comedy, however, offers an alternative vision of the *gains* of being queer and of the costs of upholding the myth of *the normal*.

Laughing forward, however, is not *straightforward*; it does not simply imagine a brighter future. José Esteban Muñoz begins his theoretical rehabilitation of the future (after Edelman's earlier declaration that there is *No Future*) with an extraordinary reimagining of the queer:

> Queerness is not yet here. Queerness is an ideality. Put another way, we are not yet queer. We may never touch queerness, but we can feel it as the warm illumination of a horizon imbued with potentiality. We have never been queer, yet queerness exists for us as an ideality that can be distilled from the past and used to imagine a future. The future is queerness's domain. . . . Queerness is that thing that lets us feel that this world is not enough, that indeed something is missing. Often we can glimpse the worlds proposed and promised by queerness in the realm of the aesthetic.[70]

I find this concept of queerness compelling and it informs many of my insights in this book. But I do not entirely share Muñoz's vision. He states that "at the center of *Cruising Utopia* there is the idea of hope."[71] *Laughing forward*, as I experience it, is not centered on hope. It is neither hopeful nor hopeless. It is *eccentric* and therefore centered on nothing. It offers no prospectus. It offers no strategy. It is a promise, but only of the kind that Derrida invokes when he writes that "a promise that cannot be broken, isn't a promise: it's a forecast, a prediction. The possibility of betrayal or perversion must be at the heart of the commitment to a promise and the distinction between promise and threat can never be assured."[72] *Laughing forward* offers no certain reward and threatens not only betrayal but also disaster. It is not optimistic but, rather, *affirmative*—and the *yeses* that it offers are open and reckless and fleeting. The queer *yes* offered by Sidney Stratton does not reside in his white suit—which unravels, as structure always does when it is ex-centered—but in the evocative and irregular sounds of his bubbling experiments that end the film and, promising nothing definite, gesture to an instability and uncertainty and *possibility* that may yet completely unravel the status quo.

It is this unfocused play of possibilities that is mistaken by some critics of postwar British cinema for apoliticism, but I find in these comedies a resistance to the strictures of structure, a neutralization of the forces of assimilation, and the projection, instead, of a sprawling vision of liberation. In this, the films offer what Eve Kosofsky Sedgwick suggests tentatively may be a definition of *queer*: "the open mesh of possibilities, gaps, overlaps, dissonances and resonances, lapses and excesses of meaning . . ."[73] At odds with Muñoz's focus on the singular, *laughing forward* creates not a "brighter future" but, as it were, *broader futures*, whose ironies, connotations, and paradoxes are too diffuse, too at odds to offer a template, a test run, or even a taste of a coherent future. *Laughing forward*, as I envisage it, is a preposterous textual dynamic whose play of indeterminacies can never be settled, even provisionally, in the present and that, therefore, keeps slipping toward a future, not in the hope or expectation of meaningfulness but in a state of continued play. This forwardness looks beyond whatever moment it encounters, offering images of funniness that collapse historical remoteness and gesture toward unorthodox futures that we are always yet to reach. In *Beyond Good and Evil*, Friedrich Nietzsche writes that "perhaps, even if nothing else today has any future, our laughter has a future."[74] The laughter of these postwar comedies has a future—or futures—because it was not settled by the reforms and revolutions of the 1960s or stifled by the conservative myths of the 1980s—and continues its subversive chortling now.

This focus on forwardness, however, runs the risk of eclipsing a valuable backwardness. There is a pastness inscribed in these films, characterized by Britain's sense of contingency as its society was reassessing its social, domestic, and sexual structures in the wake of conflict and in advance of cultural revolution. The comedy arises from a peculiarly postwar tussling over gender roles, male intimacy, dysfunctional parents, undisciplined children, unruly homes, and alarming inheritances. Although these are certainly historical specificities, like any contingencies they cannot be neatly reduced to a definitive statement about the past. Cook describes the "vice-like grip the notion of authenticity has on the historical film."[75] It is worth reflecting on how this oppressive demand for authenticity applies to films *from* (as well as *about*) history; the cinema of past eras is fashioned as a canon of historical artifacts waiting to offer up their evidence about *life back then*. A study that focuses on such evidence can be revealing about historical cultural trends and behaviors, but it applies a constraint to the texts' play of and with meaning. To remedy this (even as I lose focus on historical filmmakers and audiences) I position the films not only as artifacts *from the past* but also as artifacts *to the future*, which make visible the structures that continue to center prevailing cultural logics today. The films are not merely ambassadors for the moments of their production. *Laughing forward* shakes the films free from their burden as decodable time capsules and they become, instead, multivalent and rediscoverable semiotic spaces. The readings that I offer in this book engage with histories of postwar Britain in order to reflect on the sense of cultural upheaval and possibility and never to shepherd textual complexity and resistance into neatly meaning their moment of production. At no point do I wish to suggest how audiences do or should react to these films; this is an account of how I react to them and an invitation to others to excavate their own queer possibilities in the films. These analyses are the performance of a type of response that never seeks to totalize and, instead, looks for the fleeting, the strange, the queer, the preposterously possible.

Making Gestures

What I observe, then, is a postwar British cinema that unravels like Sidney's white suit and ends up as so many threads, tufts, patches, and tears. The elements of the films that *laugh forward* are often ephemeral and fragmentary. Eccentricity's effect of exposing the mythic fragility of a structure often begins with one of these small parts' not adding up, not toeing the line, not standing to attention within the whole. Indeed, with a film such as *It's Never Too Late* (Michael McCarthy, 1956—see chapter 2), I find very little *laughing forward* besides one momentary fragment, but that moment is enough to unsettle the conservative meanings that otherwise might dominate the film. A term that will be particularly valuable in capturing the achievements of such fleeting but significant moments is *gesture*. The intellectual history of the concept of gesture is rich and complicated, but the term is usually understood to refer to embodied forms of communication. Foucault links it specifically to embodied structures of power; when he argues that "a well-disciplined body forms the operational context of the slightest gesture," the underpinning discipline is the result of a complex cultural power dynamic that constrains the possibilities for free expression and movement.[76] Even such seemingly personal expressions as gender and sexuality are, according to theories of performativity, not a function of a presocial self but the effects of the repetitive performance of cultural gestures.[77] In post war Britain, this constraining of gesture through the disciplining of bodies could be found etched into the plans for urban rebuilding that "would repeatedly equate good urban behavior with a specific way of moving through, socializing within, and appreciating the built environment—a logic that insinuated itself across a range of spatial scales and that came to saturate almost all aspects of ordinary everyday life."[78] This conservative idea of *good behavior* included *good sexual behavior* and *good domestic behavior*.

Postwar British comedies often perform gesture in a way that challenges discipline and models the pleasures of bad behavior. What we may call *eccentric gesture* is the kind that, to borrow and extend Hornsey's image of urban planning, moves in the wrong direction, socializes with the wrong people, and disrespects the built environment. Eccentric gestures in the films are performative in that they constitute identity; they do not pretend that there is anything solid beneath the gesture. When Millicent Fritton whistles so archly in *The Belles of St. Trinian's*, the gesture draws attention to itself but not to *anything beneath*. Millicent Fritton, as I see her, does not exist as a *character* but as a series of eccentric gestures that constitute a *performance*. These gestures—the histrionic mannerisms of limb, torso, and face—are erratic and inimitable; they do not *mean* anything and yet they produce *effects*. Bertolt Brecht, in his theory of *gest*, argues that "the first condition for the achievement of the A[lienation]-effect is that the actor must invest what he has to show with a definite gest of showing."[79] A *gest*, in Brecht's theory, is a complex series of gestures that collectively reveal a discrete set of human relations, including patterns of exploitation and cooperation. The alienation effect advocated by Brecht, which draws heavily on explicitly showing the artificiality of performance, is "a technique of taking the human social incidents to be portrayed and labelling them as something striking, something that calls for explanation, is not to be taken for granted, not just natural."[80] Sim's eccentric gestures in *The Belles of St. Trinian's* offer a gest that shows the arbitrariness of the social and conceptual systems of knowledge that govern sexual, gender, and familial identity; they are part of a queerness at work in postwar British comedy that makes visible the ruptured seamlessness of heterocentric logic and calls its claims to naturalness into question. They offer exhilarating glimpses of collapse, of an after-order in which heterocentric structures look *funny*.

While gesture and eccentricity are most commonly associated with performance, I shall also explore other *formal* gestures made by the films that contribute to their ex-centering effects. To suggest that postwar British cinema is formally interesting is considered by some to be more or less heretical. Barr suggests that "one of the depressing trademarks of British cinema has commonly been a form of frozen theatricality," static and stiff, even inert, and euphemistically thought of as "a 'classically' restrained British style."[81] Such an account suggests that a routine dullness is inscribed in the films' very style. In his survey of postwar British film criticism, John Ellis observes how critics declared that "the renaissance of British films [caused by a perceived surge in quality and audience sophistication during and immediately after the war] is deemed to have more or less passed [by the end of the 1940s], and mass cinema will fall back to its old pattern of monotonous entertainment" with static visual style, formulaic narrative, and mannered performance.[82] This book hopes to reevaluate this impression of entertainment by concentrating on a formal eccentricity that is an affront to ideas of monotonous wholes. Formal eccentricity is the discordance—both irritating and enchanting—as constituent parts tumble apart rather than cohere. It is ironic, connotative, even paradoxical. It is what leaves the nagging sense that a film's logic or structure does *not quite hang together*. Sometimes this is the result of the challenges posed by eccentric performance; as chapters 1 and 6 suggest, Margaret Rutherford is a test of any editor's skill as her histrionic gestures make continuity between shots almost impossible. In such an example, formal lack (*not quite* coherent) translates into semantic excess (*not just* this or that meaning). Eccentric form's effects may often be unintended and are usually fleeting; a collapse in continuity, an awkward edit, a shudder as a camera moves, a jarring divorce between image and soundtrack, a suddenly visible boom, a clumsy use of rear projection, or a bad set's compromise of a film's illusion can offer a glimpse of instability enough to shake the security of a film's centered structure. I wish to rescue these elements from critical opprobrium and place them as the subject of my queer analysis.

Such formal eccentricity can spread through a film, even when an eccentric performer makes only a cameo appearance, disrupting confidence in the conventional institutions and systems of knowledge that underpin the imagery. The *way that they are presented* can make such obviousnesses as heterosexual monogamy, biological family, and conventional gender roles look distinctly shaky. Sedgwick notes that "the making historically visible of heterosexuality is difficult because, under its institutional pseudonyms such as Inheritance, Marriage, Dynasty, Family, Domesticity, and Population, heterosexuality has been permitted to masquerade so fully as History itself."[83] Along with eccentric performance, eccentric film form can make these pseudonyms not only visible but *laughable*. This process of making-visible is linked to the idea of artifice; as I explore in chapter 2, the heterocentric homes depicted in these films—and, by implication, the people and relationships within them—look decidedly *fake*, making the performances of heterosexual inheritance, marriage, dynasty, family, domesticity, and population spectacularly and amusingly visible. While the effects can be considerable, the gestures themselves are often small; their fleetingness tethers them intimately to the *glimpse* (and not the more sustained and dominant temporality of the *gaze*). They punctuate films, often in the form of momentary disturbances that poignantly puncture dominant logics. Such poignant glimpses are linked to a history of queer gestures that communicate meanings in times and spaces in which such meanings are impossible or dangerous. Muñoz writes that: "Ephemeral evidence is rarely obvious because it is needed to stand against the harsh lights of mainstream visibility and the potential tyranny of the fact. . . . Ephemera are the remains that are often embedded in queer acts, in both stories we tell one another and communicative physical gestures such as the cool look of a street cruise, a lingering handshake between recent acquaintances, or the mannish strut of a particularly confident woman."[84] Queer gesture represents both an absence (a *not-yet*) and a proliferation (a *not-just*) of meaning; it "signals a refusal of a certain kind of finitude" and, by momentarily punctuating seamlessness, "interrupts the normative flow of time and movement."[85] To spot such gestures requires an attentive analysis that takes close reading as its methodological foundation. While broad thematic and contextual analyses may identify comedies of consensus, close readings attuned to eccentricity glimpse also comedies of queerness. Sarah Street echoes Barr when she writes that mainstream comedies from the era are "'daydreams' of 'timeless, seamless communities' where England is a united family."[86] The film that she uses to exemplify this is *Passport to Pimlico*, which, she argues, marks "the return to wartime solidarity . . . [and] Ealing's refusal to confront the challenges and problems of post-war society."[87] As I shall show in chapter 1, the film is, in fact, punctuated by ephemeral gestures that so destabilize the family (both as heterocentric domestic institution and as metaphor for nation, corporation, and community) that it *laughs forward* a set of semiotic possibilities that *are* disruptively political.

In the chapters that follow, I am promiscuous in my use of theories and I pledge no monogamous fidelity to any one school of thinking. Some theorists are leading players; others make cameos; others make such brief appearances as to be little more than extras. Hand in hand with such a queerly eclectic troupe and with an eye to an eccentricity that evades the constraints of structure, it should be clear that the ambition of these analyses is not to offer new totalizing readings. Attempts to turn the indeterminacy of cultural texts into knowledge are too often exclusionary; I shall attempt to turn our knowledge about these films back into an indeterminacy that can embrace the queer, the contingent, and the *funny-peculiar*. By dismissing no gesture as irrelevant or unworthy of attention—including mistakes, misjudgments, and continuity howlers—I ask what we are to make of a cornucopia of gestures that have been routinely alibied away under the term *eccentric*, used by most critics with no interrogation, no precision, and little appreciation. The term has routinely become a critical end point. I believe that it should be a critical launching point, a first and not a climactic observation. It is not enough to notice that eccentricity *is*; it is necessary also to notice what eccentricity *does*. Some of my readings here may not convince readers, and I hope that those readers will take them up as invitations to add their own interpretations of these gestures to the proliferating range of possibilities. I hope, whatever else, that simply by drawing attention to gestures I make harder the reductive work of any reading that takes a thematic or contextual long view only in order to discover a mythic consensus.

Making It through this Book

The first part of this book—"Coming to Terms"—dedicates three chapters to giving a workout to the ideas that broadly underpin my analysis: *eccentricity*, *queer*, and *comedy*. In chapter 1, I explore what I call *exploding eccentricity*. *Passport to Pimlico* provides a test case for critiquing the assumption that British comic eccentricity is cozy. My close reading suggests that eccentricity in the film is a site of disruption, punctuating the text as a series of explosions, some literal, some metaphorical. The sense of danger in the film becomes clearer when viewed alongside the disturbing and eccentric short film *The Stranger Left No Card* (Wendy Toye, 1952). A historical survey of the idea of the eccentric—including the political theory of John Stuart Mill and Henri Bergson's philosophy of laughter—offers no account that adequately articulates the films' radical and unsettling effects. Ultimately, the poststructuralist writings of Derrida, which deconstruct the notion of centered structure altogether, provide the framework for this exploding eccentricity that supports the broader discussions through the book.

In chapter 2, I investigate how the idea of the *queer* operates in postwar films. Concentrating on the ex-centering of heterocentric structures, I introduce the idea of *domestic drag*. This idea, seen in the family comedies *Young Wives' Tale* (Henry Cass, 1951), *Sailor Beware!* (Gordon Parry, 1956), and *Simon and Laura* (Muriel Box, 1955), applies theories of performative gender to domestic space. The homes in these films declare their status as studio sets and this artifice, which is integral to the comedy, laughs openly at the artifice of heterocentric structures, or what one of the films refers to as "marital bliss." Domestic drag prefigures the Thatcherite idea of pretended family relationships, enshrined in Section 28, but here the pretense is firmly settled as heterosexual and monogamous, suggesting that the naturalness of heterocentric structures is a myth.

In chapter 3, I turn my attention to comedy and, in particular, to the disruptive properties of laughter. Inspired by a sequence in *The Lavender Hill Mob* in which Holland (Alec Guinness) and Pendlebury (Stanley Holloway) *laugh at nothing*, I explore images of this eccentric, unmotivated, undirected laughter that run through postwar comedies. From Lavender Hill, I journey to the streets of St. John's Wood, where Irene Handl plays a giggling neighbor who throws the film's meanings into disarray as she bursts apart a family's home in *It's Never Too Late*. Finally, I analyze how *Laughter in Paradise* (Mario Zampi, 1951) makes family inheritance into a laughing matter.

The second part of the book—"Going over the Top"—takes three recurring motifs from postwar British comedy and looks into their ex-centering effects. In chapter 4, the striking images of ruins, which dominated towns and cities and cinema screens, are analyzed in relation to Walter Benjamin's theory of porous urban life. The bomb sites that provide spaces for children's play in *Hue and Cry* (Charles Crichton, 1947) are read as sites of radical contingency, deconstructed and indeterminate. This imagery of ruination extends to the London-to-Brighton car rally in *Genevieve*, where myriad homosocial triangles and the collapsing body of a vintage car spell the ruination of monogamy. Finally, I revel in Alastair Sim's performance as a bomb-building assassin in *The Green Man* who ruins postwar plans for a leafy suburban utopia.

Chapter 5 explores one of the recurring displays of eccentric film form through an analysis of multiroling. Touching briefly on Alec Guinness's bravura turn as the D'Ascoyne family in *Kind Hearts and Coronets* (Robert Hamer, 1949), I revel in the eccentric oddness of two frame-sharing performances by Alastair Sim in *The Belles of St. Trinian's* and by Norman Wisdom in *The Square Peg* (John Paddy Carstairs, 1959). I frame this doubleness as a literalization of the state of being *beside oneself*. In chapter 6, I consider the queer possibilities represented by the more-than-human animals and wild spaces that pass through the films. In *An Alligator Named Daisy* (J. Lee Thompson, 1955), I argue that secure species boundaries are eroded as eccentricity denaturalizes the human–animal divide and human social and sexual rituals are rendered zoological. Finally, in *Alive and Kicking* (Cyril Frankel, 1958), I consider how the wild provides a glimpse of a space that exceeds the constraints of systems of knowledge and offers queer respite in images of a beauty that exists without meaning and without order. In the inconclusive conclusion, I return to the question of what really changed with *Victim* and ask whether eccentric queerness simply shut up shop as the 1960s began.

Looking at this neat summary, it strikes me as lacking eccentricity. I encourage you, therefore, to read haphazardly and out of order—preposterously, in fact. My hope is that, somewhere along the line, between here and the index, some of my fleeting interpretative gestures interest or even excite you. If they can flag up moments when these films *laugh forward* a glimpse of ex-centering possibilities, then I shall be delighted. Like Sidney Stratton's suit, I hope this book can unravel productively to reveal a queerness that lies not in dirt-repellent arguments or academic labor or intellectual capital, but in a transgressive bubbling of eccentric possibilities.

Part One

Coming to Terms

1

Exploding Ex-Centricity

Few British films from the postwar era have attracted as much critical attention as *Passport to Pimlico* (Henry Cornelius, 1949). With its bomb-blasted landscape that still bears the visible scars of the blitz, the film may be read as a visual expression of London's postwar cultural moment. Conflict echoes through the film, and it is a series of explosions—literal and metaphorical—that drives its unruly comedy. These explosions detonate in a city whose atmosphere is already pressurized by a heat wave, continued rationing, and substantial state intervention in the lives of citizens.[1] The first explosion goes up when children larking about in the Pimlico district accidentally roll a large wheel into a pit inhabited by Pamela, a leftover Second World War bomb (see fig. 1.1). The blast from this arbitrarily feminized device injures no one and uncovers a hole filled with fantasy objects: a picture of a glamorous pinup, a treasure trove, and a clutch of legal documents. These objects represent a world of possibilities in the aftermath of conflict and light the blue touch paper for the film's second—more figurative but no less deconstructive—explosion. Erupting with the unnerving tinkle of a pocket-watch alarm and the roar of a stentorian voice, Professor Hatton-Jones (Margaret Rutherford) dominates the subsequent coroner's inquiry with her revelation that this sun-scorched corner of London is, legally, part of Burgundy.

In her gleeful de-Britaining of the district, Hatton-Jones is hardly a character at all; she is a series of inimitable gestures, bound together loosely by a tweed cape and an unforgettable face. She has

Figure 1.1. The first explosion goes off in *Passport to Pimlico* (Henry Cornelius, 1949). *Source:* Ealing Studios/Courtesy of STUDIOCANAL.

no background and no future; she has ambition, but only to outsmart a galaxy of unseen intellectual rivals; the film offers her no first name, no family, no home life, and, barring some strained signifiers, no gender. Her presence is functional, and that function is to cause havoc. In his account of the film, Barr remarks that in the case of *Passport to Pimlico* and the earlier *Hue and Cry* "both adventures are 'released' by eccentrics."[2] The question that percolates through this chapter is: What should "eccentric" signify in relation to postwar British comedy? My first observation is that it marks a disturbance of the status quo. With *Passport to Pimlico* (and, indeed, the other comedies explored in this book), Barr's use of the word "released" is too weak, a fact perhaps acknowledged by his use of scare quotes. "Detonated" would be a better term. Like Pamela, the professor eccentrically rearranges the landscape and offers, when the dust has settled, a glimpse of something different.

This eccentricity is in part a result of Rutherford's remarkable physicality during the coroner's inquest that follows the discovery of the buried treasures. Rutherford once claimed, with good cause, that she had "every twitch and ripple of [her] body under control."[3] At the inquest, there is a sense of both control and abandon as she writhes and contorts her way through the sequence. She inflates; she vibrates; she is never still. As her body moves—including her jowls, implausibly both solid and liquid as their heavy matter cascades and flows with an uncanny grace—it is impossible to pin her down. She is expertise on the go. Christine Geraghty, quoting Anthony Giddens, argues that postwar "modern life . . . depends on the willingness of people to trust in 'systems of technical accomplishment or professional expertise,'" but from the mouth of Professor Hatton-Jones, this expertise is slippery and dangerous.[4] When she instructs her audience to "picture a battlefield," her history lesson declares itself as performance, its truths constituted (and not merely described) by the force of their telling. The history for which the professor is the mouthpiece is not straightforwardly *true*; with compelling charisma, she offers a histrionic performance that is *not quite* credible. And the fact that the professor's performance is able to disturb something as seemingly solid as national identity implies that those systems of knowledge through which structures of identity are understood and articulated are, themselves, elaborate social fictions. More than simply a figure of "whimsical realism," the eccentric professor is a destructive angel, an emissary from beyond the real world represented elsewhere in the film who brings glad tidings of the death of common sense.[5]

Passport to Pimlico is, by any account of the period, a major film. Nevertheless, it is often mistaken for a cozy story whose meanings ultimately validate consensus, community, and calm, an ethos of "enthusiasm and idealism."[6] It has been slackly addressed as the soft and soapy variety of quality film that lacks the panache and punch of the darker stylings of *Kind Hearts and Coronets* (Robert Hamer, 1949) and *The Ladykillers* (Alexander Mackendrick, 1955). At times, Rutherford's presence is listed as one of the film's reassuringly cozy ingredients; in postwar comic cinema she is popular and ubiquitous (a fact captured by Durgnat's reference to her simply as "La Rutherford") and, perhaps as a direct result, mistakenly thought of as benign.[7] To hail her performance in *Passport to Pimlico* as endearingly dotty would be a critical defusing of a positively explosive turn. Hatton-Jones—a force more than a character—is not (just) benign. Gone is the straightforward binary of British wartime propaganda, in which ally and foe are straightforwardly opposed to one another. Pamela, a Nazi bomb, goes up, not with the violent destructiveness of the blitz but with the din of a merry anarchy in which community and individual statuses are challenged. Hatton-Jones performs puckish *mischief* that is outside simple moral schemas and makes the naive certainties of national, familial, and sexual identities look ridiculous. In short, Pamela, the professor, and the film more generally are *eccentric*. In order better to understand this explosive mischief, it is useful to survey theories of eccentricity. A close reading of moments from *Passport to Pimlico* will then allow the testing of these theories and begin to build a more exact vocabulary for the articulation of postwar comedy's effects.

Making Trouble at Mill

What follows in this chapter is not intended as a definitive definition of eccentricity—such a thing would be both inconceivable and unhelpful. It is, instead, designed to encourage a more rigorously engaged critical use of the term. Henry Hemming points out that "originally eccentric was written as 'excentric,' meaning 'out of the centre' or 'away from the centre.'"[8] This rudimentary etymological insight will return throughout this chapter to guide an understanding of the term and what it means for postwar British comedy. Writing just four years before the release of *Passport to Pimlico*, the French journalist Pierre Maillaud identifies living "out of the centre" as a peculiarly English quality and insists on its benevolent impotence:

> A distinctive feature of English society is its ability to produce individuals who do not challenge the social order but choose to break away from conformity by singular pursuits and harmless oddities. I mean primarily the eccentrics. . . . The true English eccentric has two great merits which raise him above his foreign competitors: his eccentricity does not depend upon his wallet; and he is not an exhibitionist. He does not demand any audience but himself. Sometimes he even hides, not out of fear, but to

enjoy his hobby all the more. He is an example not only of sheer harmless individualism but of the contentment that life can offer to the wise if it is crossed on a few selected and original stones instead of by the communal bridge.[9]

Maillaud's repetition of the word "harmless" strikes me as a case of the critic protesting too much and his portrait's emphasis on reclusion, "the quixotic," and adherence to the social order does not tally with the spectacle of the charismatic, order-busting Professor Hatton-Jones.[10] There is no settled reason why onscreen eccentrics should necessarily resemble off-screen eccentrics, but Maillaud's dampening of the potential for challenging social order strikes me as performative; his words do not describe but *constitute* a form of out-of-the-centeredness whose threat to the center of power has been defused.

Paul Langford, in his study of the history of English national identity from 1650 to 1850, identifies eccentricity as one of six defining English characteristics, invented (as a politically softer variant of *originality*) in order to control potential anarchy by emphasizing that the norms existed in the form of "some 'centricity' from which the eccentric had deviated."[11] Hemming recognizes this tendency to control and defuse when he argues that the term *eccentric* encases disordering oddness "like the corpulent arms of an overbearing matron, and this, strangely, is where its power lies. It can be used to extinguish the explosive potential of a marginal person or idea by holding them close."[12] I see this extinguishing of explosive potential in Maillaud's postwar journalism and in film criticism such as Street's description of Rutherford's "ebullient, affectionate presentation of eccentricity."[13] My hope is to relax the corpulent arms of such criticism and to leave *Passport to Pimlico* to explode in an unconstrained comic display of disorder.

Disorder—or at least innovative challenges to existing order—are embraced as a defining part of eccentricity in the political theory of John Stuart Mill. Inspired by his impression of Romantic solipsistic individualism, Mill proposes that the social function of the eccentric lies in defamiliarizing the normalized, naturalized ideological patterns of a particular culture. He presents eccentricity as a socially necessary antityrannical energy; "even despotism does not produce its worst effects, so long as Individuality exists under it; and whatever crushes individuality is despotism, by whatever name it may be called."[14] He argues that conformity without idiosyncrasy is a bar to both individual happiness and social progress; the danger that he identifies lies in the fact that "the majority, being satisfied with the ways of mankind as they now are (for it is they who make them what they are), cannot comprehend why those ways should not be good enough for everybody."[15] It is in the transformation of this majority that eccentricity performs its fundamental role; "the first service which originality has to render them, is that of opening their eyes: which being once fully done, they would have a chance of being themselves original."[16] The eccentrics in postwar comedies often represent the shock of the extraordinary, a startling intrusion into the everyday. Written in the 1850s, but still resonating a century later in a postwar Britain that so often sought to cling on to the comforting systems of knowledge that had been more firmly in place before the war, *On Liberty* declares that "the despotism of custom is everywhere the standing hindrance to human advancement."[17] In *Passport to Pimlico*, the despotic custom that insists that *Londoner*, *Englishman*, and *British citizen* are all stable identities is trounced by the professor who eccentrically redesignates Pimlico as Burgundy. As Mill makes clear, such an enterprise is useful:

> Precisely because the tyranny of opinion is such as to make eccentricity a reproach, it is desirable, in order to break through that tyranny, that people should be eccentric. Eccentricity has always abounded when and where strength of character has abounded; and the amount of eccentricity in a society has generally been proportional to the amount of genius, mental vigour, and moral courage which it contained. That so few now dare to be eccentric, marks the chief danger of the time.[18]

In the postwar moment of the late 1940s, tyranny—whether by European dictators or by unaccommodating convention—remained a current concern. Echoing Mill, the British writer Harold Nicolson published a pamphlet in 1946 on "The English Sense of Humour," in which eccentric humor is pitched explicitly against the kind of totalitarianism that had devastated Europe. He shares Mill's faith in eccentricity's capacity for social critique: "the English, being by nature eccentrics, have an instinctive dislike of the adult pattern of society, and . . . they tend, not so much to attack the pattern directly, as to seek comfort and relief in the constant representation of those unconditioned members of society (the child and the naïve) by whom and which the pattern is exposed to consoling, rather than to disturbing, criticism."[19] While this account argues that such critique remains useful, it nevertheless presents it as ultimately toothless. Nicolson's image of the child—unconditioned but consoling—is at odds with the Pimlico children who blow up Pamela (or, for that matter, the bomb-slinging St. Trinian's girls), who resonate more with "the wondrous anarchy of childhood" that Jack Halberstam presents as queerly subversive.[20] Although Mill and Nicolson both make clear how crucial it is for the political and intellectual health of a society to disturb the petty tyrannies of centers (or patterns), neither writer ultimately observes within eccentricity the capacity for radical social upheaval. Nicolson's recognition that laughter is a "valuable lubricant in the machine of society" does not suggest that eccentric comedy might, instead, blow up that machine.[21]

Humiliating Eccentrics with Bergson

Nicolson draws attention to the relationship between eccentricity and humor.[22] The most sustained discussion of this relationship is in Henri Bergson's *Laughter: An Essay on the Meaning of the Comic* from 1900. Bergson argues that comedy performs the social function of bringing the inflexible or obstinate into line with the majority. Laughter—which "always implies a kind of secret freemasonry, or even complicity, with other laughers"—unites this majority in a ritual of humiliation targeted at "*mechanical inelasticity*, just where one would expect to find the wide-awake adaptability and the living pliableness of a human being."[23] Bergson makes clear that the rejection of this automaton-like inflexibility has an ethical dimension; individuals, including dramatic characters, are made rigid by vice that exists as a "ready-made frame into which we are to step" and by which we are constrained.[24] Such vice is presented as a poison that rigidifies the individual until it is "neutralised by other secretions," namely laughter, "the specific remedy."[25] This theory has much in common with a dominant theory of humor deriving from the political philosophy of Thomas Hobbes (whom W. H. Auden describes as the spokesman for "clever nasties") that suggests that humor stems from a feeling of superiority; people laugh at what is inferior to them, the process reassuringly anchoring their own status and punishing the object of their laughter.[26]

In an inversion of Mill's theory, Bergson uses the term *eccentricity* to refer to the rigidity that threatens social progress. Eccentricity is the vice corrected by laughter:

> Society will therefore be suspicious of all *inelasticity* of character, of mind and even of body, because it is the possible sign of a slumbering activity as well as of an activity with separatist tendencies, that inclines to swerve from the common centre round which society gravitates: in short, because it is the sign of an eccentricity [*excentricité*]. . . . Society is confronted with something that makes it uneasy, but only as a symptom—scarcely a threat, at the very most a gesture. A gesture, therefore, will be its reply. Laughter must be something of this kind, a sort of *social gesture*. By the fear which it inspires, it restrains eccentricity . . . and, in short, softens down whatever the surface of the social body may retain of mechanical inelasticity. Laughter, then, does not belong to the province of esthetics alone, since unconsciously (and even immorally in many particular instances) it pursues a utilitarian aim of general improvement.[27]

For Bergson, the norms that are situated at society's center must be preserved; eccentricity must be mocked into conformity. He associates this center with spontaneity and freedom, despite the regularity and routine—or what Mill calls the tyranny of opinion—that must accompany any concentric structure arranged around a shared set of centric values. Bergson links eccentricity with gesture, but this gesture has lost its fleeting strangeness and is rendered so leaden and habitual that its effects become stagnant. Bergson diminishes the political potential of these gestures until they are "scarcely a threat," although he admits to more nervousness when he concedes that eccentric automatism is something that society "must now dread."[28] The laughter that Bergson identifies as the corrective to this deviant eccentricity—which sets out to "repress any separatist tendency . . . [and] readapt the individual to the whole"—operates through fear in order to produce a "general improvement" that is a form of social homogenizing.[29] This, in the history of queer gesture, is the cruel laughter of prejudice that coerces the sexually unconventional or gender nonconforming to toe the line, and risk being punished when "he [or she] abandons social convention."[30]

Bergson's theories are not in sympathy with the instances of eccentricity that I discover in the films of postwar Britain. His theory does not apply in a postwar moment that marks a rupture in modernity's seamlessness, in which the UK's systems of knowledge previously believed to be unshakable (including the obviousness of imperial, sexual, gender, and class hierarchies) are collapsing and not yet securely replaced. In this climate of social change for the nation, the "common centre round which society gravitates" is harder to define.[31] It is instructive to test the specifics of Bergson's claims against Rutherford's eccentricity in *Passport to Pimlico*. Bergson associates eccentricity with absentmindedness, and Hatton-Jones displays this quality in a manner familiar from a thousand film depictions of academics; she is so engrossed in the historical documents that the coroner has to cough several times to attract her attention. Bergson argues that this obliviousness can mark the conflation of a person with their professional function; Hatton-Jones is largely defined by her profession, but it is not the case that she is laughed *at* for being a professor but rather that her professional platform empowers her to grandstand amusingly. Bergson describes the comic effect when "an eccentric wears an outmoded fashion," and Hatton-Jones's Edwardian stylings—her frill-fronted blouse, collared cape, and high-perched hat—do seem amusingly out of place and time in a film that opens with a shot of a young woman sunbathing in a contemporary bikini.[32] But Bergson's argument that the "inert rigidity of the covering" shrouds the "living suppleness" of the body beneath overlooks the dovetailing of bubbling frills and cascading cape with Rutherford's unpredictable, writhing body; the grandiloquent motions of flesh and cloth move independently but in sympathy.[33] She is, contrary to Bergson's insistence that a deadening repetition is fundamental to automatism and eccentricity, always adapting, changing direction both rhetorically and physically; Rutherford's repertoire of facial and bodily gestures is too diverse to allow for real repetition and any accusation of sameness is based on inattentive watching. Her eccentric body is anything but rigid, eschewing the habitual and becoming, in the process, mobile play incarnate.

Most significantly, Hatton-Jones is not humiliated. Even a potentially embarrassing moment when her watch alarm goes off passes uneventfully, suggesting an eccentric imperviousness to social awkwardness. There is a mean-spirited Hobbesianism that courses through Bergson's theory, in which laughter's "unavowed intention [is] to humiliate, and consequently to correct our neighbour" but the laughter generated by Hatton-Jones in this sequence is not spiteful as described by Bergson.[34] Nor is it sentimental. Street suggests that "what is notable about Rutherford is that . . . rather than present eccentricity to be humiliated through laughter, her performances instead generate more positive affectionate, endearing attitudes towards her characters."[35] I agree that there is no humiliation but I query the emphasis on affection. I find Hatton-Jones less endearing than impressive. The local residents laugh as she compares herself with Joan of Arc, but the comparison is not as fanciful as it first appears: she too envisions a new world and leads a revolt against a state. The locals' laughter is detonated by the historian's revelations as she, without second opinion or legal expertise, liberates Miramont Place into the freedom of statelessness. She is the master of ceremonies in a burlesque theater of threat as, unpredictable, she stirs up laughter at the heart of the sacred seriousness of a coroner's court; Bergson argues that "those engaged in ceremonies appear mechanical" but in *Passport to Pimlico* it is precisely the eccentric who startles the drab coroner out of accustomed routine to the sound of surprised laughter.[36] If Bergson's laughter makes visible the fact that our semblance of "freedom conceals the strings of a dancing Jack," then it is the eccentric professor who cuts the strings of the Burgundians, liberating them into chaotic self-determination from the manipulations of a state puppeteer.[37] I agree with Bergson's claim that all art "has no other object than to brush aside the utilitarian symbols, the conventional and socially accepted generalities," but I argue that in postwar cinematic art it is eccentricity that makes this object attainable.[38]

Neither Mill, Nicolson, nor Bergson offers a definition that can answer the question of what "eccentric" signifies in relation to postwar British comedy. None of their theories embraces the possibility that it can be a political force that dynamically dismantles centric myths—including the heterocentric. Whether a minor threat to social convention or a gentle source of innovative progress, these definitions do not embrace a potential for more deconstructive mischief. And yet watching and rewatching continues to convince me that postwar comedy films' eccentricities *do* more than this, *threaten* more than this, and that the obvious eccentric characters are not the extent of the eccentric mischief on display. The articulation of an *explosive* eccentricity, one that disrupts knowledge and identity as the professor does, requires an alternative theory.

Deconstructing the Center

Mill, Bergson, Nicolson, and Maillaud—despite the differences between their arguments—agree that eccentricity is a feature of single, definable characters. Although Hatton-Jones is an eccentric feature in *Passport to Pimlico*, the film's challenges to centric ideas are not restricted to her role. Any theory that is to provide an understanding of the term that can be profitably applied to postwar comedy cinema needs to uncouple *eccentricity* from character alone and consider film form more generally. The work of deconstructionists, and Jacques Derrida in particular, offers an approach to the idea of centered systems of knowledge that gestures toward just such an idea of eccentricity. Bergson suggests that initially, before "society avenges itself for the liberties taken with it," a reader or viewer passes through a phase of sympathizing with an eccentric character and treating them "as a playmate."[39] I want to take up Bergson's idea of play and extend it beyond his limited application; what these postwar films offer is not an inconsequential game, but deconstruction's free play of meanings. John Caputo argues that *deconstruction* itself remains an undefinable term precisely because any static definition would impose a limit on its play; "it would bring peace to all the restlessness, order to the chaos, locate the center of its eccentricity."[40] The relationship between a notion of eccentricity and the demythologizing of heterocentric norms becomes clearer if one concedes that deconstruction

> describes a world that fluctuates between steady sense and shocking surprise, between settled convention and unsettling interventions. It seeks out the eccentric rather than the center, the margins rather than the middle, the ellipsis or the hyperbole rather than the mean, the parasite rather than the host, the subversion rather than the norm, the

supplement rather than the original, the copy rather than the exemplar, the representation rather than the presence, the impossible rather than the possible, the specter rather than bodily presence.[41]

Hatton-Jones is one element of a deconstructive intervention: the unsettling, elliptical, hyperbolic, subversive representative of the impossible possibility of liberation. This play—of meaning, identity, truth—is significant in "Structure, Sign and Play in the Discourse of the Human Sciences," Derrida's first substantial engagement with the idea of the center, and so, by implication, with the idea of eccentricity. In it, he discusses a rupture in human thought that has ushered in a new sense of the concept of structure. This new awareness allows a dissection of the structurality of structure in which the operation of the center becomes visible:

> The function of this center was not only to orient, balance, and organize the structure—one cannot in fact conceive of an unorganized structure—but above all to make sure that the organizing principle of the structure would limit what we might call the *play* of the structure. By orienting and organizing the coherence of the system, the center of a structure permits the play of its elements inside the total form. And even today the notion of a structure lacking any center represents the unthinkable itself. Nevertheless, the center also closes off the play which it opens up and makes possible.[42]

The structure—of a field of thought, a system of knowledge, an individual text—is anchored by the operation of a center that holds the structure, right to its perimeter, in an organized, secure form. Such centers, as Derrida points out, have been given "different forms or names. . . . It could be shown that all the names related to fundamentals, to principles, or to the center have always designated the constant of a presence—*eidos* [essential form], *archē* [origin], *telos* [end], *Energeia* [actuality], *ousia* (essence, existence, substance, subject)[,] *alētheia* [truth], transcendentality, consciousness, God, man, and so forth."[43] Through the history of Western philosophy and art, Derrida argues, these centers have given structure to systems of thought that ultimately have limited the semantic and political play of ideas, idealities, and identities. This has included the play of the queer, constrained and curtailed by heterocentric teleologies (orientated toward biological reproduction and inheritance), archaeologies (focused back on the insistences of biological and cultural roots and creation myths that remind us unamusingly that nothing began with Adam and Steve), and truths (dedicated to a poorly grounded argument that Nature, God, and the Enlightenment idea of reasonable Man abhor nonnormative sexual desire and behavior).

Derrida's intervention is to mark the problem of all centers, a problem effaced throughout the history of Western thought. He argues that the center must be part of the structure in order to govern it, but must also be separate from the structure in order to maintain sufficient autonomy to escape the play that threatens other elements of the structure. This paradox results in structures whose centered structurality is "contradictorily coherent" and impermanent.[44] The reassurance of familiar systems of thought—around, for example, the rightness of biofamily, the parallel logics of genetic and financial inheritance, the unique value of lifelong monogamy, the natural law of private domestic property that every Englishman may defend, the British national birthright expressed through imperial conquest and management—is centered not on eternal truths but on cultural contingencies. Narratives that seek to substantiate these claims in relation to a centering God, Nature, Man, or History are ultimately spurious, offering discourse as truth. Derrida suggests that periods of "decentering" have coincided with moments of dislocation in which European culture has been "forced to stop thinking about itself as the culture of reference."[45] Postwar British comedies—not despite but, rather, as a function of their laughter—register a dislocation in the war-scarred nation. For the first time since the Enlightenment and the Industrial Revolution, Britain was becoming globally ex-centric, no longer the geopolitical center that both permitted and constrained the world's play, most obviously through the empire, which was, by 1945, in a decline that would see the pink areas of the map diminish significantly by 1960, corroding heterocentric myths of reproducing the nation.

The strength of Derrida's poststructuralist argument is that eccentricity is not understood in relation to a secure center; rather, eccentricity is *a mechanism for exploding the myth of a stable center.*

Derrida presents a history of Western systems of thought in which one flimsily contingent center replaces another, each substitution an evidence of the uncertainty of the structure: "the entire history of the concept of structure . . . must be thought of as a series of substitutions of center for center, as a linked chain of determinations of the center."[46] The certitude offered by each center, which allows cultural anxiety to be mastered, is an illusion only. And the rupture that has made this structurality visible to Derrida and other theorists coincides with a postwar moment in which conventional significances have lost their stability. For the first time in any of the theories of eccentricity, the center against which the eccentric is defined is radically destabilized. Now, the originary, teleological, robust center is reimagined as a mere substitute, temporary and additional, replacing another substitute that was, in turn, also lacking solidity: "Henceforth, it was necessary to begin thinking that there was no center, that the center could not be thought in the form of a present-being, that the center had no natural site, that it was not a fixed locus but a function, a sort of non-locus in which an infinite number of sign-substitutions came into play."[47]

Eccentricity in this theoretical model is not simply in an erratic orbit around a stable center; it is the irreverent gesture that pulls the rug out from beneath any attempt to center meaning at all, subversively chuckling as it exposes the centric as always-already mythic. In "Ellipsis," Derrida queries whether "excentricity [is] a decentering," suggesting that it is not, because there was never a center to be decentered.[48] In the light of this poststructuralist model, *eccentric* does not simply mean odd; it is, more scandalously, the deconstructive principle at work in all structures. All fields of thought, systems of knowledge, and individual texts are eccentric—that is, ex-centered—because the centers on which they rely are always only posing and always only passing. The political significance of this is profound as it is only through the insistent belief in false centers that prejudiced violence against the marginalized becomes possible. To conform to the centers in whose names discrimination occurs is to accept the constraint of free play and to trade an array of possibilities for an illusion of stability. In the fractured atmosphere of a society rebuilding itself, the postwar years gave license to a startling onscreen depiction of this eccentric world in which the familiar centering myths suddenly looked sadly funny. From my queer perspective, these comedies eccentrically undermine the stable heterocentric mythology in such a way that "traditional binary pairing . . . [such as centric–eccentric, normal–abnormal, heterosexual–homosexual, masculine–feminine, and so on] no longer functions by the privilege given to the first term over the second."[49] Just as queerness is not straightforwardly opposed to normativity, eccentricity is not that which is against, outside, or other than the centric. It is more radical than that. It is the agent behind enemy lines, the Trojan horse, which reveals that there is no line and there are no opposing forces. It is the explosive energy that blows apart the structure from within and makes visible the contingency of all centers. It is the liberation of structures into play and the collapse of the idea of total order and meaning.

In his critique of totalization, Derrida recommends instead *solicitation*. Totalization trades in the same certainties, the same mythocentric constraints on conceptual play, as totalitarianism; it seeks to describe—and dominate—the totality of a text or system of knowledge by governing it according to a reductive formula. Deriving from the Latin for *shake*, solicitation represents the alternative process of shaking a structure in order to reveal the absence on which its authority rests. With its suggestion in English of sexual nonconformity, *solicitation* becomes a valuable means of articulating how queerness interjects in the totalizing history of interpreting these texts, shaking criticism free from complacent assumptions about coziness and coyness and community-as-family, and finding, instead, an eccentricity that "obeys the principle of discontinuity" and marks a "*rupture* with totality."[50] In step with the restless questioning of the myths of identity in the postwar period, this demands "a dislocation of our identity, and perhaps of identity in general . . . [as] the origin or alibi of all oppression in the world."[51] The figures, whose dance through the worlds of postwar comedy leave those worlds shaken and ex-centered, eschew clear identity; Hatton-Jones cannot be pinned down according to any social group or type. Such characters are not defeated or denied and the laughter that surrounds them is a reckless and subversive laughter that shakes the structures that might constrain them. What I am preposterously calling *laughing forward* opens up proliferating possibilities that amount to an "infinity (as infinitely other) [that] cannot be violent as is [finite, limiting] totality."[52] The futures that are made glimpsable by eccentricity are futures in which systems of thought and the behaviors that they condition no longer cohere around a false center. These are the futures that I glimpse in *Passport to Pimlico*.

Taking a Stranger Route Back to Pimlico in *The Stranger Left No Card*

Whether this deconstructionist theory of eccentricity can ultimately help to illuminate a reading of postwar British comedy can only be determined through testing. This process necessarily involves close reading, attentive to the ex-centering gestures through which a structure's centered structurality is shaken (or solicited). This testing will see a final visit to Pimlico, but only after a detour to the unnamed town of *The Stranger Left No Card* (Wendy Toye, 1952). This film is not typically regarded as a comedy and its final reveal as a form of murder mystery seems to constrain and not open out meaning. I wish, however, to suggest that the film displays the danger that eccentricity poses to systems of knowledge. Derrida argues that a totalizing centered structure "*takes on meaning* by anticipating a *telos* . . . [and] risks enclosing progression . . . [by] stifling force under form."[53] *The Stranger Left No Card* offers a useful opportunity to explore this constraining teleological form that will, in turn, allow a new and more eccentric reading of the climax to *Passport to Pimlico*. Christopher Norris notes that hermeneutic interpretation typically regards itself as "a quest for order and intelligibility among the manifold possible patterns of sense which the text holds out to a fit reader."[54] The readings in this book are on a different quest; to glimpse the alternative, uncentered futurities that flicker through the films.

The Stranger Left No Card is a twenty-three-minute-short film that tells the story of a *funny-peculiar* stranger (Alan Badel) who arrives in an unnamed English town and signs into a hotel under the name "Napoleon." He delights the local population with his unpredictable and wacky antics until he finally and shockingly commits the crime for which he has come to the town. Very little has been written about the film, despite the fact that Jean Cocteau called it a masterpiece and it won the Cannes Film Festival's Palme d'Or du court métrage. William Fowler and Vic Pratt have reclaimed it as a gem from "the lesser-explored territories of British film."[55] They place the film within a postwar eccentric tradition that attempts "to come to terms with social advance and anxiety, fearing conformity and homogenization, amidst the strangeness of an uncertain future."[56] Despite a conviction in eccentricity's ability to "throw the potential for a more conformist future into relief," they still identify a clear binary between "the exciting and the eccentric . . . [and] the bland backdrop of the everyday."[57] I read the film differently, as a more radical dismantling of this everyday backdrop and an ex-centering of both social convention and film form.

The film, despite its violent climax, plays with comic form. For much of its length, its seemingly somewhat directionless narrative winds through the streets of the town as the eponymous stranger clowns his way into the affections of the townspeople. His movements are aligned with the rhythms of Hugo Alfvén's *Swedish Rhapsody No. 1*, whose cheery strains set the film's tone, even when they are starkly, shockingly at odds with the violence that unfolds. Despite the careful coordination of Badel's movements with the soundtrack, the stranger does not appear like the automatons described by Bergson. His eccentricity is unpredictable; it innovates, improvises, and creates. Both the music and the character are rhythmic without being reliable, and both reserve the capacity to surprise. It is appropriate that the music, which so defines the film, should be a rhapsody; as the name suggests, its expression is extravagant and its form free. A rhapsodic mood increasingly comes to define the whole town; the crowds of townspeople who gather laugh along with the stranger, even when he parodies esteemed military institutions in the form of marching soldiers. This small act of rebellion against the soldiers' masculine performance (which is, contrary to Bergson's insistence, both entirely conventional *and* entirely automaton-like) is approved by the watching bystanders as they become complicit in the first glimmerings of the stranger's anarchic tendencies. The crowd's laughter is made unnerving not only by its unpatriotic target but also its formal presentation; the film lacks synchronized sound, and the absence of audible laughter leaves an uncomfortable sense of at-oddsness between soundtrack and image track.

Intimations of anarchy run through the film. Alongside the music, the soundtrack is dominated by a voiceover from the stranger that opens with the seemingly innocuous statement that he arrived in town on a windy day. This windiness, however, which has blown him into the lives of the townspeople, will ultimately prove destructive as the stranger transforms into a kind of retributive storm. His first action is to perform a magic trick for children, making an egg disappear in a shower of paper fragments. Having performed the trick, and because he "had no wish to be interviewed," the stranger's broad, hypnotic smile transforms in an instant into a frightening frown that makes the children run away. These crude emotional signifiers—smile and frown—are histrionically performed; both their scale and their rapid change suggest no underlying emotion. In the street, people begin to follow him, a fact that he attributes to their belief that he is "peculiar looking." This visual peculiarity is partly sartorial, but it extends to a whole set of gestures that, despite the wild extravagance of sweeping arm movements and enormous strides, remain unsettlingly indeterminate. He robs objects of their customary function, signing a hotel register with the ferrule of his umbrella; he offers a distorted performance of a theatrical cliché by carrying a rabbit beneath his top hat; he responds illogically to his conditions, extending a hand to test for rain and raising his umbrella despite the fine weather; he abandons the convention of film performance and gazes directly into the lens. These gestures do not center character but, rather, mark out the space in which a character would conventionally reside but where all that can be found is *contingent performance*. The gestures have no meaning, but they do have an effect; they enchant the townspeople and draw them into unconventional behaviors of their own: ogling, spying, cheering, laughing in an ecstatic silent uproar of abandoned mirth. As the stranger pretends to wield a gun, a respectably suited citizen dodges the bullets with the commitment of a playing child. With comic understatement, the stranger says that "I didn't make much of a furor. No more than an earthquake." The danger that he represents is seismic and has the capacity to destroy structures but, even as the town's sense of stability is ex-centered and the residents dance to the stranger's jaunty tune, the extent of the risk remains obscure. Fowler and Pratt suggest that the film presents such an "innocent world that it's hard to conceive of anything going quite so drastically wrong."[58] But this innocence is a myth exploded by the film's gestures; the stranger is both innocent (in more than one way) *and* guilty in a tale in which responsibility and retribution are confused beyond distinction. The townspeople are wrong to imagine him "harmless, quite harmless" not only because he commits a crime but because he threatens to derange all the structures of their familiar systems of knowledge.

The Stranger Left No Card is useful to my study of eccentricity because it makes visible the danger that eccentricity poses to social structure. This is not "scarcely a threat" as Bergson suggests.[59] At the film's halfway point, the narrative changes direction. The charmingly funny fable of an eccentric visitor metamorphoses into a violent revenge tale. It is clear on a second viewing that the revenge is always-already an element of the earlier whimsy (as the stranger violently skewers an apple with his umbrella, for example), but the climactic violence is also a continuation of the first half's eccentricity. The revelations, such as they are, of the final scene are not *answers to* but *amplifications of* the earlier eccentric strangeness that is as harmless as an earthquake. The stranger goes to visit Mr. Latham (Cameron Hall), a local businessman who has appeared only fleetingly in the film up to that point. Precisely halfway through the film, standing in Latham's office, the stranger laughs; it is a laugh made grotesque by a sudden close-up that both reveals and conceals, effacing the space around him and making his face the frame-filling extent of the world for a moment (see fig. 1.2).

Figure 1.2. Eccentric laughter in *The Stranger Left No Card* (Wendy Toye, 1952). *Source:* Meteor Films/Courtesy of STUDIOCANAL.

He performs a series of magic tricks for Latham, repeating them in close-up and gazing steadily into the camera with manic focus. His final trick is to free himself from a pair of handcuffs. He asks Mr. Latham to try the same trick; the businessman drops his initial reluctance and becomes enthusiastic, but he finds himself trapped by the manacles. The stranger then proceeds to remove his outlandish outfit, revealing himself as an ordinary-looking man called Smith who went to jail for a crime committed by Latham. The stranger's coup de grâce is to remove his umbrella's ferrule and stab Latham with an exposed blade. The stranger slips out of the office, seemingly disguised by his new lack of disguise, and boards a train away from the town.

This ending seems to run entirely contrary to my theory of eccentricity. After an initial period of uncertainty, the film appears to resolve in a denouement whose revenge-orientated structure gives meaning to everything that has preceded and reveals that beneath eccentricity lurks something recognizable and identifiable (albeit criminal). The eccentric Napoleon is centered on the killer Smith, complete with backstory and motivation, and the eccentrically aimless comedy is centered by the generic shift into crime story. But such a reading does a disservice to the film's manifold and unruly strangenesses. The scene in Latham's office, as Napoleon slowly evaporates to make way for Smith, plays ironically not only with expectation but also with meaning itself. The stranger's macabre pantomime performs murder as a magic trick. As he begins to change his clothes, he sings one sustained note, a bewildering gesture that has no *sense* to it and only disconcerting *effect*. Many of his clothes are not removed and replaced but inverted and subverted: his waistcoat is changed into a bag, his coat is reversed, and the lining of his top hat is transformed into a trilby. These objects are deranged in a state of eccentric becoming, in which neither appearance nor function is permitted to limit the play of their identity. The stranger's dialogue assumes a kind of childish punning so that language is destabilized like the clothes. As he performs the top-hat-into-trilby trick, he tells Latham that "I never wear a top hat. I mean, not normally." "Normally" floods the conversation with its indeterminate senses of *habitually*, *conventionally*, and *sanely*, threatening the coherence of what is being said. More disturbingly, the repeated refrain "You wouldn't recognize me now, Mr. Latham" finally—and ironically—coincides with the moment in which Latham does recognize him as Smith. The film form plays along with this metamorphosis: Alfvén's *Rhapsody* disappears for a time before returning transposed into a minor key and ultimately beginning a slow crescendo, once more in the major key, which accompanies the remainder of the film as the stranger leaves the scene of the crime and comic levity is obscenely reinstated.

Even as objects, language, and music conspire in this eccentric destabilization of meaning, the film's climax still appears to concern the discovery of solid *identity* beneath assumed *eccentricity*. I wish to suggest, however, that the free play of the stranger is not constrained by Smith and, indeed, that the revelation that Napoleon is not himself does not offer stability but, instead, shakes the very systems of knowledge that typically ground interpretation. Smith cannot stabilize Napoleon because Smith is a self-declared "mere nobody." He is unnoticeable, unmemorable, and disposable. Even his name is too generic to reassure; had he signed the hotel register as *Smith* instead of *Napoleon*, the name would have been no more credible, given that Smith is the time-honored alias under which illicit lovers sign in to hotels. The Smith who undresses in front of Latham loses focus with every layer of clothing he removes. The backstory that he narrates—gratuitously, given that Latham should know their shared past—is inadequate. It is unclear what the crime was, whether Latham deliberately framed Smith, and what made the eloquent Smith unable to accuse Latham at his trial.[60] Before he decides to double as Napoleon, Smith—an "innocent bystander"—was already Latham's patsy, a kind of double who is made to take the blame for someone else. Given the status of homosexuality as still illegal in 1952, the intimacy between the two men and their shared past of criminal practice, is suggestive. Smith—just like the stranger Napoleon—is seemingly without family, without spouse, without children; now, he has even lost the grounding logic of a distinctive name and personality. The climactic scene is of Smith undressing for Latham—and what he uncovers is not a man beneath the costume, but a *space* where the expected centers of name, or family, or history are conspicuously absent. This ending is more unsettling than settled. This is eccentricity; however much a system (whether a town or a text) insists on the knowability of its elements and the teleological inevitability of sense, their meaning remains in play.

The ending of the film retains a final twist, although it, too, is ultimately inscrutable. As the stranger arrives at the train station and boards his train, his voiceover says that "the perfect crime was over. Never in a million years would they guess that the little man who left town that day was their bearded village halfwit. Never in a million years. Never in a million years. Never in a million years." The stranger appears not to notice that his bag—the erstwhile waistcoat—is spilling the little shreds of paper that became his hallmark when he was performing the role of Napoleon. This telltale clue to his double identity is spotted by children. A centric reading might insist that Smith's complacency is ironic, that he is suspected, and that justice will provide a dramatic and moral center to the story. But this is not quite what the film depicts. In Latham's office, the revelation appears to be that Napoleon *contains* Smith, that the ordinary Smith *centers* the extraordinary Napoleon. Beneath the playful surface, Napoleon and his anarchic free play seem ultimately to become *comprehensible* according to a system anchored by Smith's past and his desire for revenge. But the ending reverses this idea. Smith now *contains* Napoleon; the extraordinary Napoleon *ex-centers* the ordinary Smith as he leaks these impossible quantities of paper fragments that are now the nearest thing he has to a solid core. Derrida argues that "play is the disruption of presence" because presence is only ever a result of signification and substitution and not a fully centered status.[61] Smith reels in "the play of absence and presence" as he flickers in and out of existence both beneath and around the fragmentary Napoleon.[62] Now, as Smith boards the train and hemorrhages these ephemeral traces of his alter ego's strangeness, the film confronts the more disturbing fact that Smith is not a coherent structure; he and his detailed plan become incomprehensible again as the film's earlier dream logic reasserts itself and questions the status of everything.

Smith's final speech, delivered as he boards the train chuckling to himself, is *laughing forward* into a future that extends "a million years." The children, who look thoughtful but who pointedly do not share their suspicions with a grinning policeman, for a moment share this future. The film offers it also to its viewers. This is not a fixed future from which policy, practice, or principle can be extracted. It is not a statement in favor or condemnation of vigilante justice or revenge. It is something more enigmatic than that. Latham—representing "the policy-makers, the planners, the intelligentsia, the readers of Penguin specials" who dominated postwar towns across Britain—is exorcised through violent death.[63] Smith is also a planner, and he, too, is exorcised, deposed as center by the paper-fragment traces of Napoleon that he will continue to leak for a million years. The futures that I glimpse in the dangerous and disordered ending of *The Stranger Left No Card* are ones in which identity functions as *mise-en-abyme*, in which planning gives way to chance, in which the individual is liberated from their reputation, and in which childish lack of comprehension is less frightening than the foolishly grinning authorized knowledge of the policeman. If this is a "postwar anti-morality tale" its stance is not simply oppositional but, rather, reveals morality to be yet another contingent substitute that fails to center securely.[64] The film outrageously, eccentrically makes murder into a magic trick and, amid the uncomfortable tension of lingering laughter (seen but not heard in the dismaying spectacle of unsynchronized silent imagery), transforms a moral framework into a hollowed-out center. Uncomfortable for some, this dethroning of conventional morality also allows a glimpse of alternative ways of living unconstrained by centric mythologies; the stranger, who is never just Smith in funny clothes, performs his unassimilable queerness in full view.

Blowing Up South London in *Passport to Pimlico*

The South London area of Miramont Place houses no vengeful killers, or at least none revealed in the course of *Passport to Pimlico*. This, however, is not to say that the film's eccentricity is not deconstructive. I have already suggested that the film is arranged as a series of explosions, the first two of which are the detonation of the German bomb Pamela and the scandalous revelations delivered by Professor Hatton-Jones; the explosion becomes the film's fitting metaphor for unadulterated eccentricity, marking the display of a force that displaces false centers and disarranges the conceptual landscape of structures. In order to understand better the concatenation of explosions that ripples through to the film's conclusion, it is useful to consider carefully the precise achievements of the scene in the coroner's court. Barr, who divides Ealing comedies into cozy daydreams and more radical nightmares, places *Passport to Pimlico* into a mainstream canon of films that celebrate characters and communities who are "quiet, friendly, feet solidly on the ground."[65] This attitude to community is born, according to Barr, of an attitude within the UK to postwar idealism that "could not sustain the energy needed to translate that first fine, careless rapture of 1945 into successful forms"; as the initial optimism under the new Labour government began to wane during the years of privation, rationing, and peculiarly bitter weather, Barr suggests that "Ealing's vision contracts as Britain's vision contracts."[66] Barr tethers this reading to the attitudes and policies overseen by Michael Balcon, head of Ealing Studios and a formidable player in postwar British cinema. But a producer is a false center whose authority does not need to be allowed to constrain the play of a film. This contraction of vision is not what I see when I watch *Passport to Pimlico*. It is perhaps telling that Barr does not devote any attention to the coroner scene; its eccentric gestures and glimpses of proliferating alternative futures would sit uneasily with the image of "cosy parochialism" so often associated with the film.[67]

The first glimpse of the professor, as the coroner coughs to attract her attention, is obscured by the open lid of an ornate wooden chest. The professor, who is rummaging around in the chest, is positioned centrally in the frame but the lid eclipses her face. She appears, Alice-like, to be attempting to climb inside the box. Her failure to acknowledge the coroner is not simply absentmindedness; rather, she is not immediately attentive to his authority. He is expected to provide a centering authority to the court, but she does not at any point permit him to constrain her play (as, later, the Burgundians will not allow the Whitehall representatives of central government to rain—or, indeed, reign—on their parade). When the coroner's cough succeeds in attracting her attention, Rutherford's gesturality becomes visible for the first time. This is gesture not as meaning but as meaning's displacement; it radiates out from the body in a series of flailing limbs that point nowhere and accomplish nothing except to show unruly mobility. The documents, whose translation she is responsible for, are brandished with a kind of abandon that is neither reverential nor simply emphatic. With such gestures—which are the sole ingredients of this performance—she undulates dangerously throughout, her body a quivering playground that, despite its solidity, lacks definitive structure. It is the miracle of Rutherford's screen allure that she should be so instantly recognizable, so always herself, and yet so mobile and unpredictable.

The professor's testimony takes an immediate potshot at history as an authoritative discourse as she disputes the accepted view of "all the major historians." With contempt for authority, she announces that "with the aid of this most exciting document, I am now able to change the course of history." As she screws her face and brandishes the document, a cut reveals the smiling faces of the local residents, seemingly delighted by her theatrical oddness. This moment marks the beginning of the locals' undoing; the professor's extraordinary present-tense changing of the course of history is not speaking only of her discovery about the historical Charles VII but also of undreamed possible futures that will, in their turn, change the course of the history of Britain. As she relates her reimagined story of Charles VII, she assumes the role of storyteller, revealing the narrational process that official history typically effaces. Her storytelling style abandons claims to objectivity and makes merry with rhetorical flourish and theatrical gesture instead. As she segues from the gruesome details of "9481 frozen corpses" slain in battle to the question of whether the duke himself lies among them, her bosom thrashes, casts aside the lapels of her cape and, accentuated by the ruffled blouse, erupts. There is nothing in this gesture of Bergson's insistence on the rigidity of eccentrics; Rutherford is a phenomenon of the moving image, undulating expressively but without clear meaning. The effect of this erratic and unignorable motion is amplified by a cut from the professor with bosom expanded in medium shot to her with bosom contracted in long shot; continuity collapses as the edit cannot keep pace with the unreliable, explosive movements of the professor (see figs. 1.3 and 1.4).

The sequence runs on as a parade of eccentric gestures from the professor. She brandishes the document, whose ability to unlock history assumes a kind of magic, so expansively that she has to lean back at an alarming angle in order to accommodate the movement; she silences the chimes of her pocket watch with a certain sheepishness before continuing as though the interruption never happened; and as she enunciates every syllable of "indubitably" she writhes and cascades, screws her eyes into points, brandishes the documents, and sets her liquid chins in motion. The effect of these gestures is to make the professor hollow; she is gesture without depth. She is a character who exists as performance and it is inconceivable to me that she has a life beyond the narrative of the film. Others may disagree, but I cannot imagine sympathizing with her; structures of sympathy and identification are displaced by disorders of dynamic energy that are amusingly baffling. Harper's objection that "the only ratified conditions

Figures 1.3 and 1.4. Continuity collapses as eccentricity gestures in *Passport to Pimlico* (Henry Cornelius, 1949). *Source:* Ealing Studios/Courtesy of STUDIOCANAL.

[for female characters in Ealing films] were virginity or respectable conjugality . . . [and that] any departure from these norms met with severe punishment" is set into confusion by the professor.[68] She is, as far as can be determined, not conjugal, but it is meaningless to think of her as virginal either. Her existence as a series of eccentric gestures explodes all the terms—misogynistic or otherwise—with which we might discuss her gender or sexuality. Speculation is risible because any answer is unknowable. Like the Fool in *King Lear*, she is summoned into existence according to her capacity to make things visible to others. And, like the Fool, her eccentricity leaves her strangely affectless but affecting; she is unconstrained by shame, and is beyond simple ideas of good and evil, but her words and gestures send shock waves through the small world of Miramont Place. She exorcises the familiar centers of court authority, national boundaries, and capital-h History.

For me, however, the coroner scene is not ultimately about Professor Hatton-Jones herself but, rather, her effect. Her legacy of shaken structures and degraded systems of knowledge does not stop at the gesturing boundaries of Rutherford's performance but defines the remainder of the film. If eccentricity were to be yoked exclusively to (that is, centered in) one particular character, a conservative and cozy reading would become possible; eccentricity, in that case, would be a question of amusing, even distracting, cameos. But this is not the case in *Passport to Pimlico*. Radiating out like ripples—or, perhaps, tidal waves—the professor's impact soaks the entire logic of the film's world. As soon as the professor ends her oration, P. C. Spiller (Philip Stainton), his arms folded and his eyebrows raised, delivers the gag that ends the sequence: "Blimey, I'm a foreigner." This line is largely overlooked by Barr and many other commentators (as is the coroner scene generally), possibly because its comedy seems to be built on an obvious incongruity that needs no further unpacking. But a deconstructionist account of eccentricity invites a return to the notion of incongruity as evidence of the breakdown of a binary logic that insists that a thing simply *is the opposite of whatever it is not*. The laughter that P. C. Spiller's line evokes is a disorientating one—because the line is an outrage to binary logic. The word "foreigner" necessarily means only those people who are *not-I* (and not part of the I-extensions of *family* and *community*). The *I* cannot both retain its integrity and be *foreigner*. The line is a logical paradox, exacerbated by the word "blimey" (a contraction of "blow me") that is still haunted by its function as an imperative, but one directed at no one. In her discussion of national identity, Cook invokes Freud's theory of the uncanny to argue that "the safety of home (*heim*) is inseparable from its strangeness . . . [and that] the place to which we belong is also foreign to us."[69] The radical implication of this is that Home—with its intimate stakes in family, marriage, inheritance, nation—is never a reliable center because it is always also not itself. Cook makes only one fleeting reference to *Passport to Pimlico* as one of the "quintessentially English Ealing comedies . . . [that] are impelled to test national boundaries."[70] I argue that P. C. Spiller's line gestures to more than a testing of national identities; it explodes them in a display of eccentric paradox.

The sequence's ending reinforces the point that Hatton-Jones is effect more than character as a slow pan across the agitated faces of the crowd dissolves into a shot of Whitehall. Throughout the film, the heart of British government is not presented as a place of personalities; Straker (Naunton Wayne) and Gregg (Basil Radford), two Home Office types who are charged to negotiate with the Burgundians on behalf of the government, are cardboard bureaucrats and the well-known figures of Winston Churchill and Clem Atlee are reduced to silent images on a newsreel. Whitehall is an institution, a system of knowledge and power whose authority as the center of state is threatened by the eccentric happenings in Pimlico. Whatever the film's conclusion, the mere fact of the ex-centering of governmental power is a radical stroke that *laughs forward* the possibility of anarchic localism and the rejection of centrally administered constraints. Eccentricity corrupts the strict centrism of the way the British understand power and leaks out into abstract systems of knowledge. Professor Hatton-Jones, then, is not the *site* of eccentricity but its *distributor* and eccentricity is not a personal quality but an explosive energy that reveals the contingency of structures. The danger of character-centered readings—which have overwhelmingly defined studies of eccentricity in films—is that they substitute a *new center*. Hatton-Jones makes for a poor center, not least because she more or less evaporates from the film at this point, reemerging fleetingly on two further occasions in order only to stoke more eccentric deconstruction. In my search for eccentricity, the eccentric character is never a destination and always a complication.

This complication is felt throughout the film, spilling out in a series of comic gestures that give glimpses of eccentric futures. Gallic sexuality is visible in the seduction of Shirley Pemberton (Barbara Murray) by the duke (Paul Dupuis) whose talk of Temples of Love is only interrupted by the intimate sounds of someone gargling and spitting before going to bed; Mrs. Pemberton (Betty Warren) speaks a nonsensical parody of what are understood as British values when she says that "we always were English and we always will be English and it's just because we're English that we're sticking up for our right to be Burgundians"; freedom from rationing is paradoxically maintained through the introduction of rationing with Molly (Jane Hylton) as the smiling new Burgundian minister for food; the devastated modernity of London ruins is made stranger by the spectacle of Frank Huggins (John Slater) searching for water with an anachronistic divining rod; the Burgundians' liberation is also captivity and conservation as dialectic editing draws a parallel with seals in the zoo; the scraps of food lobbed across the "new iron curtain" of barbed wire and checkpoints that surrounds Miramont Place are both sustenance and missiles, showering down on the Burgundians' heads and almost braining Bert (Charles Hawtrey); the upper deck of a bus whose side reads SAVE FOR PROSPERITY is used as the platform from which to hurl food to the hungry Burgundians in an act of unmanaged decadence; and the signs erected to mark the end of the tensions read, nonsensically, WELCOME HOME BURGUNDY and are overseen by Professor Hatton-Jones. There is no fixed locus of eccentricity here; it pops up in diverse ways in diverse places, scattered through the film in the form of paradox masquerading as comic incongruity. This assault on stable knowledge is distilled into the results of a democratic poll about the creation of a lido in Pimlico: 3 percent for, 3 percent against, and 94 percent "don't know." The sphere of the knowable has contracted in this eccentric world.

There remains, however, the problem of the ending. Barr sets the tone for discussions of the film's conclusion when he identifies it as "a deep-rooted nostalgia for consensus" and "a cosy retreat, a soft option, operated not by harnessing and redirecting energies, but by denying them."[71] He concludes that the deal struck between Pimlico and Britain, in which Pimlico loans Britain its gold and the border is dismantled, is "a compromise" symbolized by the celebratory return of "ration book and identity card"; he insists that "never was a message made more explicit" than when Mrs. Pemberton acknowledges that they were better off with restrictions.[72] Barr argues that "the prime 'fantasy' of the film, which caught the imagination so firmly, is not—whatever [the film's contemporary] publicity might suggest—the dream of release from rationing and restrictions. . . . The more potent dream that takes over from it is of a return to wartime solidarity, which means an intensification of rationing and restrictions: in the course of the film, these become truly romanticised."[73]

The image of order restored through the restitution of the previous status quo has defined criticism on the film. Amy Sargeant argues that "eventually, order is restored when the bank loans its treasure to Britain—and even the weather returns to normal."[74] Sarah Street suggests that the film stands in "opposition to post-war restrictions and institutions, [offering] a cosy middle-class outlook and nostalgia for wartime 'community.'"[75] Tim Pulleine suggests that "a supposed celebration of the jettisoning of the wartime restrictions becomes a nostalgic evocation of the wartime spirit of solidarity."[76] But the ending is not so simple as these descriptions of nostalgic reverse or return suggest, because reverse and return have been complicated by the eccentric dismantling of the systems of knowledge that these critics suggest remain intact. Andrew Higson implies some of this complication in his argument that the film goes "to great lengths to reproduce the war-time conditions of siege and insularity and to assert and explore the idea of community, represented by a proliferation of narrative protagonists and a multiplication of incidental narrative lines."[77] Even here, however, proliferation and multiplication ultimately serve the reproduction of community, a lost-and-regained center. My object is not exactly to argue that *Passport to Pimlico* is not a conservative or cozy film but, rather, that it is *not just* a conservative or cozy film. Norris suggests that, in Derrida's work, "the concept of structure . . . functions as a *metaphor* to contain the unruly energies of meaning."[78] I argue that the structures of normality, and community, and solidarity evoked by the critics do not need to be allowed to contain the unruly energies of the fleeting gestures that could ex-center them and preposterously *laugh forward* new possibilities for our future.

The film ends with a celebratory feast. As the film's characters sit to enjoy their alfresco meal, behind them lies the water-filled bomb crater with a sign reading PIMLICO ~~BURGUNDY~~ LIDO (see fig. 1.5).

Figure 1.5. Burgundy *sous rature* in *Passport to Pimlico* (Henry Cornelius, 1949). *Source:* Ealing Studios/Courtesy of STUDIOCANAL.

The crossing-through of Burgundy is an eccentric gesture. Burgundy is not gone but nor is it present; it remains as a trace, disrupting the possibility of Pimlico's replacing it as the anchoring center to the community. In Derrida's terms, this crossing-through places a word *sous rature*, under erasure. Gayatri Spivak explains that "the gesture of *sous rature* implies 'both this *and* that' as well as 'neither this nor that' undoing the opposition and the hierarchy between the legible and the erased."[79] She explains simply that "since the word is inaccurate, it is crossed out. Since it is necessary, it remains legible."[80] The mere fact of a part of London becoming Burgundian is not eccentric. The eccentricity of the situation lies in the fact that Miramont Place is both London and Burgundy, a space beyond identity and without clear boundary. The literal signpost at the film's close gestures to *both* Pimlico *and* Burgundy; neither *Pimlico* nor *London* nor *England* nor *Britain* can recenter this space because it remains also Burgundy, defying structure as it continues, even for a million years, to bear the trace of its own otherness. The final moments of the film lay on a feast of eccentric gestures. The meal does reunite the citizens with their ration cards, as Barr points out, but only as the place settings on a table opulently strewn with lobster and other delicacies. The atmosphere of privation is reembraced, but only alongside shocking waste as the meal is abandoned when rain comes. The rain marks the end of the heat wave, but it cannot erase the unruly possibility of heat that Pimlico will always bear as trace. The image of the diners at a long table beside both blitz-scarred ruins and a duck-inhabited lido is almost surrealist in its confusion of opposites.

Bergson suggests that laughter is the correction of eccentrics. Eccentricity, however, cannot be corrected so easily as it spills out from individual figures and ultimately confuses an entire landscape. In such a landscape, centric structure is visible as myth. *Home*—in the form of Pimlico and Burgundy and England and Europe—is neither the origin nor the destination of the film; it is a space in which the self has lost its self-sameness and the group has become its own other. As the film laughs its way to an ending, the absence of grounding center is not encountered as loss but as ecstatic possibilities. It is, in Derrida's term, Nietzschean and affirmative:

> Turned towards the lost or impossible presence of the absent origin, this structuralist thematic of broken immediacy is therefore the saddened, *negative*, nostalgic, guilty, Rousseauistic side of the thinking of play whose other side would be the Nietzschean *affirmation*, that is the joyous affirmation of the play of the world and of the innocence of becoming, the affirmation of a world of signs without fault, without truth, and without origin which is offered to an active interpretation. *This affirmation then determines the noncenter otherwise than as loss of the center*. And it plays without security. For there is a *sure* play: the *substitution* of *given* and *existing*, *present*, pieces. In absolute chance, affirmation also surrenders itself to *genetic* indetermination, to the *seminal* adventure of the trace.[81]

It is not nostalgia that declares itself to me in *Passport to Pimlico*. Nor is the film "strictly a period piece."[82] Rather, it offers glimpses of an affirmative world at play, without security, where everything and everyone bears the trace of their own other, becoming both *I* and *foreigner*, in an adventure that *laughs forward* to a time that is still not yet here, in which shameless eccentricity displays itself in genetically indeterminate performances of nationality, class, gender, desire, and place—and norms are become so mobile that correction has no reliable standard. Barr sees "the *containing* of violence and personal emotion," which is true if only interpersonal violence is considered, but the shaking—*soliciting*—of institutional structures of identity and knowledge is its own kind of violence.[83] Caputo suggests that the spectrality that Derrida discusses at such length lies, in part, in a political imperative to consider potential futures: "Our beliefs and practices, our constitutions and institutions, can flourish only by being spectralized—that is, exposed to a future they themselves resist."[84] The spectralizing of institutions in *Passport to Pimlico* sees the explosion of both the local council's plan for profit and Pemberton's plan for a heterocentric family lido; what is made visible, through the dust and debris, is a future that includes the erosion of national boundaries and a becoming-French, the privileging of the group over the family, and the rejection of British law (including, necessarily, the statutes that still criminalized homosexuality, abortion, polygamy, and so many other forms of sexual unorthodoxy). Barr presents *Passport to Pimlico* as a nostalgic and escapist daydream of consensus, but I see a tapestry of ex-centering gestures and spectral possibilities that give glimpses of the limitations of systems of knowledge in both 1949 and today, more than seventy years later. This exercise in escapism is neither grounded in nor divorced from reality; it critiques reality precisely by escaping its inescapable logics.

2

Doing the Domestic Drag

THE LIMITATIONS OF HETEROCENTRIC systems of knowledge can be glimpsed in the domestic comedies that were a staple of British cinema during the late 1940s and 1950s. These popular films have received critical attention under a variety of names, including "family comedies" (see Landy 1991) and "comedies of marriage" (see Bell-Williams 2007). Much of the critical focus has been on gender. Melanie Bell-Williams positions the genre as a space in which "to explore post-war ideas about the 'companionate marriage' and the emergence of a 'modern' British society" including "anxieties about the 'new' and the 'modern' [that] are displaced onto the female protagonists."[1] She identifies "a degree of gender radicalism" in the films but sees this as ultimately serving a model of monogamous marriage through narratives of "heterosexual couples who face a crisis in their relationship which has to be resolved for domestic harmony to be restored."[2] Ultimately, the critical impression of the subgenre is as formally and politically conservative. Marcia Landy argues that the films' "popularity can be attributed to a convergence of factors: official and media encouragement of familialism in images designed to strengthen family relationships; sociological concerns about crime and juvenile delinquency traced to inadequate family bonds and care of the young; a concern about broken homes—more generally, a retreat from the public arena into the home; the rise of television as a form of family entertainment; and the film industry's attempt to woo straying audiences."[3] In this way, domestic comedies are thematically aligned by critics with other popular films that present flourishing heterocentric homes as a means of social restoration.

These critical snapshots indicate how discussions of domestic comedies have overwhelmingly focused on their relationship to the political context of their production. This context, in relation to the domestic sphere, is complex and ambivalent. The Second World War had substantially upset existing family structures in Britain and the self-evident heterocentrism of monogamous heterosexual marriage had been thrown into a certain amount of confusion. While Lynda Nead argues that British culture associated the symbolic family home with "all that had been fought for during the war and much that was desired and expected of the future," she also presents a country in which "identities and relationships that had been torn apart during the war were now being reassembled, but it was not a straightforward process and everyday emotional life could be messy and conflicted."[4] The homosocial intimacy enjoyed by men in the services, prolonged male absence from the home, women's pleasure in increased professional and social self-determination, and city children's independence cultivated during evacuation to rural parts of the UK all posed challenges to the unassailable national logic of the hierarchical biofamily. Martin Francis gives a snapshot of a historical moment in which anxieties about the future of marriage became firmly linked to anxieties about moral and national degeneration. He outlines how there was "a preoccupation in Britain in the immediate post-war years with the viability of family life, as experts evaluated the long-term consequences of wartime dislocation and sought to explain a recent dramatic rise in the divorce rate. Clergymen, psychologists, eugenicists, social purity advocates, sexologists and social workers, all were mobilised in what [David] Mace [in his 1948 book *Marriage Crisis*] histrionically described as 'the battle of the family.'"[5] In a reimagining of domestic hierarchies, married couples increasingly aspired to equality between the partners (although whether this model of equality permitted women to work outside the home was often somewhat hazy and the extent to which the ambition extended beyond the middle class is unclear). Bell-Williams, citing Judy Attfield, details how research indicates that "many women exercised considerable agency in relation to the home, challenging the figure of the housewife and housework as conceptualised by male, and female, designers."[6]

This is, however, not to argue that British women's limited roles had been entirely revised; the postwar years were a transitional period before the more mobilized, dynamic women's liberation movements of the 1960s, and through the 1940s and 1950s there remained "the dominant notion of woman as wife and mother as perpetuated within 'official' British discourses such as the Beveridge report" and the 1949 Royal Commission on Population, which "understood the wife to be the husband's companion."[7] Although "considerable changes were taking place in British society regarding the manner in which heterosexual marriage was imagined," the impression that heterosexual monogamous marriage was fundamental to any definition of the home remained hegemonic.[8] Estella Tincknell argues that companionate marriage was conceived as "the 'solution' to male desire and its most effective management" and that the postwar period retained a sense of "the necessity of marriage and procreation, especially to the rebuilding of Britain as a unified nation."[9] Critics of the cinema of the period tend to see this hegemony reflected on the screen in narratives about female characters who, Geraghty suggests, range between the unappetizing stereotypes of the "childish, silly and vindictive or valorised and saintly."[10] Although Francis argues that "cinematic representations at the close of the war revealed a [substantial] degree of female ambivalence about the return to domesticity," his examples include no comedies.[11]

Given monogamous marriage's continued hegemonic function in postwar Britain, neither the broader sociopolitical landscape nor the domestic comedies that reflect it seem to offer substantial promise of eccentric queerness. Tincknell, in her study of "compulsive heterosexuality" in cinema, suggests that, rather dispiritingly, the cinema of this era presents marriage as "the 'true career' which women are supposed to desire and the fate that men must both resist and ultimately succumb to, with, in the case of the comedies, a degree of hearty joshing about the loss of valued homosocial bonds"; comedy, Tincknell argues, "works to endorse the ideal."[12] Such readings made in the light of prevailing cultural attitudes of the period offer important insights into the gender and domestic politics of postwar Britain but they do not explore the fuller range of possible meanings made available by the films to twenty-first-century audiences watching back. I find in the films an abundance of images of domestic disarray and I am not as confident as Bell-Williams that they prioritize the restoration of harmony.[13] I argue that these narratives, when dislocated from their contemporary discussions of the companionate marriage, offer up queerer domestic portraits that give glimpses of sexual and gender nonconformity, interrogating domestic conventions by positioning marriage and parenthood not as *happy-ever-after* endings but as institutions to be laughed at.

Seeing Queerly Now

Part of the challenge posed by these queer domestic portraits arises from the challenge of situating precisely what is meant by the term *queer*. Queer theory both suffers and benefits from the eccentric elusiveness of its ought-to-be-central term. Among its many senses, *queer* has referred to: anything that is odd, unsettling, or ruined; LGBT+ individuals and groups (as slur, reclaimed slogan, and identity statement); a form of relationship, which may or may not include marriage; a nonbiological approach to kinship; a focus on friendship; a range of unconventional approaches to sex, including sex work, BDSM, and even bestiality; an account of the natural that blurs the easy lines between species; a challenge to, redefinition of, or escape from the disciplining apparatus of normativity; a potential market for neoliberal capitalist forces; a trendy marketing tool for films and other commodities; a politics of identity or of desire; a rejection of identity and a complication of desire; a set of performative ways of being in the world; a site of shame (as disparaged or reclaimed affect) and pride (as galvanizing or rejected affect); a productive type of failure; a history of protest, marginalization, and loss; the inadequacy or impossibility of history; a nonlinear understanding or experience of time; future as impossibility or idealization. *Queer* does not mean everything but nor does it mean something in particular. And, with its perverse polysemy, it gives the indistinct impression that there is nothing that falls entirely outside its erratic parameters. As noun and adjective, it can seem to gesture to identity and status; as verb, it withdraws from any semblance of stability and implies a making strange. Like *eccentricity*, *queer* struggles against clear meaning and often becomes more about effect; it is an epistemological thorn in the side of assumptions about sex, sexuality, gender, desire, identity, and reproduction, and the social institutions of family and inheritance.

Doan points out that "the very fluidity and openness of 'queer' has attracted scholars who have discovered its usefulness in dealing with sexualities of the past and the present (and, at the same time, has confused and even angered some nonacademic LGBT audiences who yearn for a usable past)."[14] A straightforwardly *usable* past is beyond the ambitions of this book, but I do hope to suggest that the past of these films is *dynamic* not in its clear vision of *how things were* but in its fleeting glimpses of *how things might yet be*.

With such an unmanageable, irreconcilable plurality of senses, the term *queer* openly proclaims its distinctive *eccentricity*, uncentered by either stable meaning or fixed function. This is, perhaps, unsurprising given the commingling histories of these two terms; "in the nineteenth century, 'queer' designated eccentricity as well as possession of a pronounced character."[15] This streak of unconventionality blossoms into a destabilizing effect that in chapter 1 I argue could be articulated through the poststructuralist terms of Derrida's deconstruction. Christopher Norris describes deconstruction's eccentricity as the "task of dismantling a concept of 'structure' that serves to immobilize the play of meaning in a text and reduce it to a manageable compass."[16] Heterocentric understandings of sexual *orientation* may be seen as a discourse that insists on ideas of manageable compasses. Eccentricity, on the other hand, abandons such mapped structures in favor of what Lee Edelman describes as "the disorientation that queer sexualities *should* entail."[17] Sara Ahmed suggests that sexual *disorientation* "may be the source of vitality . . . [and] giddiness" as it deviates from what José Esteban Muñoz describes as the "normative map of the world."[18] As I suggest in the introduction, this wandering from the straight and narrow is not simply *antinormative*. Eccentric queerness, as I am losing myself in it, is a recognition that this "normative map of the world" is always a work of performative cartographic mythmaking; the normative world does not exist before or beyond the map. Expressing a protoqueer sentiment, Mill writes in the 1850s that:

> In our times, from the highest class of society down to the lowest, every one lives as under the eye of a hostile and dreaded censorship. Not only in what concerns others, but in what concerns only themselves, the individual, or the family, do not ask themselves—what do I prefer? or, what would suit my character and disposition? or, what would allow the

best and highest in me to have fair play, and enable it to grow and thrive? They ask themselves, what is suitable to my position? what is usually done by persons of my station and pecuniary circumstances? or (worse still) what is usually done by persons of a station and circumstances superior to mine? I do not mean that they choose what is customary, in preference to what suits their own inclination. It does not occur to them to have any inclination, except for what is customary. Thus the mind itself is bowed to the yoke: even in what people do for pleasure, conformity is the first thing thought of; they like in crowds; they exercise choice only among things commonly done: peculiarity of taste, eccentricity of conduct, are shunned equally with crimes.[19]

Mill's account of the unnatural home ("they have no nature to follow"), which is devoid of both eccentricity and (queer) inclination, is presented in the minor key of despondent social commentary.[20] The films in this chapter play with the same ideas, but in the major key of popular comedy. The homes in these films are as artificial and as stultifying as the homes in Mill's description, but they are presented as *absurd* rather than sad. Through the fine but disorientating mist of this absurdity, the films ex-center their neatly mapped-out heterocentric structures. They make the workings of heterosexual convention visible by denaturalizing its "institutional pseudonyms" and not allowing them to "masquerade so fully as History itself."[21] Marriage, dynasty, family, and domesticity are eccentrically exposed as flimsy performances that can easily and farcically fall apart. Without dismay or despair, heterocentricity is shown, in a cavalcade of laughable domestic spaces, playing with itself.

This play is naughty. It is both sexy—all the comedies in this chapter are, in their 1950s ways, sex comedies—and violent. Derrida writes that "one could call *play* the absence of the transcendental signified making play boundless, that is to say [a] shaking up."[22] The sexy, violent play of these comedies shakes up the structure of the home in the absence of the transcendental heterocentric signifieds that might otherwise have constrained them. These signifieds may be understood as the cluster of ideas that gather under the term *heteronormativity* and that have historically had "a totalizing tendency" and been mistakenly thought of as present and meaningful.[23] Heteronormativity has been in a constant state of redefinition since it was discussed in Michael Warner's *Fear of a Queer Planet* in 1991. Warner describes how "the logic of the sexual order is so deeply embedded by now in an indescribably wide range of social institutions, and is embedded in the most standard accounts of the world."[24] Given the extraordinary scale of this normative force, Warner suggests that being queer "means being able, more or less articulately, to challenge the common understanding of what gender difference means, or what the state is for, or what 'health' entails, or what would define fairness, or what a good relation to the planet's environment would be."[25] Warner and Lauren Berlant clarify further in 1998 with a definition that stipulates that heteronormativity refers to the "institutions, structures of understanding, and practical orientations that make heterosexuality seem not only coherent—that is, organized as a sexuality—but also privileged . . . as the basic idiom of the personal and the social; or marked as a natural state; or projected as an ideal or moral accomplishment."[26] They trace heteronormativity in "love plots and sentimentality . . . , in marriage and family law, in the architecture of the domestic."[27] It is this architecture of the domestic that is at stake in postwar domestic comedies. I am sympathetic to those viewers and critics who find in these films only further evidence that "homophobia and heterosexism may be read in almost any document of our culture."[28] But I suggest that the play of these comedies also generates a laughter that *shakes* the architecture of the domestic significantly. Heteronormativity—a collective name for the force and effect of heterocentric mythologies—is not straightforwardly stabilized by the comedies but, rather, ex-centered by a series of punctuating gestures that explode any claim to easy restoration of domestic harmony.

It must, however, be admitted that the architecture of the domestic in these films does not, even as it shakes nearly to pieces, fully accommodate the homosexual. For some, such an omission must always leave the postwar films languishing behind later British cinema, which, in the wake of *Victim*, openly speaks the love that hitherto dared not speak its name. I would counter, however, that these comedies do give glimpses of promiscuity, polyamory, and pansexuality, expressions of desire that remain taboo in the UK of the twenty-first century. The films do not suggest these as new norms, new centered elements accommodated by a revised structure. Instead, they suggest that they are disruptive traces always inherent in the domestic structures of fidelity, monogamy, and heterosexuality. The queer does not trade in new exclusivities, new *either/or*s, but in the giddying inclusivity of *both/and* forms that permit no neat concentric structures. The homes in these films are both model homes and domestic disasters; they are both lifelike and artificial; they are both harmonious and discordant. Their signifiers bear the absent-present trace of their own opposites, undoing the totalizing myths that underpin heterocentric prejudice. The queer is the *both/and* at work in the disruption of any play-constraining structure. Laughing at *nice families* is not politically feeble; making their setup look ridiculous is resistance of a high—and often very enjoyable—order. The comic punctuating of cinematic homes with traces of queerness is an act of domestic sabotage that may not champion homosexuality explicitly but does *laugh forward* a queer eccentricity that can still undo twenty-first-century domestic convention.

Misbehaving with Nanny in *Young Wives' Tale*

This queer eccentricity can be seen at work in *Young Wives' Tale* (Henry Cass, 1951). Based on a successful West End farce, the film is a comedy of two marriages. Compromised by postwar housing shortages, Sabina and Rodney Pennant (Joan Greenwood and Nigel Patrick) share a London home with Bruce and Mary Banning (Derek Farr and Helen Cherry). The histrionic Sabina has given up her job as an actor in order to take charge of running her portion of the home and raising her toddler, Valentine. She is domestically unsuccessful: largely unable to manage Valentine, to prepare meals, or to maintain order. Rodney is a writer who works from home and is usually in a state of frustration with his wife's failures. He is, nevertheless, glad to have a wife who does not have a paid job and is therefore a "really womanly woman" with a "fluffy mind" and "no modern nonsense" about her. Mary, in contrast to Sabina, is a successful career woman who hires a nanny to tend to her baby daughter Elizabeth and to oversee the running of the house. She is cool and efficient. Bruce is dismayed by his wife's coolness and, particularly, her career-mindedness; he expresses his envy of Rodney's situation. Mary's one apparent source of consternation is Sabina's reckless habit of irritating the nanny. Because of a somewhat archaic stipulation that a single nanny should only look after biological siblings and not the cohabiting children of different parents, Mary and Bruce's nanny is employed only to care for Elizabeth; Sabina, however, in her disorder, regularly calls for nanny to look after Valentine as well. When Nanny Blott (Fabia Drake) becomes so affronted by Sabina that she quits, Mary takes to the park to find a replacement. She is ultimately successful and employs Nanny Gallop (Athene Seyler). In order to ease Sabina's domestic load, the two couples pretend to Nanny Gallop that Elizabeth and Valentine are sister and brother. Complications arise when Sabina and Rodney have a row, and she, in a fit of pique, kisses both her seedy friend Victor Manifold (Guy Middleton) and Bruce. When Nanny Gallop walks in on Sabina and Bruce kissing, she presumes that they are the parents of the two children. The attempts to maintain the deception in order to retain their nanny while processing their feelings of betrayal and jealousy play out as farce and the household ends up in chaos.

This rather lengthy synopsis demonstrates something of the range of competing tensions in *Young Wives' Tale*: the question of whether women should stay at home or go to work; the disturbances resulting from infidelity; the stresses felt by families sharing one home; the pressures on housing in the years that followed the war; and the challenges of finding and maintaining domestic help. The film has not attracted a substantial body of criticism, but what criticism there is has concentrated on it as a time capsule, an index of postwar debates about gender. In a short entry on the film, Landy argues that it "portrays misalliance and the discontents of professional and domestic women" and "the oppressiveness of all alternatives available to women."[29] In a more developed case study, Melanie Bell presents the film as "a satirical take on the competing demands of work and career from a female perspective."[30] Bell-Williams identifies a gendered and stereotyping binary at work in the use of "the common narrative device of doubling between the central female characters, whose representation is based on the dualism of art and science; the emotional versus the rational."[31] Her driving question is an uncertainty over what made the film a box office failure in 1951 and she concludes speculatively that it was "out of step with the cultural consciousness of post-war cinema audiences."[32] This out-of-stepness stems apparently from the film's lack of "double consciousness," a necessary feature of all popular postwar cinema; Bell-Williams argues that *Young Wives' Tale* lacks ambiguity on the question of gender resulting in the audience, "still largely anchored to the ideologies of gender underpinning the figure of the 'buxom wife' [being made] uncomfortable by the depictions of gender and modernity at play within the film."[33]

Landy and Bell-Williams both produce readings that, while compelling, view the film squarely within the period of its production. It has no meaning in such a reading beyond being an articulation of 1951 concerns. Bell-Williams concludes that "the film, and its commercial failure, stand as a valuable historical document about the extent to which gender norms could be challenged in Britain in the early 1950s."[34] Such a reading structures the film around the seemingly settled center of History, forming a structure about which knowledge can be assembled. My reading, however, is of a film that does not offer such epistemological clarity. It is perverse in its free play with paradox. Roland Barthes presents paradox as the corrective for a "formulated, intolerable" doxa, that is, "a popular opinion."[35] Paradox—along with rhetorical tropes that generate semiotic instability such as irony, allegory, and catachresis—dismantles the orientated structure of *either/or* in favor of a more bewildering *both/and* in which a sign means both itself and its own other. The regime of centered structures does not welcome such reckless freestyling. The paradoxes of the film, played as comedy, unhinge orthodox—postwar *and* twenty-first-century—British opinions concerning gender, sex, family, and reproduction. Reading *Young Wives' Tale* as a stable piece of evidence of a coherent and definable History permits heterosexuality "to masquerade so fully as History itself" and limits the play of the film's paradoxes by overlooking the specificity of contradictory gestures.[36] Allowed the full play of their instability, these gestures remain uncentered and ex-centering. Paradox is the play of queer *both/and*ness that reveals that meaning is more plural and more inconsistent than conventional cultural logic suggests.

One of the representative sites of queer *both/and*ness is drag. Drag upsets heterocentric mythologies by combining aspects of gendered experience that, according to the commonsense logic of these mythologies, should be mutually exclusive. Heterocentric models of home and family naturalize a particular relationship between anatomical sex, gender identity, and gender performance, in which the terms *male-man-masculine* and *female-woman-feminine* are aligned and reproduced in familiar patterns of heterosexual monogamy, division of gender roles, and child-rearing. In a classic statement on the politics of drag, Judith Butler argues that "if the anatomy of the performer is already distinct from the gender of the performer, and both of these are distinct from the gender of the performance, then the performance suggests a dissonance."[37] Drag can mark the play with dissonant paradox. The startling conclusion in Butler's analysis ex-centers gender from its position as one of the familiar centers for identity; robbed of its essential status, gender is seen as the performative repetition of learned gestures that constitute, and do not reveal, identity. Butler writes that "performativity is a matter of reiterating or repeating the norms by which one is constituted; it is not a radical fabrication of a gendered self. It is a compulsory repetition of prior and subjectivating norms, ones which cannot be thrown off at will, but which work, animate, and constrain the gendered subject, and which are also the resources from which resistance, subversion, displacement are to be forged."[38] Elsewhere in this book, I look at films that contain explicit drag performances (see chapter 5). That is not the case in *Young Wives' Tale*. I am, however, interested in the film's presentation of a parallel to what Butler describes as drag's potential to expose "the failure of heterosexual regimes ever fully to legislate or contain their own ideals."[39] This potential in the film is not activated through a drag that produces "imprecise and exaggerated imitations of masculinities or femininities" but through an alternative form of performance that I am calling *domestic drag*.[40] Domestic drag is any performance of a *home* that makes the reiteration or repetition of domestic conventions visible. It arises when a nonhome (typically a studio set) *poses* as a home. This drag complicates the assertion that the home is a natural space centered on self-evident heterocentric principles of monogamy, reproduction, and inheritance. The visible artificiality of domestic comedies presents domestic life as a crisis of paradoxical *both/and*ness—natural and unnatural, genuine and fake—undermining the centered structure of the home. Gestures and the spaces in which they are performed are unconventionally aligned in such a way as to reveal the absence of a natural and reliable center to justify and control the play of meanings. The house shared by the two couples in *Young Wives' Tale*—with all the declared artifice of a set on a sound stage—is also not a house.

The domestic drag of 1950s domestic comedies begins with the open declaration of artifice. The attributes of a home—decor, function, personalities—are presented, but as exaggerations or travesties and not as credible imitations. The studio aesthetic has been criticized as the unconvincing substitution of stage for world. Domestic drag embraces this incredibility and, through ironic play, inverts the significance and implies that the world is a stage on which scripted social norms are performed. *Young Wives' Tale* has a clear and developed visual style, despite Bell-Williams's insistence to the contrary. She acknowledges that "the focus of a single setting recalls the film's theatrical origins" but also argues that the effect is "realist . . . , not symbolic . . . [and] neutral."[41] As I read it, however, "unobtrusive" camerawork and editing does not naturalize the action and the film's stagy world does not entirely convince.[42] Even in an age in which studio artifice was commonplace because its controllable conditions were routinely favored over locations, the sets in *Young Wives' Tale* look *dressed* rather than lived in. The realist home in the film is always also its own anonymous, artificial other. The glimpses of the street and the garden compound this effect by announcing their fakery. I do not see the "smoothness and seamlessness that was a feature of modern domestic design in this period"; I see signs of fracture and unruliness in a wider British fantasy of the heterocentric *home* as security and fulfillment, a fantasy that still persists in the twenty-first century, despite being rendered unconvincing by the Second World War and the subsequent decades of falling marriage rates, rising divorce rates, falling birth rates, and rising numbers of same-sex and unmarried straight couples cohabiting.[43]

Even Sabina's disorder looks stage-managed: her clothes driers draped with laundry resemble stage flats; she handles props, such as the telephone (whose ring she ecstatically imitates at one point), with deference, as though they are loaded with dramatic significance; and she moves through the cluttered rooms with an exquisitely choreographed grace that negotiates obstacles impeccably.[44] Bell-Williams argues that this choreography "capture[s] the piecemeal nature of housework" but I suggest that it gestures to a more general discrediting of the home as a natural space. Bell-Williams also suggests that "Sabina's flitting and fluffiness, evocative of her erratic, unpredictable nature, is echoed visually in the *mise-en-scène*," but this emphasis on the *nature* of a character so committed to artifice and performance is misleading.[45] Discussions of the film that insist that Sabina has given up acting (as my synopsis earlier in this chapter mischievously does) are incorrect; she is only ever acting. Bell-Williams acknowledges that Joan Greenwood's "performance style comprises the flamboyant use of exaggerated and expressive gestures" but does not pursue the queer implications of so histrionic a style.[46] Greenwood's consummate vocal performance uses emphasis, tempo, rhythm, and color to derange every line, drawing out both the comedy and the theatricality in the dialogue. Durgnat recognizes the eccentric vocal gestures of her "suavely plummy voice [that] enriched so many comedies with its ironies and its mockingly sexual gravity"; this generalization is compelling, but it is useful to look at her delivery in *Young Wives' Tale* in detail.[47] Having rowed with Rodney and ruined the dinner, she comes downstairs in a beautiful evening gown (see fig. 2.1). She explains her change of clothes to her husband by saying: "You can't imagine the effect it has on a woman going about all day looking like a drab. Putting on real clothes and doing one's face has the effect of—well, of a champagne supper." This is one of the pinnacles of Greenwood's performance as domestic drag queen, giving the performance of a housewife in order to make visible the cultural and artificial elements of the role. Nothing is left

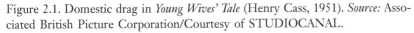

Figure 2.1. Domestic drag in *Young Wives' Tale* (Henry Cass, 1951). *Source:* Associated British Picture Corporation/Courtesy of STUDIOCANAL.

to chance. Everything is poise and pose. Her eyes are almost closed, downcast and accentuating the sensual line of her lashes. Her chin is slightly raised, part of her general sense of elegance, except when it sinks in studied sympathy with her description of "looking like a drab." For most of the exchange, she looks away from Rodney, positioned at an angle that favors an implied audience out front more than her interlocutor. Her hands pulse with the pace and cadences of "putting on real clothes," setting the diaphanous material of her gown's long sleeves into slinky motion. The "well" is transformed from a mere filler through outrageous delivery; it is a performance of improvisation that is so mannered, so unimprovised that it lacks any sense of the sparklingly spontaneous. The words "champagne supper" are delivered on a breathy exhalation characteristic of Greenwood; deep and sonorous, the exquisitely cracking syllables confirm the impression that her descent down the stairs is a dramatic entrance. As in the case of Margaret Rutherford in *Passport to Pimlico*, the impression that these are lines *being delivered* ex-centers character. In a witty acknowledgment of this artifice, Rodney later writes some fruity dialogue for a play of his based, verbatim, on a conversation he has had with Eve (Audrey Hepburn); when he reads it to Sabina, she says that it is beautiful but that no one would ever speak like that.

One of the gestures that pulses most emphatically through *Young Wives' Tale* is kissing. The film seems to confirm the uncontroversial assertion that kissing is a legitimate and necessary signifier of the heterocentric home, signifying the special status of the privileged relationships between husband and wife and parent and child without becoming indecorous and lewd; Nanny Gallop sees it as the evidence of appropriate marital affection between what she describes as two "love birds." Kissing in *Young Wives' Tale*, however, is scandalous and shakes the structures of partnership and parentage: Victor kisses Sabina and is caught by Bruce; Sabina kisses Bruce and is caught by Nanny Gallop; Sabina kisses Bruce again and is caught by Rodney; Rodney kisses Eve and is caught by Sabina; Sabina kisses Rodney and is caught by Nanny Gallop; Bruce kisses Mary and is caught by Nanny Gallop. Just as drag aligns anatomical sex, gender identity, and gender performance unconventionally, domestic drag produces queer misalignments between sexual desire, married status, and the performance of physical intimacy. At moments, the characters indicate that they are in on this metatheatrical wheeze and recognize that physical intimacy is a question of domestic drag: Mary is far more angered by the possibility of losing a good nanny than the news of her husband's infidelity and Rodney says, having kissed Eve, that "there was nothing personal in it—I just had to kiss something." The unconvincing space of the film set and the histrionic acting style gesture to the quasi-theatrical conceits that routinely discipline heterocentric domestic relationships. This is reinforced by the link between kiss and discovery, which is established so firmly in this epidemic of intimacy that it seems that, in a house crowded with people and desire, kissing is catching; these kisses are there to be seen. Individual events in this giddy partner rotation are choreographed with the precision of a dance and performed with archly comic style: as Victor kisses her, Sabina gently attempts to fend him off, but the pulse of her gesture of resistance weakens as she capitulates; as Sabina kisses Bruce, her abandoned performance of passion overwhelms his performance of embarrassment; after her kiss with Rodney, Eve glows at Sabina with smug satisfaction as she leaves to darn his socks. These gestures are always *both* expressing passion *and* going through the (theatrical) motions as a series of mannered actions.

This artifice does not mark the film's failure but its achievement. The domestic drag of *Young Wives' Tale* critiques the heterocentric home by deranging its claims to naturalness. The conventional domestic pillar that seems to have the most unimpeachable claim to naturalness—biological parenting—is dragged up by the film with the same eccentric energy as monogamous marriage. Nanny Gallop's belief that Bruce and Sabina are the married parents of Valentine and Elizabeth results in a sequence in which Valentine rides Bruce, his acting father, while Nanny Gallop hums the *William Tell Overture*, breaking off periodically to shout "Hit him, hit him!" Not only is Valentine playing merrily (and with convincing Oedipal violence) with a second father, he is being encouraged by Nanny Gallop, an additional mother. Neither Bell-Williams nor Landy expresses any substantial interest in the role of the nannies in the film, but this overlooks their significant contributions to the domestic disorder of the film. When Nanny Gallop arrives, she tells the taxi driver that she has "been mother to forty-five children"; inside the house she refers to "my nursery" and "my babies" before she has seen either. Mother *and* stranger, master *and* servant, bringer of peace *and* disruption: Nanny Gallop is an eccentrically *both/and* character. Bell-Williams passingly observes the nanny's commitment to structure in the form of "regulation and planning" with "'rhythm and regularity, regularity and rhythm' as the cornerstone of child care."[48] But this analysis does not consider the more unsettling motion suggested by the nanny's surname as she careers round the house causing havoc. Athene Seyler's turn is too eccentric to represent only order, reveling in the *both/and* domestic drag of implausible gestures that suggest that she, too, is more performance than character.

In chapter 1, I argue that eccentricity is not defined in opposition to a stable center but is the disruption of centric logic altogether. Here, I argue that the queer is, similarly, not the straightforward repudiation of heteronormativity but the subversive energy that reveals the limitations in logic and function of heterocentric myth. Nanny Gallop's eccentricity does not lie in a lack of convention; indeed, unlike the progressive devil-may-care antics of the two couples, her behavior is bound by a conventional sexual morality, expressed as outrage when she walks in on acts of what she takes to be infidelity and cries out "Sex maniacs, the lot of you!" The fact that the other characters feel compelled to orbit her, sacrificing their own self-determination in order to perform alternative married and parental relationships, seems to position her as a static and disciplining domestic center. But in a home deranged by domestic drag, all centers become unstable. Sabina's final exhilarating condemnation of the sexual despotism of Nanny Gallop accuses her of being "a shapeless, snooping, sanctimonious old bag"; the nanny, whose expressions change so mercurially through the film, has no definite shape or structure. Her moral heterocentrism is unable to accommodate the proliferating intimacies that spring up around her and she becomes, in fact, the architect of much of this confusion. The two kisses that she denounces as obscene are, in fact, the only kisses in the film between married people. Nanny Gallop, as the embodiment of collapsing heterocentric logic, strains and twitches, her facial and bodily gestures never in repose. Armored in her starched pinafore, she oversees a house of infidelity and she smiles—albeit unknowingly—upon it. Her own centric relationship with the world spills over in a display of "the failure of heterosexual regimes ever fully to legislate or contain their own ideals."[49] In short, Nanny Gallop becomes a queer agent, conspiring with the other inmates of the house to make the heterocentric home look both *funny-ha-ha* and *funny-peculiar*.

Nanny Gallop exits, dragging herself away after the revelation that she has no shape and cannot provide a moral center to the house. After her departure, chaos descends. Bell-Williams interprets in this sequence a clear pattern of cause and effect; "narrative disruption occurs when the couples briefly swap partners and lose their nanny. Equilibrium is tentatively restored when the couples are reconciled but the film ends in chaos as the children flood the house and the neighbour's dog steals the Sunday roast."[50] This account underestimates the scale of the chaos: a neighbor's dog, unseen in the film to this point, steals in and takes the joint of meat; Sabina gives chase into the garden and fights the dog for the meat; Rodney follows Sabina and smashes his hand through a glass door; the kettle screams; Valentine plays behind a locked bathroom door as the bath overflows and begins to pour through the ceiling of the room below; Eve, watching Sabina from her bedroom, drops a sash window and smashes the pane; Eve runs out onto the landing and knocks Rodney down the stairs, who crashes into Mary and Bruce; Elizabeth wails. Meanwhile, the radio, replete with BBC accent and significant irony, says that "home security cannot be achieved without peace at home. The Minister of Food said in Birmingham last night, this country can never repay the debt it owes the British housewife." The film ends as a boys' marching band passes.

The scale of this disorder is almost outrageous. The excess amplifies the effect of the film's *laughing forward*, as the domestic drag intimates a nebulous set of possible futures. It would be easy to associate the chaos with the departure of Nanny Gallop, but this would be to overlook the deranging effect that she has had throughout the film. By the time she leaves, she is "shapeless," a spent center exposed as a mere substitute for a previous center that will, in turn, be replaced. I suggest that the chaos is a response not to her leaving but to the imminence of the film's ending; a text that is so self-consciously aware of its own artifice may design its action with an awareness of such structural concerns and build up to an obvious—and obviously contrived—climax. The chaos that ensues is a chaos that threatens the very structure of the house itself; the water pouring through the ceiling and the smashed windows both weaken the fabric and boundaries of the space. Sabina, in addition, is dragged outside. Mary, Eve, Bruce, and Patrick fall down the stairs, landing near the front door. And the house is filled with the external sounds of a radio broadcast and a band that is passing by. The movement here is all centrifugal, pulling away from the ostensible center of the home, which is beginning to collapse. This collapse is a defense against the threat posed by the reconciliation of the two couples—that the household's domestic life will continue orbiting a series of inadequate centers, quite possibly in the form of yet another nanny. The domestic drag, which climaxes in collapse, makes alternative, additional queer futures glimpsable. These futures include polyamory, collective parenting, sexual freedoms for women, and communal living, each of which remains largely taboo within the UK's monolithic twenty-first-century model of the heterocentric home. *Young Wives Tale*, in its ex-centering domestic drag, *laughs forward* futures in which such a home collapses around an exiled and shapeless moral center and makes room for queer play.

Discovering that Every Nice Boy Loves a Sailor in *Sailor Beware!*

Many of the domestic comedies of the 1950s were based on popular plays and the transfer from stage to screen typically consolidates the effect of domestic drag: the homes look like play sets. As I have explored, this aesthetic of realistic artifice can be understood as a queer commentary on the artifice of the hegemonic heterocentric myth of the naturalized home. I hope to present the films as significant historical artifacts, not in the sense of sealed time capsules offering glimpses of a remote past but as indictments of the still-happening history of heterocentrism, showing up the logical gaps in the discourse that become visible—and indeed gape wide—under the pressure of eccentricity. It is the spectacle of these gaps widening that continues to make me laugh and that offers glimpses of not-yet-reached but still-possible futures of sexual eccentricity. The films and my readings of them do not ignore or avoid heterocentric myths; rather they make a joke of them. Bergson's theory of comedy (see chapter 1) proposes that eccentricity is the static force that mobile convention must correct through laughter. The domestic comedies invert this model; the static and unconvincing sets are the product of exclusive and moribund convention and it is eccentricity that introduces play. The characters who operate as agents of this eccentricity often, though by no means always, perform gender unconventionally. Emma Hornett (Peggy Mount) in

Sailor Beware! (Gordon Parry, 1956) is such an agent, upsetting conventional standards of femininity by rejecting orthodox uxorial duty and deference and substituting explosively imperious tirades. The sheer volume of these outbursts makes them multidirectional, but many of the choicest are reserved for her submissive husband, who is usually to be found showing his maternal side in caring for newborn ferret kits in the garden shed.

Emma Hornett is preparing for the wedding of her daughter Shirley (Shirley Eaton). Shirley is marrying sailor Albert Tufnell (Ronald Lewis), a young man who was raised in an orphanage and has negligible experience of domestic life. Emma is helped little by her husband Henry (Cyril Smith), but she is supported by her sister-in-law Edie (Esma Cannon), who is a constant source of irritation to her. Edie is nervy and haunted by her experience of being jilted at the altar. Her tendency to become distracted results in her committing such domestic transgressions as indelibly marking polished sideboards with hot dishes. When Albert arrives at the Hornett home with his best man Carnoustie (Gordon Jackson), he is made to feel unwelcome by Emma, who would rather her daughter were not marrying a sailor without a family. Albert ignores her gripes until Edie inadvertently lets slip that Emma and Shirley have conspired to put a deposit down on a house three doors away. Shocked by his fiancée's deceit, Albert does not turn up at the church for the wedding ceremony. The bridal party returns home in a state of distress. Albert returns to the house and explains that staying with the Hornetts has been his "first taste of home life and if what I've seen in this house is honest to God home life then all I can say is give me the Salvation Army." He and Shirley resolve to decide their own future and rearrange the wedding for later that day. Emma overhears her husband defending her as a good wife; she becomes emotional and commits to being gentler with her family. As she and Henry walk from the church to the reception, however, she begins to bellow again: "But the one thing I will say and I don't care who hears me—are you listening, Henry?—if Shirley's marriage turns out wrong, to my dying day I shall say you were to blame."

The domestic comedies of the postwar era often present narrative scenarios that are not obviously funny. The narrative of *Sailor Beware!* could have been played as social drama or melodrama. Its comedy—which is a mixture of slapstick, innuendo, punning, and social humiliation—has been discussed as being ultimately at Emma

Hornett's expense. Such readings present the film as a feature-length mother-in-law joke. Durgnat, in praise of the film, describes Emma as "champion, apotheosis and fortissimo of all possible mothers-in-law, modulating from buzz-saw to fog-horn and back, and carrying, not only her namesake's sound, but its sting."[51] It is, however, important to note that the trajectory of the narrative is not toward the humiliation or taming of Emma; she continues bellowing at the end. I read her as less monstrous than monumental. Her daughter Shirley, although bearing the good looks of a film star, is insipid by comparison, and it is Emma who—despite her rather shapeless housecoats, unstyled hair, and hard grimaces—demands to be looked at. She occupies the center of the home and center of the film. I suggest a reevaluation of the film's trajectory, not toward her taming but toward her *displacement as center*. When, toward the end, the vicar (Geoffrey Keen) says that he wants to talk to Shirley and Albert alone, Emma does not immediately leave the room; when the vicar makes it clear that she should go, her response is to ask "Do you mean alone without me?"—clearly astonished by the idea that any discussion should go on in her absence. *Sailor Beware!* is the story of the ex-centering of a matriarchal center.

Even as Emma bellows at Henry as the film ends, the sound of her voice becomes electronically distorted and is lost as the music of the closing credits rises; she and Henry have escaped the confines of the house and are in a street, into whose on-location distance they disappear from view. Shirley and Albert, absent from the film's final scene altogether, are moving away and will no longer orbit Emma. Henry, even as he endures another barrage of verbiage, has shown his own capacity for explosive interventions when he defends his wife to Albert and Shirley. The calamities of the film's narrative do not arise strictly from Emma's personality, but from the impossible pressure of one figure acting as the cohering center for a home. The question shifts from being about whether heterocentric structures expel or exclude some subjects to whether or not anyone is able to embody the oppressive ideals circulated as domestic convention. In the film's opening scene, Albert describes his idea of marriage in a comically naive image of "a wife and a dear little house—a home—that's what married life means to me: home sweet home." This ingenuous litany of heterocentric propaganda becomes laughable as the image of optimistic Albert dissolves to a shot of a tapestry reading HOME

SWEET HOME in the Hornetts' living room where Emma is dusting aggressively and bellowing. The gag appears to be that Albert offers a fantasy of home life and Emma is the reality; but Emma Hornett and her sound-stage home are no less mythic than Albert's chocolate-box nonsense. Both are heterocentric conceits, one a myth of masculine order and the other a myth of the monstrous matriarch, and both are presented as fitting subjects for domestic drag by the film. The sentimental sailor and the tyrannical termagant are both fakes conjured up within a theatrical space. By the end of the film, liberated from the burden of monolithic centricity, Emma has begun to enter a state of free play in which she can vary herself; her booming ire is not lost, but it has been complicated by a new capacity for tenderness, shame, and affection.

The displacement of Emma as domestic center is effected by a number of ex-centering forces at work in the home. The first and most richly comic of these is Esma Cannon's Edie. Edie could easily have been a figure drawn from melodrama: the retiring unmarried woman, jilted at the altar and now bleakly depending on the kindness of unsympathetic relatives and the scant consolations of astrology. Cannon, however, endows the role with an eccentric theatricality that softens the pain of her situation through a riotous domestic drag. Geoff Brown associates the rings—which fill the Hornett living room as a result of Edie's careless placement of hot pans—with realism, displaying the film's "sharp nose for lowly detail"; Albert, however, points out the perfectly symmetrical arrangement of these marks, suggesting choreography more than chance.[52] The space is set up theatrically, with its draped curtains at the proscenium between living and dining rooms and myriad doors providing performance frames for the action. Although the film ventures out on location for a handful of short sequences, the backyard and ferret shed—where alternative reproduction is celebrated—have the smooth, grimeless sterility of a studio set. Edie is as much a creature of this domestic drag as bellowing Emma, although she operates at a different frequency. Comprised of twitching gestures and vocal squeals and yelps, Edie is an unstable, mobile form. Emma accuses her of "trailing around the place as though you wasn't all there, which you're not"; being *not all there* (assisted by the disorientating juxtaposition of the denial of "as though" and the negative confirmation of "which you're not") suggests that something—the grounding center of sanity—is missing.

Edie flits between an endearing girlishness and histrionic despair. As Albert, on his arrival, affectionately swings her around, she giggles and coyly covers her face; Cannon's tiny stature and soft voice gives her an agelessness in comic contrast with Mount's solid maturity. The childish glee quickly dissipates as she performs shrill despair at the sight of her tealeaves, which prophesy a "bleedin' broken heart." This phrase runs as a refrain through the remainder of the film, each time scoring comically because of Cannon's delivery of the ironic "bleedin,'" both an image of violence and a gentle swear word. Had the part been played for sympathy, it could have shut down laughter; had it been played only for laughs, it could have risked the discomfort of callous misogyny. Cannon's performance is pitched delicately; Edie says that she has experienced "shame and humiliation," but the acting style is *shameless* and somehow steely. Neither mocked nor pathologized, Edie is an eccentric thorn in the side of Emma's centricity.

As Emma is dislodged as center, the question of who might replace her arises. The strongest contender is Albert, who asserts his right to determine where his new home should be. But Albert is not the heterocentric model he may seem to be. As I watch it, the film's eroticism is not to be found in the rather limp dynamic between Albert and Shirley, but in the more intimate relationship between Albert and Carnoustie. I argue throughout this book that the queerness of a film is not dependent on explicit depictions of same-sex desire; eccentricity can, without such overt representation, still work its mischief on monolithic heterocentric structures. But in *Sailor Beware!* there is a homoeroticism that I find striking. Albert and Carnoustie represent, for me, a portrait of charmingly tender male intimacy, replete with a kind of eroticism that was stifled but not uncommon in postwar Britain.

Because of confusion in the neighbor's house where they were due to be spending the night, Albert has to share a single put-you-up bed in the living room with Carnoustie. Their tight naval uniforms are difficult to take off, and Carnoustie helps Albert to get undressed. Then, while Carnoustie is in the kitchen washing, Shirley comes in and she and Albert say goodnight; she withholds the information about the new house despite Albert's gentle probing, and their relationship enters a crisis of secrecy. When she is gone, Carnoustie returns; reassured that they will receive no further visitors, he removes his trousers. This simple act is performed with a remarkable wiggle in which Carnoustie gratuitously shakes his hips, accentuating the bottom-hugging snugness of his trousers and the shape of his own body (see fig. 2.2). The gesture, in its gratuitousness and playful eroticism, is repeated several times through the film. It is a gesture played for laughs, and sweetly sexy laughs at that. With the histrionically mannered comic device, Carnoustie performs his uniform as he removes it; a postwar memoirist remarks that British "sailors had the advantage of having a genuinely erotic uniform. . . . The trousers must have been made to titillate. They were very tight around the waist and bottoms. . . . If the sailor wore no underwear then very little was left to the imagination."[53] Carnoustie, with his wiggle and his tight trousers, gives a glimpse of something beyond the home, something beyond marriage. The scant criticism on *Sailor Beware!*, always faithful unto the awesome spectacle of Mount's mother-in-law, entirely overlooks Carnoustie's provocative wiggle and the scene in which two men undress each other and share a bed.

Figure 2.2. Sailors wiggling in *Sailor Beware!* (Gordon Parry, 1956). *Source:* Romulus Films/Courtesy of STUDIOCANAL.

Albert and Carnoustie's night together is interrupted by a short and unnecessary scene between Emma and Henry in their matrimonial bedroom upstairs. The sequence, dominated by her anger at his drunkenness, is given rhythm and energy by editing, close-ups, and a moving camera. When the film cuts back to the living room, Albert and Carnoustie are in bed together, smoking cigarettes; both the camera and they are still, seemingly enervated, resembling nothing so much as postcoital exhaustion. The dialogue also gestures to a homoerotic frisson:

CARNOUSTIE: Albert.

ALBERT: Yeah?

CARNOUSTIE: You'll drop me a wee line when you're on your honeymoon and let me know how you're getting on?

ALBERT: Yeah, sure.

CARNOUSTIE: No details, mind—just the general outline.

ALBERT: I suppose you'll be thinking of me.

CARNOUSTIE (coughing uncontrollably on his cigarette): I'll keep my imagination well under control.

The unspoken specter of queer desire haunts this exchange between two men in bed as one contemplates imagining the other having sex with his new wife. The sequence ends as Carnoustie, having put the light out, jumps onto the bed and it collapses, leaving the two undressed men in a heap together as the image fades to black. This is the halfway point of the film, marked by the spectacle of two men under bedcovers together and disappearing into a fade that draws a discreet veil over who knows what activity. When the dawn is subsequently heralded by a fade-up and the arrival of the milkman, Shirley is shown asleep in her room with a picture of Albert beside her; Albert meanwhile lies asleep downstairs, smilingly embracing Carnoustie's naked legs (see fig. 2.3). The images of both Shirley/photograph and Albert/Carnoustie are accompanied by a lush romantic melody on extradiegetic strings. The camera tracks in on the sleeping

Figure 2.3. Sailors cuddling in *Sailor Beware!* (Gordon Parry, 1956). *Source:* Romulus Films/Courtesy of STUDIOCANAL.

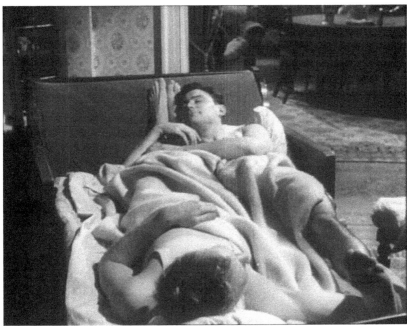

Shirley, narrowing the frame in response to her aloneness; conversely, the camera, in a broadening gesture, tracks out from Albert, revealing by contrast his togetherness with his best man. As heterocentricity, in the form of Mr. and Mrs. Hornett, begins to bellow upstairs, the two men wake, startled, and embrace each other. The sequence can be read as a homophobic joke that invites laughter at the spectacle of a sleeping man dreaming of his beautiful fiancée while he mistakenly hugs the hairy legs of his best friend, but the film does not insist on such a response. The intimacy between Carnoustie and Albert is sweetly presented, and their physical closeness is not framed by explicitly comic music or any other marker of the bathetic or absurd.

The intimate homosociality between Albert and Carnoustie—which is on a spectrum that includes the possibilities of comradeship, friendship, and sex—complicates domestic comedy with a glimpse of a "routine service comed[y]."[54] Whereas domestic comedies are heterocentric, service comedies are typically homosocial, drawing on the male–male intimacies of war or national service. Albert, lied to by Shirley and cuddling Carnoustie, represents a common phenomenon of what Francis describes as "post-war male restlessness and a yearning for the all-male camaraderie of service life," which men were reluctant to surrender when they married.[55] Francis goes on to suggest that "fed by demographic anxieties and claims of a post-war moral decline, and given legislative possibility by Theobold Matthew's tenure as Director of Public Prosecutions, filmmakers would have been very careful to avoid the suggestion that an all-male environment might create opportunities for the expression of queer sexualities or sensibilities."[56] This is no doubt true, but *Sailor Beware!* does show male physical closeness. Even when the homoeroticism is veiled, connoted rather than announced, comic rather than tragic, the ex-centering domestic effect is not wholly dissipated; indeed, the threat to heterocentric convention can become more subtle and dangerous. Sinfield notes that in the postwar period in Britain homosexuality was "too dangerous to be spoken directly" and this unspoken menace acquires a particular quality when its threats of domestic destruction and dissolution are delivered laughingly, are played in a comic key against an artificial backdrop and a catalog of domestic clichés.[57]

In his study of postwar male restlessness and its link to cinematic images of homosociality, Francis (2007) discusses many films but none of them is a comedy. Domestic comedy seems so self-evidently to exclude the possibility of homoeroticism that the homoeroticism implicit in two men embracing in bed slips beneath the surface of the noticeable. But comedies, even as they resist the dramatic rhetoric that positions nonconventional sex as *issue* and *social problem*, do address these same specters of unruly and unauthorized desire through an eccentricity that privileges gesture and glimpsed possibilities, rather than the more leaden certainties of identity. Carnoustie's gestures—the awkward stumble as he discusses imagining Albert on his honeymoon, the smoking in bed, the instinct to hold Albert—are made theatrical and do not attain definite meaning in the distorting generic light of domestic comedy's drag, which is, in return, colored by the specter of desire between the two men. Carnoustie's sexuality remains eccentric and enigmatic, allowing him to avoid being either pilloried or pitied. Definitive knowledge of his desires is impossible. In the opening scene of the film, aboard ship Albert hints at something when he tells Carnoustie that "the sooner you're married and out of danger the better." What this danger is remains unspoken. It may include homoeroticism's "barely apprehensible threat of destruction and dissolution," which Carnoustie continues to pose as the representative of a life of masculine camaraderie and adventure that Albert has known and may continue to know, even if only as fantasy, as a married man.[58] If the film's trajectory is to unsettle Emma's position as center of a world, it is also to imply that an artificial heterocentric structure will not be able to constrain the homoerotic play that arises from Albert's life of service.

My argument, then, is not that Carnoustie is gay, but that his erotic uniform, his sexy wiggle, and his intimate relationship with Albert—a relationship whose boundaries are unmappable and may or may not include the sexual—threatens the monolithic centricity of the new marriage between Albert and Shirley. Francis argues that "while the existence of an apparently flourishing homo*sexual* subculture certainly cast a troubling shadow over the discourses of postwar domesticity, it was homo*social* desire that was to play the most profound part in accounting for male ambivalence about marriage and family at this time."[59] Carnoustie ex-centers the marriage by fragmenting Albert's affection and devotion and signifying the horizons of possibility that sailing (or cruising) continues to offer. This eccentric effect would have been only compromised by more explicit representation. In postwar British cinema—and arguably still in the twenty-first century—the homosexual presented explicitly is a figure used to reinforce and not to disrupt structures. Carnoustie could have become a figure centered around his own inescapable and shameful sexual identity, against whom the *normal* Albert could define and defend his own position. Instead, he is a figure in motion, neither heterosexual nor homosexual, and as a result *both/and*. He kisses Shirley's cousin Daphne (Joy Webster), but only with an extraordinary awkwardness (reinforced by Webster's mannered performance, in which her puckering up to kiss Carnoustie resembles a grimace). Doan highlights the dangers of "practices in historicizing sexuality, in particular practices that position the homosexual or queer subject near the center of investigative curiosity."[60] Such practices—whether celebratory or pathologizing—generate new centricities, diminishing the ex-centering unruliness that queer subjects can unleash. Carnoustie, in defiance of such practices, never becomes a homosexual subject and steadfastly, perversely represents possibilities more than identity. But those possibilities are, it seems to me, emphatically erotic; the two men and their fantasies allow laughable heterosexual marriage an alternative. Carnoustie, collaborating with the domestic drag of studio-set artifice, suggests that the heterocentric home is not the only option. This is the *laughing forward* that I see at work in *Sailor Beware!* Not primarily a mother-in-law gag, the film offers a glimpse of the companionship and touch between men in (and out of) uniform. It presents the possibility that such an intimacy—in fact and imagination—might continue as complement and not challenge to a mixed-gender marriage. The joyful laughter here arises from the glimpse of a marriage of abundance in which erotic homosocial friendship, complete with tantalizing wiggle, is not ruled out but fondly embraced.

Being Divinely Dull in *Simon and Laura*

The postwar comedy that performs its domestic drag most explicitly is *Simon and Laura* (Muriel Box, 1955). This popular film was another West End transfer to screen. In it, Simon and Laura Foster (Peter Finch and Kay Kendall), a glamorous acting couple, are asked to play versions of themselves in a television drama about their idyllic marriage. Complications arise from the fact that the television producers believe the couple to be the perfect rendition of utopian heterocentric myths of the happy home, when they are, in fact, on the verge of an acrimonious divorce. Their television appearances bring them fame, but tensions increase as they each suspect the other (quite wrongly) of infidelity. The program descends into chaos when the couple reveal their hostilities live on air. Laura decides to leave Simon but, thanks to the interventions of their fellow performers, they are ultimately reconciled. The plot revolves explicitly around questions of the media's responsibility to reinforce positive images of companionate, monogamous mixed-gender marriage. The Television Controller (Richard Wattis) instructs producer David Prentice (Ian Carmichael) to "see that the script stresses the solidarity of the home: peaceful, happy atmosphere of marital bliss." This solidarity depends on the centric structure of the *nuclear family*, a term first used in 1924 according to the *Oxford English Dictionary*; deriving from the Latin *nucleus* meaning *kernel* or *core*, the twentieth-century biologically defined and state-sanctioned family is built on a centric image. The nuclear family itself is centered on a shared core and, as a social unit, it provides a center around which wider society can revolve. Barr describes how postwar British cinema can present the family as a synecdoche for broader structures, including community-as-family, profession-as-family, and nation-as-family "whose members share common standards and loyalties."[61] This shared loyalty leads to what Durgnat sees as a lack of bite in a cinema that "rarely [criticizes] the more central characters, the happily married children of Hillcrest and Hornblower. The reason is obvious. The criticized figures represent marginal attitudes. . . . Criticism of the 'mainstream'—the public-school-and-money nexus—has to wait for the angry young men and satirists of the period following."[62]

I am unconvinced that British cinema was exclusively a paean to the heterocentric nuclear family. As I see it, the family of the domestic comedies is a unit in crisis. Both *Young Wives' Tale* and *Sailor Beware!* gesture toward escape routes from the heterocentric constraints of monogamy and child-rearing. Jeffrey Weeks identifies in the postwar British cultural imaginary a family seen "both as 'natural' and permanent and as fragile and threatened."[63] The domestic comedies, as I see them, explode the impression of naturalness through their domestic drag; the spaces, situations, and personalities that make up a family have all the permanence of cardboard and the vitality of cliché. The squalor and hardship represented by the New Wave in the years that followed, feted as a more credible account of family life, do less to announce this artifice; they are, despite their depictions of sexual nonconformity, in this regard more invested in identity and less queer. It is usually assumed that the irony at play in *Simon and Laura* is that the TV Controller wants images of "marital bliss" and receives, instead, images of marital discord. This is one irony, but it is not the only one. He is also looking for natural reality (openly expressing the view that the audience and critics must *believe* in the relationship) but transmits, instead, a real fake. Like most other critics who have written on the film, Geraghty is principally interested in its commentary on television, but she does remark on "the theatrical style of acting and the dramatic arguments between the 'real' Simon and Laura [, which] are contrasted with the cloying family intimacies of the television script."[64] It is difficult to read Simon and Laura's acrimony as real when their arguments are strikingly stagy, complete with wordplay, perfect enunciation, and carefully regulated movement that acknowledges the camera's position. Early in the film, after just such a row ends with Simon's histrionic cry of "trollop," the word projected as though for those in the back row of the stalls, Laura hurls a glass dish at him, delaying her throw by a beat as though to allow him the chance to catch the missile in this *game* of matrimonial hostility.

This domestic drag is partly the product of the couple's theatrical acrimony, but it is also, and more interestingly, a function of the artificial sets through which they move. Even the vaguely verisimilitudinous washing of *Young Wives' Tale* and burn marks of *Sailor Beware!* are absent, replaced in *Simon and Laura* by the unhomely and drafty acres of a townhouse with less reality than a show home. The drag of this nonhome masquerading as home is made resplendent by the diegetic play with television sets; the house mocked up in the BBC studio for their series is indistinguishable from the *real* thing. At first, the humor seems to gesture to the film's belief in the natural but uncivilized qualities of family life; when David is pitching the series to the Television Controller he recommends a writer called Janet Honeyman (Muriel Pavlow), whose suitability is defined by her earlier work on the series *Insect Life in British Ponds*. This joke quickly gives way, however, to an alternative line of comedy that runs through the film and mischievously, mercilessly chips away at the claim that family is a natural structure at all. If the Fosters' home is a pond, it is a highly ornamental one populated by plastic insects. When David first visits their apartment, he strides around with all the camped-up energy of a man playing at being a television executive, checking shooting and lighting angles and walking out the cast's movements. When the set designer (Alan Wheatley), whom Stephen Bourne describes as "swishy, over-the-top," visits the house, he flamboyantly pronounces "my dears, what a divine room."[65] His claim that "nobody could possibly invent anything like this" sounds like an endorsement of the producers' rhetoric of the natural home, but the character's histrionic style suggests an ironic complication to his lines; he sweeps around the space, all hand-on-hip poise and stressed vowel sounds, periodically striking poses, including one close-up in which he uses his half-opened folding rule to frame his chin. He is ultimately responsible for reinventing the real-but-fake-looking townhouse as a real fake in the real (but fictional) television studio.

As with the other domestic comedies, I find the nuclear family *laughable* in *Simon and Laura*. Landy traces a transgressive streak in the work of its director Muriel Box: "In the context of the 1950s cinema, devoted so often to reestablishing the family and women's position within domesticity, her films, while set in a similar context, provide a different perspective."⁶⁶ I wonder, however, whether Laura can really be said to be "trapped in poverty, violent and negligent familial relations, and constraining marital relations" like other protagonists from Box's films.⁶⁷ She is, it seems to me, trapped only by the artificial image of the ideal family. This reaches its absurd pinnacle when the topic of children is raised. Even Simon and Laura, for all their apparent happiness, are considered inadequate. David says it is a shame that they do not have children "to complete the popular conception of real domestic bliss." In this, he echoes the sentiments of the real-world Archbishop of Canterbury who, "addressing the Mothers' Union in 1952, voiced a widespread official view that: 'a family only truly begins with three children.'"⁶⁸ David hopes that if the program runs long enough, the stars may have the chance to produce some offspring. Simon may say, "I thought we were being engaged for a television series, not to boost the birth rate," but others working on the program see those two activities as the same thing.

The couple's childless domestic dynamic represents an affront to reproduction, a social priority in postwar Britain that continues to be privileged today; such reproduction is credited with not only making a home but also "in its widest social sense, of producing a healthy workforce."⁶⁹ Unlike the multigenerational procreative homes in *Young Wives' Tale* and *Sailor Beware!*, Simon and Laura are at odds with what Warner calls "reprosexuality—the interweaving of heterosexuality, biological reproduction, cultural reproduction, and personal identity. . . . Reprosexuality involves more than reproducing, more even than compulsory heterosexuality; it involves a relation to self that finds its proper temporality and fulfillment in generational transmission."⁷⁰ To facilitate transmission of both the generational and the televisual kind, the BBC provides Simon and Laura—at least for the purposes of the series—with a child; Timothy (Clive Parritt) is introduced as the couple's nephew. Later, in a scripted scene played out in front of the television cameras, Simon and Laura are playing Happy Families with the boy; as he succeeds in acquiring all of Mr. Bun the Baker's family, Laura delivers the toe-curlingly saccharine line "Timothy's so good at making happy families, isn't he?" and announces that they have arranged to adopt him. She invites the boy to begin calling them *daddy* and *mummy*. As the television cameras cut, the adults walk quickly away, Laura saying that she thinks she is going to be sick. I share her sensation.

Timothy's arrival coincides with a crisis for the program and reveals how the term *domestic drag* can suggest not only artifice and performance but also *dullness*. Simon and Laura become a *drag*. At the halfway point of the film, the TV Controller reads out a set of audience comments that repeat the point that the program has become *boring* because of the couple's relentless performance of *happiness*. One review describes Simon and Laura's marriage as "divinely happy and divinely dull," while a correspondent (or as Richard Wattis camply delivers the line, a *woman* correspondent) remarks that "Thank God we're not all as happily married as Simon and Laura." Later, as an executive watches an episode of the series, he nods off, his head lolling and tumbling as he struggles to remain interested in so predictable a spectacle of marital bliss. The artifice of the ideal marriage with its fake home and its scripted characters, this domestic drag, is such a drag that it has become not only nauseatingly saccharine but also unwatchable.

The series regenerates its audience's interest in its episode for Christmas, that season of goodwill and miraculous birth, when Simon and Laura (along with David and various other behind-the-scenes figures) end up brawling in front of the camera and tearing down the flimsy set (see fig. 2.4). This spectacular self-destruction, however, is not the end of the film. Ultimately, the film does not offer Simon and Laura (or me) a glimpse of different futures, but uses television as a "vehicle for reconciling family discord": Timothy (along with the couple's servant Wilson [Maurice Denham]) stages a stunt with cameras in which Simon's conversation with David (in which they confess their love for Laura and Janet) is broadcast live to a control room in which Laura and Janet can overhear.[71] The two women run to the studio floor and kiss their partners. The neatness of this resolution may be so arch that it parodies certain schmaltzy clichés from the heterocentric playbook, but it remains trapped by the spectacle of sustaining and committed monogamy. Simon's hymn to his wife's virtues—"She's down to earth, and honest, and practical; she's good fun; she's highly decorative; she's good to have around the house; she's—well, she's my sort"—feels clumsy and dated and *dull*.

Simon and Laura performs domestic drag exquisitely, but I find that it lacks the explosive *laughing forward* of *Young Wives' Tale* and *Sailor Beware!* It is bold enough to suggest that heterocentrism is boring, but it does not articulate more interesting options. But in this defeat, in this pessimism, lies the film's particular brand of queerness.

Figure 2.4. Collapsing heterocentricity in *Simon and Laura* (Muriel Box, 1955). *Source:* Group Film Productions/Courtesy of ITV Studios.

The film's metacinematic ending sees Wilson (ostensibly speaking to Timothy, who is still operating the television camera) say "Cut" before stepping aside and revealing a diegetic title card that reads THE END. The camera tracks in on these words—signifying both the end of the film and that heterocentric romance is so dull, such a *drag*, that it marks THE END of narrative. In *Young Wives' Tale*, polyamorous kisses are catching; in *Simon and Laura*, heterocentric kisses are terminal. The fundamental achievement of domestic drag in these postwar domestic comedies is to make heterosexuality *visible as an image*. It is no longer the natural obviousness that underpins society, history, and narrative; it is sets of clichés performed on sets of cardboard that can be—that *are*—dull except when allowed to go rogue, to fall apart, to show themselves in disarray. Calvin Thomas suggests that "heteronormative sex is teleologically narrativized sex: sex with a goal, a purpose, and a product."[72] In *Simon and Laura*, however, heterocentric sex and romance—with their repetitions and conventions, with their lack of dynamic tension, with their twee expressions of a happiness that makes even the central characters feel sick—have nowhere left to go and are THE END.

In the introduction, I discuss both the opportunities and the limitations of a critical approach that privileges spotting LGBT+ identities on display onscreen; it offers the consolation of some historical continuity but it risks perpetuating the insistence that queerness is bound up with particular identities. The queerness at work in domestic comedies is not predicated on sexual identities (even in the case of the enigmatic Carnoustie) but on foregrounding gestures that announce the reality of their own artifice. While a number of these gestures are tied up with histrionic performance (the Sabina drawl, the Carnoustie wiggle, the Laura chuck, and so on), domestic drag most importantly transforms design and *mise-en-scène* into a series of effective gestures. Bell-Williams insists, in relation to *Young Wives' Tale*, that "the film does not derive meaning from a strong visual style. The realist *mise-en-scène*, coupled with a neutral camera style, means that the ideas of the script are broadly supported."[73] The effectiveness of the *mise-en-scène* in domestic comedies, as I laugh at it, is that it is a *scandalous* realism in its suggestion of the mythic underpinnings of reality. The performances in the films happen within sets and not homes. Harper and Porter argue that "the problem for 'fantasist' designers was that realist methods had scooped the pool by early in the decade," but this sets up a misleading binary between realism and fantasy; the artificiality of these films' realism marks reality as a kind of collective cultural fantasy.[74] Domestic roles—of spouse, parent, child, nanny, neighbor, and servant—are made up. This is gesture made, as Brecht suggests it should be, with "a definite gest of showing."[75] Domestic drag is performed whenever a home *shows itself* not as a neutral or a natural space but as a stage on which performance happens. If queer marks an ex-centering solicitation of the myths that naturalize mixed-gender monogamy, biofamily, reproduction, and inheritance, then domestic drag's unconvincing design shows up the heterocentric home as an illusion that, seen in high-key lighting, is scarcely convincing. These films can be read as conservative and mawkish portraits of conventional families living conventionally (barring a few comic hiccups). But in order to feel really secure, such a reading must overlook the punctuating gestures that mess things up. Totality is shown to be fragments; certainty is shown to be possibilities; morality is shown to be conventions and dull clichés. It is in the fleeting moments when the house collapses, the matriarch is faded out, and kissing is shown to be THE END that domestic comedies are extremely—queerly—funny.

3

Laughing at Nothing

TWO MEN HURTLE DOWN THE stairs of the Eiffel Tower at alarming speed. In successive shots, the frame is consumed by disorientating abstraction, a geometric chaos of canted angles filmed with a turning camera; this Eiffel Tower is both an iconic real-world location and a mass of diagonal lines of uncertain symbolic significance. Meanwhile, giggling schoolgirls descend the tower in a lift, a moving focus in a frame in which no fixed center can be found. While the man out in front charges on, his hat flies off and falls into the tower's central abyss; moments later, his companion's coat is caught on the railing and is thrown after the hat. As the men continue their race downward, the first man gasps air in through a slack mouth, keeps his eyes screwed tight shut, and fixes his left arm to the coil of rivets that run down the staircase's central column. Behind him, the second man begins to laugh (see fig. 3.1). It is a hearty laugh. It does not suggest anything of the men's predicament. Head back, suitcases held out at arm's length in an expansive sweep, the man laughs with a deep, throaty, ecstatic gurgle. The ominous, even discordant strains of the extradiegetic score up to this point are overtaken by a lighter, more syncopated rhythm that dances through the more serious refrain in sympathy with the laughter. His friend, as the geometrically crazy world around him continues to spin, looks confused, then glances back and shouts irascibly: "There's nothing to laugh at." Immediately the words have left his mouth he, too, begins to laugh. As they run on, nearing the ground, the sound of laughter

Figure 3.1. Laughing at nothing in *The Lavender Hill Mob* (Charles Crichton, 1951). *Source:* Ealing Studios/Courtesy of STUDIOCANAL.

continues (even when it seems at variance with the image of their faces). It becomes increasingly wild, even distorted, until it finally subsides as the friends spin out dizzily at the bottom of the tower and slowly recover their sense of balance.

This sequence is from *The Lavender Hill Mob* (Charles Crichton, 1951). It remains one of the most popular Ealing comedies, celebrated as an example of what Charles Barr calls the "daydream" films of Ealing's mainstream, in which viewers are offered "a fantasy outlet" for their postwar social anxieties.[1] Robert Murphy toes the Barr line when he states that there are "few dark shadows here."[2] These critical responses are affectionate, but they overlook some of the specific gestures at work in the film. This omission seems to stem from an assumption that the film is simple (albeit polished) and will not repay such close reading. But, for me, this assumption does not survive the Eiffel Tower. Holland (Alec Guinness) and Pendlebury (Stanley Holloway), two friends from a South London boarding house, plan the robbery of £1,000,000 in gold bullion. Holland's work as a clerk for the Bank of England provides them with access to the gold and Pendlebury's foundry, in which he makes souvenir metal paperweights, provides them with the means of melting down and disguising the gold. In the shape of Eiffel Tower figurines, the gold is transported to Paris along with Pendlebury's usual consignment of standard lead paperweights. Holland and Pendlebury travel to France in order to check the safe arrival of the spoils of their crime, only to discover that the person responsible for storing the stock has ignored instructions and is selling the bullion Eiffel Towers. Six have been sold to some English schoolgirls. It is in pursuit of these girls that Holland and Pendlebury charge wildly down the stairs of the Eiffel Tower.

That chaotic descent, in ways that I shall explore in this chapter, plays with the same kinds of eccentric, antistructural ideas that have been discussed through this book so far. Not least, it offers one of the preeminent examples of a trope that is familiar in postwar British comedy: the spectacle of characters laughing uproariously. More than simply a way of alerting the audience to the presence of a joke, this laughter is often queerly and destabilizingly *funny-peculiar*. I am interested particularly in that kind of uncontrollable laughter in which the laughers seem to laugh principally because they are laughing, in a mirthful feedback loop in which the participants lose physical and intellectual control. I have always found such laughter both wonderful and awful, ecstatic in its disorderliness. Nowhere is it stranger than here, on the steps of disaster, where Holland cries out that "there's *nothing* to laugh at" even as he begins to laugh. The questions for this chapter are what this laughing at nothing is, and whether it can provide a route to understanding what I shall think of as *eccentric laughter*.

Coming to Terms with Comedy

In part 1 of this book, I have been attempting to unpack the concepts that I think intersect in postwar British comedy to make it so interesting. This process is imagined as a combinative one; chapter 2's queerness, which displaces heterocentric myths through its play of domestic drag, mixes with chapter 1's explosive eccentricity, which solicits the secure structurality of structure. This combinative strategy will continue with the third term to which I now come: *comedy*. Comedy is as tentacular a term as *eccentricity* and *queer*. It has its own hydra-like history that coils and writhes in unexpected directions and makes clarity of meaning or purpose all but impossible. One of the defining theoretical understandings of the term is as a cinematic, theatrical, and literary genre, complete with conventions and rules, generally revolving around the idea that a narrative's complications should be resolved happily, typically in marriage. Such a view of comedy privileges centering structural ideas about form and theme and stipulates that a text's operation depend on the heterocentric myth that reads *happy ending* as synonymous with *resolution in mixed-gender matrimony*. As Andrew Stott points out, however, such a definition "falls far short of describing all that comedy can be."[3] Although Laraine Porter and I. Q. Hunter argue that "comedy is the most popular of all genres in British cinema," it remains tricky to work out precisely what it is.[4]

The term needs to be flexible enough to address such different forms as burlesque, caricature, dark comedy, drag, drawing room comedy, farce, gross-out, impersonation, pantomime, parody, pastiche, satire, sitcom, sketch comedy, slapstick, and stand-up. In her summary of British comedy film, Marcia Landy adds the specifically cinematic modes of "romantic comedies, comedian films, musicals, genre parodies, comedies of manners, family comedies."[5] It is difficult to locate a set of stable structural conventions as common ground for these different styles. It may feel more secure to argue, instead, that they are linked by the operation of *humor*, which Noël Carrol defines as "what comic amusement is properly directed towards."[6] Far from resolving the problem of definition, however, this simply introduces further challenges. Like *comedy*, the meanings of *humor* quickly proliferate. In his postwar account of *The English Sense of Humour*, Harold Nicolson distinguishes between "the ludicrous, the ridiculous, the quaint, the droll, the jocular, the facetious, the waggish, the bantering, the farcical . . . [as well as] wit, irony, satire, sarcasm, fancy, mockery, joke, quirk, pun, tomfoolery, clowning, glee, the burlesque, the mock-heroic and what is known as 'innocent mirth' . . . [plus] 'grim humour,' 'kindly humour,' 'wry humour,' 'pretty humour,' 'sardonic humour,' 'salacious humour,' 'sly humour,' 'macabre humour,' 'pert humour' and 'gay humour.'"[7] Such a list can only hope to be partial, although this iteration has already assumed sufficient scale to become *laughable*.

As is becoming clear, it is not possible to arrive at a definitely definite definition of *comedy*, any more than of *queer* or *eccentricity*. It is also not desirable. This is not because, in Andy Medhurst's colorful terms, "the analyst of comedy is the definitive killjoy, literally so: the assassin of enjoyment, who takes what was life-affirming and renders it inert, or the slaughterer of laughter, hauling the still-warm body of comedy into the analytical abattoir before felling it with the deadening blows of uber-scrutiny and eviscerating it with the scalpels of hyper-analysis."[8] No cultural mode that matters—as Medhurst acknowledges—should be overlooked because of critical squeamishness; comedy is too important not to be discussed. My reluctance to enter the fray and attempt a definition of comedy is because I hope, through this book, to celebrate the slipperiness of critical terms rather than to attempt to turn them into totalized centers that constrain a text's play. I wish to allow the gestures that I am calling *eccentric*, *queer*, and *comic* as much latitude as possible to undo stable meaning. This attempt is aligned with the body of critical and theoretical writing on comedy that identifies humor's capacity for subverting expectation and making hierarchically arranged power look ridiculous. As a critique of assumptions, this kind of comedy works as the rib-tickling partner to eccentricity and queerness, each of them fleetingly revealing the fragility of the mythologizing category of the *normal* and giving a glimpse of something else. Humor—benignly or maliciously, but always mischievously—pokes fun at the flawed, cracked, incongruous, contradictory, defunct, paradoxical, inadequate structures that govern social and political lives. One of the structures that British comedy has routinely mocked is the network of heterocentric myths around marriage, family, children, gender, and sex.

John Morreall suggests this political function when he argues that humor represents "a jolt to our picture of the way things are supposed to be."[9] This *supposed to be* marks the site at which a contingent attitude has been repeated and reproduced so often within a culture that it has come to seem natural and been transformed into a center that constrains the play of possibility, consolidating a society's hierarchical structure in which power is not evenly distributed. Jokes wriggle free of such centers. Even a simple joke such as "Marriage is when a man and woman become as one—the trouble starts when they try to decide which one" provides a modest jolt to the clichéd image of marriage as the metaphysical transformation of two beings into one flesh. It embeds a heterosexist assumption that marriage is between a man and woman, but it yokes this structure to the unruly word *trouble* (which starts but does not, as far as the joke lets on, ever stop) and uses direct repetition of *one* to show some of the absurdity of the heterocentric myth of monogamy. The cumulative effect of a whole film's worth of jokes can be seismic. "When we look at our own culture with a sense of humor," writes Morreall, "we see our customs, which we often take for granted as the natural way to do things, as just one possible way of doing things."[10] In any rhetorical process through which the *obvious* becomes merely *an option*, other possibilities become available, even if they are not explicitly stated. In the joke above, the absurdity of the metaphysics of matrimonial *oneness* raises the specter of alternative possibilities, from the banal deromanticized view of marriage as the companionate contract between two independent individuals to the more transgressive shout-out for polygamy or adultery (which explode the two-become-one model), or homosexuality (which redefines the marriage = man + woman formula).

Terry Eagleton describes humor as "a minor outbreak of anarchy . . . [which disturbs] our rigorously taxonomising impulse."[11] He lists the comic strategies of "irony, bathos, puns, wordplay, ambiguity, incongruity, deviation, black humour, misunderstandings, iconoclasm, grotesquerie, out-of-placeness, doubling, absurdity, nonsense, blunders, defamiliarisation, quick changes and hyperbole" as disturbances of a world that "suddenly ceases to be as self-consistent as it appeared a few moments ago."[12] This assault on the ordered world of meaning is the point at which comedy intersects with the eccentric and the queer as I have been presenting them; they each represent the scandalous moment at which a "grim-lipped insistence on congruence, coherence, consistency, logic, linearity and univocal signifiers, ceases to fend off unwanted meanings and unconscious associations, [which] allows us to revel in a playful diversifying of sense."[13] And this play, as with explosively eccentric queerness's rearrangement of heterocentric myths, is politically charged; Steve Neale argues that mythoclastic comedy is "a narrative process in which various languages, logics, discourses, and codes are, at one point or another—at precisely the points of comedy itself—revealed as fictions."[14] Comedy joins eccentricity and queer, with their shared work of denaturalizing structures, in the conditional mood. They each displace what *is* with the fantastic possibilities (however fleetingly glimpsed) of what *could be*, what *should be*, and *what would happen if*. . . .

The most well-known statement on this kind of eccentric comedy, whose function is to expose the absurd contingency of familiar myths and give a glimpse of alternatives, is Mikhail Bakhtin's theory of the carnivalesque. Bakhtin's account of the medieval festival locates the comic as a radical spirit, stifled by the privileging of seriousness in the periods that followed, which can invert and subvert the hierarchical structures of a society through the dynamic exercise of fun. Bakhtin's work provides a historical commentary on how, in the words of Allon White, "the authority to designate what is to be taken seriously (and the authority to enforce reverential solemnity in certain contexts) is a way of creating and maintaining power."[15] The carnival is opposed precisely to such seriousness, undermining any authoritative attempt to impose power. Bakhtin writes that: "As opposed to the official feast, one might say that carnival celebrated temporary liberation from the prevailing truth and from the established order; it marked the suspension of all hierarchical rank, privileges, norms and prohibitions. Carnival was the true feast of time, the feast of becoming, change and renewal. It was hostile to all that was immortalized and completed."[16] This concentration on the mirthful interruption of "norms and prohibitions" indicates the carnivalesque roots of much queer activism and theory, especially given Bakhtin's concentration on the profane and the erotic, which includes, as Morreall summarizes, "the breaking of sexual taboos."[17] The carnivalesque is the suspension of "laws, prohibitions and restrictions that determine the structure and order of ordinary, that is noncarnival, life", this everyday structure is the "hierarchical structure and all the forms of terror, reverence, piety and etiquette connected with it—that is, everything resulting from socio-hierarchical inequality."[18] Bakhtin explicitly invokes the idea of eccentricity as fundamental to his theory. Adrian Stevens highlights this, suggesting that in Bakhtin's work

> eccentricity represents "a special category of the carnival sense of the world" because it permits "the latent sides of human nature to reveal and express themselves"; and it is through the eccentric capacity to overturn repressions and break with taboos that the grotesque comedy of mismatches or "carnivalistic mésalliances" is generated. All things which

are, in Bakhtin's words, "self-enclosed, disunified, distanced from one another" by the normative (and characteristically decent and decorous) hierarchical worldview pertaining outside carnival get "drawn into carnivalistic contacts and combinations." In its celebration of mismatches and misrule carnival "brings together, unifies, weds, and combines the sacred with the profane, the lofty with the low, the great with the insignificant, the wise with the stupid"; it dramatizes the "sense of the gay relativity of prevailing truths and authorities"; and the comedy it generates in the process of destabilizing norms is the anarchic, transgressive, topsy-turvy comedy of a world turned upside down and stood on its head.[19]

In many ways, the postwar Britain of the comedies explored in this book can be read as carnivalesque. In the shock of a peace that had to articulate itself in the absence of many of the certainties that had underpinned society before the upheaval of conflict, many "decent and decorous" assumptions had been disturbed. Arising from the slow end of austerity and the first gleaming hint of affluence, *The Lavender Hill Mob* is a "topsy-turvy comedy of a world turned upside down." Its heroes—Holland, a self-declared "nonentity" and Pendlebury who must "propagate British cultural depravity" through his production of tacky tourist souvenirs—claim a little of the opportunity that has always been denied them. Barr writes that "both the worms turn; they decide to grab their chance at wealth."[20] The wild descent down the Eiffel Tower by these two turning worms smacks of a kind of carnivalesque abandon.

Bakhtin's notion of the carnivalesque, at its most transgressive, complicates "the relations of subject and object, agent and instrument, husband and wife, old and young, animal and human, master and slave."[21] In the form of the carnivalesque identified by Barr, however, this complication is merely a kind of inversion, namely the (temporary) flipping of the power dynamics within a binary: powerful/nonentity. This process of inversion ultimately preserves unequal, concentric binary structures; the center may shift, but the basic structure remains fundamentally intact. As Derrida expresses the point, "because such a scheme of reversal could only repeat the traditional scheme (in which the hierarchy of duality is always reconstituted), it alone could not effect any significant change."²² This does not seize the radical potential of Bakhtin's rejection of inversion and, instead, "brings together, unifies, weds, and combines" opposites.²³ Eagleton agrees, arguing that "Bakhtin recapitulates *avant la lettre* many of the leading motifs of contemporary deconstruction" and describes how "only the rumbustious carnivalesque spirit, joyful, fearless and free, is audacious enough to affirm reality in all its volatile, provisional, unfinished, unstable, open-ended character, and thus to dispense with stout foundations, metaphysical guarantees and transcendental signifiers."²⁴

This vision of the carnivalesque, at odds with Barr's worm-turning, is reminiscent of the eccentricity that, as I argue in chapter 1 in relation to *Passport to Pimlico*, is not the inversion but the *explosion* of binary structures. The Pimlico police constable's realization that "Blimey, I'm a foreigner" does not reinforce the dichotomy self–other but unceremoniously shatters it. Similarly, domestic drag (see chapter 2) does not simply chuckle over the reversed structure of the binary real–artifice but confuses it entirely; the *real* home—whose reality is both guaranteed by and, in turn, the guarantee of its naturalness—is always also the *fake* home because the very idea of *home* is understood through the fictions of heterocentric mythology. In *The Lavender Hill Mob*, hierarchized binaries are not simply inverted in gestures of worm-turning topsy-turvydom. Holland and Pendlebury's fall from the Eiffel Tower is characterized by a more subversive carnivalesque energy; the men are both winning and losing, both successful and defeated, both heroes and villains, both safe and endangered. In their uncentered state of uncertainty, they have not been caught, but they are no longer free; they are chasing, not being chased, and yet they cannot escape the schoolgirls who have made off with the incriminating Eiffel Towers; the men are together, but they begin to fall apart. Their success displays its trace of failure, but their failure always maintains a trace of success. They are lost according to the structured, orientating map of their culture, and, in their lostness, they laugh—*at nothing*.

Laughing at—What?

Bakhtin argues that in the world of mediaeval carnival "laughter was as universal as seriousness; it was directed at the whole world, at history, at all societies, at ideology."[25] This laughter, which expresses a playful subversion of political structure, has points in common with the laughter imagined by George Orwell as the Second World War ended: "A thing is funny when—in some way that is not actually offensive or frightening—it upsets the established order. Every joke is a tiny revolution. If you had to define humour in a single phrase, you might define it as dignity sitting on a tin-tack. Whatever destroys dignity, and brings down the mighty from their seats, preferably with a bump, is funny. And the bigger the fall, the bigger the joke."[26] Like the carnivalesque, this understanding of the funny collapses hierarchy by upsetting established order. Orwell's vision, however, is of a specific facet of carnivalesque comedy, one defined by what Alex Clayton refers to as "the acerbic bite of satire"; it shows its teeth to its target, but more as snarl than smile.[27] Roger Rawlings identifies postwar British comedy films (including *Passport to Pimlico*) not as "mere 'comedies' but great achievements of high satire," allowing the filmmakers and their audiences "to address the social trauma and define a new age . . . [in order] to understand where they were."[28] Satire is often a "sourish meditation on British institutions."[29] Although, according to Rawlings, it "question[s] the moral certainties and absolutes of those (often insular) groups that held sway and power for so long," in order to do so it has to recognize the logic of the system that it is interrogating.[30] Satire relies for its legibility on recognizable structures, with films such as *Private's Progress* (John Boulting, 1956), *Brothers in Law* (Roy Boulting, 1957), and *Lucky Jim* (John Boulting, 1957) recognizing—even as they laugh at—the structures of the army, the legal system, and higher education respectively. Satire's play may lampoon structures, but its freedom is nevertheless constrained by the individuals and institutions that are its object and continue to center it. Satire is always laughing *at* (and *around*) *something*.

While I agree with Rawlings that many postwar British comedies (including those that I am exploring in this book) have satirical elements, I argue that a more radical subversion of meaning results from the ex-centering of the structures that the satire depends on. Rawlings suggests that "satire is lethal, it seeks to destroy, to burn away the rot of what it sees as the virus decaying society" but its ambition is to produce "a newer, purer" world, to replace the *something* that it laughs at with *something* else.[31] Eccentricity questions the idea of both newness and purity; this singular world imagined by satire is too stable, too centered to be an eccentric fantasy of proliferation, indeterminacy, and open possibilities. Rawlings quotes Northrop Frye's argument that satire's "moral norms are relatively clear, and it assumes standards . . . to give form to the shifting ambiguities and complexities of unidealized existence"; images of clear norms and definite form may articulate political programs, but they diminish the queer possibility of ambiguous, complex eccentricity.[32] In *Brothers in Law*, satire is represented by Ian Carmichael's and Richard Attenborough's silly ass turns as barristers, operating within conventional hierarchical institutions in a way that makes them look ridiculous. Eccentric comedy, on the other hand, is represented in the film by Irene Handl's tiny cameo as a witness who explodes those institutions by failing to register the centric authority of the court and giving testimony as a hilariously meaningless string of ambiguous pronouns (*it*, *what*, and *that*) in place of useful detail. Rawlings suggests that comedy "ultimately lets the community off the hook"; I disagree, and argue that its incorrigible plurality of possibilities is more destabilizing because less directed than the dream of satire "to destroy the world so a new one can be born from its ashes."[33]

As Holland and Pendlebury are careering down the Eiffel Tower, they are satirizing nothing. Their laughter is not caused by or directed at anything in particular. They are not even satirizing the conventions of the crime film; their later chase with an infantry of policemen and then a fleet of police cars may be generic parody, but the Eiffel Tower sequence is too idiosyncratic to be satirizing a recognizable genre. They are not laughing specifically at the conventions of the crime film, the habits of the Parisians, the silliness of the British police, or the chilling grown-upness of British private schoolgirls. They are *laughing at nothing* for the simple reason that *there is nothing to laugh at*. As a gesture, this laughter *expresses* without fully *meaning* anything. Such disturbing images of meaningless and undisciplined mirth have underpinned a history of philosophical and cultural unease about laughter. Plato presents it as "a lack of rational self-control" and a comparable prejudice coils forward through centuries of religious prohibitions.[34] Addison argues that it is a result of Original Sin and a kind of Fall from grace.[35] Baudelaire discusses it as "a damnable element born of satanic parentage."[36] Its effect on the body "dissolves good posture, contorts the face, causes physical abandon (such as incontinence), and generates loud, extra-linguistic sounds."[37] It has been seen as "a respiratory convulsion . . . [which] is not something which we can undertake voluntarily."[38] It can consist of involuntary actions that are "little more than physiological reactions."[39] Clayton, more lyrically and more affirmatively, describes it as "that surge of exhilaration that, for shorthand, we call laughter."[40] Laughter, and especially undisciplined laughter at nothing, is exhilarating, explosive, and dangerous.

This danger lies in the fact that laughter *at* nothing is not laughter that *does* nothing. The laughter on the Eiffel Tower, unlike the directed laughter of satire, has no object (that is, no external target). When the laughter audibly continues despite Holland and Pendlebury's faces showing no signs of laughing, it is also divorced from a clearly laughing subject. Such a disruption of the subject–object binary is observed by Bataille, who regards laughter as "that place where nothing counts anymore—neither the 'object,' nor the 'subject.' "[41] Without either subject or object to anchor itself around, the laughter becomes eccentric. It is also ecstatic. It is a laughter that is without scorn because it is without target, and is a display of neither agency nor loss. Unlike satirical laughter, it runs no risk of consolidating any structure because it is itself structureless. It is a point of intersection between the *funny-ha-ha* and the *funny-peculiar* and represents a kind of logical misbehavior that makes a joke of such heterocentric apparatuses as *grown-up common sense*, *masculine reason*, and *feminine deportment*. Giggling at nothing shows the same kind of irreverent disregard for convention as other displays of childish silliness. It is unproductive. Some viewers may seek to argue that the two men on the steps of the Eiffel Tower are not laughing at *nothing*, but spontaneously as a result of their own lightheaded dizziness or anxiety. I suggest that the explanation is *not just* this banal, and that Holland be taken at his word. To insist that he has overlooked *something* is to take a sequence—whose visual grammar, shifting soundtrack, and narrative gratuitousness all resist centering—and to impose a center. It is to introduce structure needlessly to a sequence that offers no such structure. It is, therefore, to diminish the free play of elements and to overlook a display of preposterous *laughing forward* of the vision of an eccentric world.

Comic theory has often struggled to accommodate such unaccountable laughter. The three most durable totalizing explanations for laughter have been the superiority theory, the release theory, and the incongruity theory. The first, originating in the work of Thomas

Hobbes, argues that laughter arises from a sense of physical, moral, or intellectual superiority in the laugher; this superiority can be relative to the humorous object (which is humiliated) or the laugher's sense of their own earlier self (which is mocked as ignorant or foolish). The second theory, associated with Freud's psychoanalytic writings, argues that laughter is the audible sound of relief at the laugher's release from repressive convention into temporary play with taboo; when the "energy used for the inhibition has now suddenly become superfluous and has been lifted, [it] is therefore now ready to be discharged as laughter."[42] The third theory, expressed in works by Kant and Schopenhauer, argues that laughter is the result when hierarchical structures are disrupted by the absurdly incongruous mixing of the high with the low. Each of these theories has received sustained critique, and generally it is accepted that none is able to explain all humor.[43] None provides a mechanism for reading eccentric laughter in *The Lavender Hill Mob*. Each, in a different way, reinforces structures and does not ex-center them: a comic sense of superiority depends upon rigid hierarchies to underpin its judgments; a comic sense of release depends on the structure of norms against which the momentary freedom can be measured and to which the laugher must return after the fleeting catharsis of the taboo laugh; and a comic sense of incongruity must have a sense of where things belong in order to see the laughable absurdity of their new position. As the two running men laugh, there is no one for them to feel superior to, no reason for them to feel relief from convention, and, while their situation may be unusual, there is no humorously incongruous meeting of dissimilar elements.

The two questions that course, helter-skelter, through theories of laughter are: What do we laugh *at*? and What do we laugh *for*? As I read the sequence from *The Lavender Hill Mob*, both questions are answered eccentrically: there is nothing to laugh at and they laugh for no reason. This, it should be stressed, is not a perverse reading, but a reading in good faith, one that accepts the testimony of a character who has no reason to dissemble. This leads me to ask what laughter is when it is *at* nothing, and what such laughter does. Theodor Adorno and Max Horkheimer offer a pessimistic theory of eccentric laughter in which they rather party-poopingly pronounce that "fun is a medicinal bath," diagnosing laughter as a symptom of a culture industry that treats mass entertainment as a vacuous placebo to distract its audiences from the emptiness of their lives.[44] Audiences watch films and laugh in place of meaningful experience; this process is a mechanism through which capitalism maintains its central dominance within a culture. But *The Lavender Hill Mob*, in a daring gesture, introduces a metalanguage in which the emptiness of the laughter is not effaced (as Adorno and Horkheimer argue that it is) but declared. It is not just the audience laughing, but also the characters. And Holland *admits the absence of meaning*. The frame—which twists and turns and confuses with the almost abstract diagonals of the Eiffel Tower—does nothing to relieve this semantic emptiness. The sequence's politics stem from the subversive admission that the laughter is a gesture beyond meaning.

Poststructuralism models a response to laughter at nothing that permits a more productive eccentricity than Adorno and Horkheimer's theory of the culture industry. In this model, laughter—like gesture more generally—marks a site of semiotic insufficiency. Rather than a confirmation of the structures of knowledge that underpin our sense of language's capacity for communication, the laugh is slippery, expressive but ultimately not meaningful. It disrupts the reductive binary meaningful–meaningless. This laughter is an "extra-linguistic bark signalling a lack of understanding."[45] Eagleton describes it as "a pure enunciation that expresses nothing but itself . . . lack[ing] intrinsic sense" and suggests that "at its most riotous and convulsive it involves the disintegration of sense, as the body tears one's speech to fragments."[46] This derangement of sense, in which something is expressed but nothing is meant, "represents a momentary respite from the tyrannical legibility of the world, a realm of lost innocence which pre-dates our calamitous fall into meaning"; "the literally meaningless sound of laughter enacts this hemorrhage of sense . . . [as it] bleaches [the universe] of coherent meaning altogether."[47] In a preposterous echo of Holland on the Eiffel Tower, Mikkel Borch-Jacobsen argues that laughter is "representation, necessarily pathetic and miniscule, of NOTHING . . . NOTHING is the impossible, the impossible to present, and thus its presentation can be nothing other than a comedy, risible and ridiculous."[48] This is not a complicity with capitalist structure as observed by Adorno and Horkheimer; it is, rather, the grave of structure altogether. Outside structure, this eccentric laughter is outside the possibility of clear representation. It is unconstrained play, directed at and opposed to nothing, resisting any attempt to coerce it into final meaning. Outside of any possible binary, both fun and deadly serious, it is the *un*reasonable rendered in sound as an affront to understanding and logic. The question *Why do Pendlebury and Holland laugh?* must produce such an ungainly infinity of speculations, all based on the assumptions of the individual viewer, that it ultimately remains unanswerable.

Descending for the Final Time in *The Lavender Hill Mob*

Like eccentric gestures more generally, the laughter in *The Lavender Hill Mob* creates an effect even as it disturbs the seeming solidity of systems of knowledge. The Eiffel Tower sequence generally is a tour de force of imaginative direction and design that stands within the broader film in a position of both central importance and total gratuitousness; the film both hinges on it and does not need it at all; it is the decisive shift in direction toward disaster and the absence of any actual narrative event. It is a center that is not the center—and yet it is. The camera tilts, and reels, and spins—each gesture coordinating with a vertigo that is not only a response to heights and circular motion but also to the collapse of Holland's plan, which has structured the narrative till this point. With a couple of minor hiccups, the plan has run as it was designed to. The mob—whose members include Lackery Wood (Sid James) and Shorty Fisher (Alfie Bass), the career villains who aid Holland and Pendlebury—has respected the plan's integral structure. Lackery wobblingly learns to ride a bicycle in preparation for the robbery and the endless (somewhat erratic) circles that he describes on the wobbling bike mark the mob's attempts to remain concentric around the stable center of Holland's scheme. But at the Eiffel Tower, this plan evaporates as a structuring center and the two men are lost. The abrupt ex-centering of narrative and thematic structure is accompanied by a suddenly feral camera, liberated from the constraints of a British postwar cinema that typically favors more sedate cinematography.

As the men begin their descent of the staircase, the editing shifts the frame between a range of impossible vantage points, accentuating the strange geometries of the structure, with its acentric diagonals. When the two men begin to laugh, spinning vertical shots through a mass of eccentric steel amplify the sequence's liberation from conventional screen grammar. The binary static–mobile is disturbed by a frame in which it is difficult to identify which parts are moving and which are still: the camera, locked on a crane, drops in a vertical shot, moving on a consistent line; the central column and the staircase, which pretend to be still, spin anticlockwise while the two men run clockwise at a slightly faster rate; meanwhile, moving footage of a Parisian view intersected by the geometrically outrageous girders of the Eiffel Tower turns nauseatingly in rear projection on a still screen. I laugh, even as I reel vertiginously at the absence of a center for the frame; the men, the central column, the background, and the tower itself are all too mobile to anchor the confusing spectacle. As each element moves in a different direction and at a different rate, both space and time become unreliable. In a virtuoso flourish of unconvincing realism, the film is speeded up as the men continue down the tower; the deranged rear projection fairly gallops past them, like the backdrop to a static fairground ride designed to create the sense of movement. Once more on solid ground, the camera, parodying the men's fall-about dizziness, tilts and pans and spins in an unfocused, unstable reel. Blurrily, Holland and Pendlebury watch as the schoolgirls are driven away, their faces distorted through the windows of the car. The audacious sequence of *trompes l'oeil* eschews realism for something else, which is not quite fantasy and not quite surrealism and which I call eccentricity.

If the sequence exists in order to make sense, it is inept. This is Harper and Porter's view when they argue that such formal elements as rear projection were "deployed [by Ealing] in an increasingly ham-fisted manner: *The Lavender Hill Mob*, for example."[49] Such a verdict is predicated on the belief that the ambition of British comedies in the postwar era must be verisimilitude, but it is difficult to understand why this sequence should be read in these terms. If it exists, instead, to mock sense and to explode (with a level of visual panache that director Charles Crichton is not given full credit for) narrative order, it is sublime. From this point, the film's story, which has lost a center to "orient, balance, and organize the structure," becomes unpredictable and unstructured.[50] The Eiffel Tower sequence ex-centers all that follows in the film and, retroactively, all that has come before. Narrative, thematic, and tonal coherence decay as gestures begin to dismantle the certainties that can no longer underpin the film. This eccentricity is largely overlooked in critical responses to the film. In particular, analysis has insisted that the framing narrative *settles* the film and organizes its structure absolutely. The film begins in Rio; Holland, a social success, flirts with Chiquita (Audrey Hepburn) and gives money to good causes. He smokes a cigar, wears a nice suit, and beams with satisfaction. He shares his table with another man and begins to tell him the story that the film dramatizes. After the climactic police chase in which Pendlebury is caught, Holland gives the police the slip in the City of London by Bank tube station as the strains of South American music incongruously begin. The film returns to Rio via a slow dissolve in which, for a handful of exquisite moments, bobbies and bowler-hatted bankers outside a London tube station merge and play with the cigar-wielding Holland and a bongo-beating samba band (see fig. 3.2).

Twelve months are folded into this destabilizing dissolve, acknowledged but unshown, a period whose excesses of ribald play can only be imagined; Holland suggestively refers to Brazil as a "gay sprightly

Figure 3.2. Dissolving boundaries in *The Lavender Hill Mob* (Charles Crichton, 1951). *Source:* Ealing Studios/Courtesy of STUDIOCANAL.

land of mirthful ease." Compounding the strangeness of the dissolve, Holland says that "changing as usual at Charing Cross, I came straight on to Rio de Janeiro," skipping over the challenges—not to say the impossibility—of such an escape. A brief interlude with the British ambassador (Michael Trubshawe) reveals that Holland has done more for British prestige than a battleship. Holland sits for a still moment of inscrutable reflection. The man with whom he is sitting asks if he is ready; Holland says that he is; they stand and leave, revealing that the film's hero is in handcuffs. It is this twist—revealed with the force and timing of a punch line—that has resulted in criticism's conviction that the film is ultimately a consensus picture of impeccable conventionality: Barr suggests that it "continually endors[es] the 'social' values"; Landy that "the narrative, utilizing the comic mode of the world turned upside down, turns not to a utopian solution but to a sober restoration of law and order"; Geraghty that it is "a conventionally moral ending"; Harper and Porter that it "entertains the idea of a challenge to order, but it . . . is playful and inconsequential"; and Rawlings that "authority may prevail in the end, a conventional device to keep the censors satiated."[51] Barr and Geraghty agree that the film plays with an image of attractive unorthodox behavior, but that ultimately the lack of "risk"—by which they mean violence and nastiness—"reasserts order."[52]

This, however, is a needlessly narrow definition of risk. As I see it, that Parisian laughter, which echoes through the film, risks everything. Holland and Pendlebury, even in the moment of their greatest danger, not only laugh at nothing but *laugh together*. Their group laughter compounds the disruption to the self–other binary while a kind of infectious joy undoes the boundaries between them; capturing the sense of both energy and explosive risk in such laughter, Morreall describes it as being "like atomic fission."[53] Eagleton presents it as a "Dionysian force [that] garbles sense, confounds hierarchies, merges identities, scrambles distinctions and revels in the collapse of meaning."[54] In this, it recalls queer theory's interest in sex's "self-shattering" effects; eccentric laughter has an erotic *jouissance* that "involves the transgression of the supposed boundaries between self and other, subject and object, inside and outside, active and passive, power and powerlessness."[55] It resembles the carnivalesque laughter that Eagleton summarizes as "a 'dialogic' decentring of the discrete subject that explodes the authoritarian solemnities of monologue . . . [and leaves] the subject caught up in a pleasurable play of shifting solidarity with others."[56]

By *laughing together*, Holland and Pendlebury become fluid; they lose their stabilizing centers and their own definition. The demotic sounds of their laughter merge and become indistinguishable. Their bodies become, in the intimacy of their shared danger and exhilaration, "unfinished, open-ended, perpetually in process . . . a riposte to the timeless, absolute status of official ideologies."[57] As the images of their running down the stairs in Paris are projected at an accelerated rate, Holland and Pendlebury are hardly bodies at all; they are blurry motion filmed in long shot, unbounded bodies that make even the iconic solidity of the Eiffel Tower spin. It is the echo of this boundary-blurring laughter at nothing that later allows Holland, across a dissolve, to transform from a London nonentity into a Rio man who is "better than a battleship." And the ghost of this explosive queer laughter is visible in Holland's smile as he talks to the arresting officer in the Brazilian bar. The situation cannot adequately explain the smile. Nor can it justify the officer's decision to sit with Holland long enough to hear his complete story, his hand buried in Holland's lap (which cannot credibly be justified as an attempt to hide the handcuffs). Their unaccountable companionship and Holland's smile recall the iconography of the *date* more than the *arrest*. (In a 1950s in which plainclothes police officers in the UK solicited men in order to arrest them for homosexual offenses at ever-increasing rates, dates and arrests could easily be confused.)[58] This intimacy—in which handcuffs trouble rather than reinforce the boundaries between the two men and make them look as though they are holding hands—explodes hierarchized binaries.

The heterocentric conventions of culture are caught in the blast of this explosion. In a surprising parallel, the laughter of Holland recalls the laughter that Hélène Cixous sees on the face of Medusa. Cixous advocates an antipatriarchal, antiheterocentric writing that is able "to smash everything, to shatter the framework of institutions, to blow up the law, to break up the 'truth' with laughter."[59] This is the creation of a new and destructive "chaosmos" that enjoys "the taste of free air" not by negotiating a new position within existing structures but by ex-centering and queering them and exploding the insistent hierarchies of conventional thinking; Holland's smile-at-nothing at the moment of incarceration gestures to this freedom outside the logic of law and manacle.[60] Woman, in Cixous's essay, "has always functioned 'within' the discourse of man, a signifier that has always referred back to the opposite signifier which annihilates its specific energy and diminishes or stifles its very different sounds, so it is time for her to dislocate this 'within,' to explode it, turn it around, and seize it."[61] Holland and his mob, in parallel, have lived their lives within a heterocentric language that cannot accommodate them and their homosociality, that has reduced them to the status of "nonentity," and—whether caught or not—their ebullient, meaningless laughter has liberated them by refusing to work within a semiotic system that can acknowledge, let alone celebrate, their unorthodox intimacy. This mob intimacy represents a kind of self-shattering, a boundary-detonating intimate friendship that overrides class to reveal the "fragility . . . of the symbolic order seen as an orderly structure of kinship roles, governed by a set of rules for their appropriate combination"; conventional heterocentric kinship is experienced only as constraint, as seen in the ways in which Lackery is constrained by his responsibilities as a married man whose wife won't allow him to travel to Paris.[62] On the Eiffel Tower, in the mob's earlier raucous celebration, and even in the smiling scene of his own arrest, Holland discovers a homosocial kinship that dissolves character (quite literally in the gesture of the slow transition between Holland-as-nonentity outside Bank station and Holland-as-battleship in Rio) and reduces heterocentric meaning to the explosive bark of a laugh at nothing.

The Lavender Hill Mob, for my money the funniest of all postwar comedies, is all risk. I disagree with Barr and Geraghty who find it cozy. It is a film that *laughs forward* a glimpse of the ecstatic liberation that comes as plans collapse. This is in sharp distinction to postwar Britain's commitment to planning, in which cities, health, families, and kindness (as welfare) were all subject to the schemes of the architects of the New Jerusalem. This planning, socially important though it was, was necessarily always within structures that excluded many. *The Lavender Hill Mob* finds its laughter in the very spaces outside planning, spaces in which something disordered can arise. This is not the same as the unregulated free market dreams of the postconsensus 1980s; it is the image of a mob whose liberation is from the broader social logic that heterosexual romance (culminating in children) and wealth accumulation are compulsory. The triumph of Guinness's performance in the final scene is in the gesture of that enigmatic smile, even as he is about to lose his life of cash and Chiquita. It is the same smile that he shares with Pendlebury earlier as they hold the first of their golden Eiffel Towers and proudly—and homosocially—christen it their "first born." The smile is a gesture of semiotic insufficiency that defiantly resists the moralizing efforts to read his homecoming as the collapse of his pleasure. *The Lavender Hill Mob laughs forward* the image of homosocial love and the structure ex-centering laughter that marks the grave of meaning at the point at which there is nothing to be said.

Ending Up in Stitches in *It's Never Too Late*

In the remainder of this chapter, I consider two films that end in images of onscreen laughter. The laughter in these instances coincides with cinema's terminal slogan—THE END—to become a sound that is, structurally at least, at the very limit of the film's meaning-making. The first is from *It's Never Too Late* (Michael McCarthy, UK, 1956), one of the preeminent examples of 1950s domestic drag. Based on a play and set within the artifice-admitting studio setting of a house in St. John's Wood, it tells the story of the Hammond family. Materfamilias Laura (Phyllis Calvert), with the unflappable good grace and gentle glamor of so many onscreen domestic laborers, carries the worlds of her family members on her gently padded shoulders: she keeps house for her husband Charles (Patrick Barr), babysits for her stepson John (Richard Leech) and stepdaughter-in-law Anne (Sarah Lawson), soothes her daughter Tessa (Susan Stephen), and makes endless cups of tea for her sour mother (Jean Taylor Smith). This family, rubbing along together in an enormous townhouse, takes Laura for granted. When publisher Stephen Hodgson (Guy Rolfe) expresses interest in a novel that she has (miraculously) written in her spare moments and secures an enormous deal for the film rights, Laura takes a break from her family and jets to America to work on the screenplay. In her absence, Charles has an affair with neighborhood vamp Madge Dixon (Delphi Lawrence), John and Anne employ a sadistic nanny, Tessa is harassed by a lecherous film producer, and Grannie gets no tea. Laura returns to England but, in order to avoid the distractions of her demanding family, stays in an apartment arranged by Stephen. She is, however, unable to write and realizes that her creative inspiration depends on domestic pandemonium. She returns to the family house and is reconciled with her husband.

It's Never Too Late is, for my taste, a very unfunny comedy. Its domestic drag is less arresting than the films discussed in chapter 2—not least because of the fairly extensive amount of location filming in gorgeously sun-drenched London streets—and this makes it a less effective critique of the artifice of heterocentric structures. The camerawork is imaginative and more varied than in many British films of the period, with extensive use of traveling shots. The editing is expressive and unexpected; as Charles tells Laura that she is becoming very like her mother, an extraordinary J-cut introduces an explosive sound that is only explained seconds later as the image dissolves into a plane propeller before, in turn, dissolving into a series of spinning newspapers bearing headlines about Laura's trip to Hollywood. Despite these moments of visual flair, many sequences offer such outmoded images of gender performance that it is hard to imagine that they were ever intended to be funny. Stepdaughter-in-law Anne, denied either discernible character or narrative function, is reduced to a vase-flinging depiction of *unreasonable womanhood*; her arguments with her husband—because he wishes to escape "this atmosphere of nursery rhymes and wet napkins" and is thwarted by the fact that she has "those damn children on the brain and can't think of anything else"—end in unpleasant violence, including slapping, hitting, and shoving. When Grannie witnesses this violence, she smiles. Charles is no better; he admits that Laura looks harassed but, even as she begs him to listen to her, he lurks behind his raised newspaper in a gloom of misogyny. As the film begins, Tessa is rehearsing the part of Cordelia; this is an appropriate role, as like *King Lear*, *It's Never Too Late* addresses the question of how love should be expressed and how power should be distributed. Also like *King Lear*, it has very few laughs.

When I refer to this absence of laughs, I am not only making a comment about my response as a viewer. The diegetic worlds of the Hammonds' home and Hollywood are also both markedly devoid of laughing characters. Laura periodically attempts to laugh, but she is typically censored by the acerbic figure of Grannie: the older woman glowers when Laura begins to laugh at Tessa's histrionic threats never to eat again and tells Laura that she "fail[s] to see what is so amusing about that" when the old woman mistakes Stephen for a bank manager. When Laura and Tessa share a joke about a shared memory, the laughter is constricted and forced. There is a freer laughter among the family when Laura, returning from Hollywood, gives the gift of a whisky-concealing statuette to Charles, but it is quickly choked when Laura reveals that she is not moving back into the house. Finally, when Laura's magic solution to her daughter's problems with the lecherous film producer is to conjure up her drippy ex-boyfriend (Peter Hammond), the stage is set for a totally mirthless heterocentric resolution. When the young couple become engaged, Tessa declares unsmilingly that they will move into the family home together and, despite no desire of her own, have children; her comment that "I suppose we shall have them—people always do" hints at the heterocentric pressure under which nuclear families are constructed.

The film's lack of performed laughter marks the lack of eccentric levity permitted in this home. The ending of the film, however, in an extraordinary gesture, introduces an unaccountable laughter that interrupts speech and complicates signification. As the uncomfortably reunited Laura and Charles sit on the stairs—a spot that is both architecturally central to the home and a liminal space of coming and going that is not really a place in its own right—a black dog runs through the open door and disappears into the garden. The dog is wonderfully shaggy, their flowing hair rendering them almost no more definite than a shapeless black mark on the filmstrip. In the open doorway, following her dog, appears the Hammonds' new neighbor (Irene Handl). The neighbor utters some seemingly innocuous words—"Oh, excuse me. I'm awfully sorry to intrude, but I seem to have lost my dog. I've taken the Dixon house next door. I'm your new neighbor." Laura and Charles exchange a glance and begin to laugh. The laugh is snortingly, convulsively helpless. The neighbor, apparently affronted, says, "Well, really." The film ends with an image of the Hammonds laughing, their tenuous family reconciliation seemingly predicated on an exclusionary laughter directed at someone from outside.

This laughter does not seem to be the boundary-disturbing laughter of the Eiffel Tower, which undoes clear division and merges identities. This is a laughter that builds on exclusion. Unlike the directionless laughter at nothing, it forms community by aiming its laughter at a ridiculed outsider. It helps to reinforce a concentric structure that has community at its center and rings of exclusion held in check around it. Poststructuralism rejects this idea of community, as summarized by John Caputo:

> After all, *communio* is a word for a military formation and a kissing cousin of the word "munitions"; to have a *communio* is to be fortified on all sides, to build a "common" (*com*) "defense" (*munis*), as when a wall is put up around the city to keep a stranger or the foreigner out. The self-protective closure of "community," then, would be just about the opposite of what deconstruction is, since deconstruction is the preparation for the incoming of the other, "open" and "porous" to the other, which would of course make one poor excuse for a defense system.[63]

The laughter-at-nothing of *The Lavender Hill Mob* is deconstructive in the capaciousness of its laughter, which explodes boundaries, makes its bearers porous and open to one another, and can even bestow smiles on arresting officers. The laughter of *It's Never Too Late*, on the other hand, is deferred until the very end and seems to be designed to chalk out the boundary line between the Us of the Hammonds and the Them of the rest of the world. Like homophobic, misogynistic, and xenophobic laughter, this sounds like an exclusive laughter. Medhurst writes that jokes "can wound and damage as much as they enthral and delight, and . . . if you belong to the group being vilified so that those who occupy another space of belonging can feel validated, the niceties of textual exegesis are not liable to be at the top of your agenda."[64] Such humor reproduces and reinforces heterocentric structures of power that are anything but eccentric and it is certainly not my hope to use textual exegesis to exonerate the mean-spiritedness of the Hammonds. This is Bergsonian laughter as a mechanism for social correction (see chapter 1); the neighbor's vocal affectations and unconventional physical gestures mark her out as an eccentric and the laughter may be read as a strategy for humiliating her into orthodoxy. It is the laughter of superiority, of disparaged incongruity, and of release from the taboo against mocking others. The word *humor* originally signified the idiosyncratic individual, the eccentric; even as its sense developed, the word retained some of the suggestion that oddity is laughable. This laughter is normalizing, consolidating cultural norms by laughing at deviations. It establishes distances, builds walls, and patrols boundaries. It is a mean-spirited resistance to otherness, and insists that difference can always be articulated in binary terms that presuppose a hierarchy of legitimacy. James English suggests that "comic practice is always on some level or in some measure an assertion of group against group, an effect and an event of struggle, a form of symbolic violence. The inescapable heterogeneity of society, the ceaseless conflict of social life, the multiple and irreconcilable patterns of identification within which relationships of hierarchy and solidarity must be negotiated—these are what our laughter is 'about.'"[65] It seems an unanswerable charge: Laura and Charles Hammond's laughter is about confirming their happy-ever-after heterocentric intimacy by performing its absolute exclusion of the stranger who lives next door; she—bizarre, unglamorous, and foolish—is *laughable*.

The account that I have given of the sequence, however, omits some important details. These details consist of a series of gestures performed by Handl. The film's first glimpse of her is in long shot, standing in the open doorway of the Hammonds' house, dressed extraordinarily in a bold floral print dress with lime-green bows. Elbow-length gloves complete the ensemble and help to emphasize her staginess; this is a domestic drag entrance. She is *The Comic Neighbor* as dramatic type rather than character. She has no name, no background, and no future, and her mannerisms, like Rutherford's in *Passport to Pimlico*, do not add specificity to the character portrait but draw attention to the fact of performance. On the words "awfully sorry to intrude," Handl performs an outrageous wiggle (as ecstatic as Gordon Jackson's in *Sailor Beware!*) that begins in an extreme lateral tilt of the head, cascading down into a multidirectional roll of the bosom and a swing of the hips. The skirt of her dress billows and tumbles. Her delivery of the line milks it for comic potential, finding a happy stress on the word "awfully," which becomes not only an intensifier but also a descriptor, suggesting both the awe-inspiring and the terrible. A brief shot of Laura and Charles bewildered ends with a cut back to a medium shot of the neighbor for the line "I'm your new neighbor." As the tighter shot begins, the absurd grandiloquence of Handl's pearl choker and earrings becomes clear; Handl writhes and ripples through the line, finally drawing in her chin as she finishes speaking, the seeming coyness of the gesture undone by the asymmetrical garishness of the lime-green bow. Laura and Charles exchange a glance and begin to laugh. The neighbor, again in medium shot, purses her lips, aspirates the extended, deranged syllable "Well" with all the showy outrage of a drawing room comedy. The sound out, she looks defeated, deflated. The Hammonds, again in their own exclusive medium shot, continue to laugh. But, in a return to the medium shot, the neighbor, initially looking forlorn, performs an extraordinary, scandalous shift: Handl takes a half step to frame right, her shoulders, chin, and eyes rising and falling with the movement, as she delivers the word "Really" and her pout twitches into a smile. This gesture (conveying both the irritated offendedness of the line and pout and the conviviality of the grin) defuses the targeted aggression of the Hammonds' communal laughter without censoring it. They laugh on and in a final shot of the neighbor, this noncharacter, who arrives only in order to provoke laughter in an unlaughing household, also laughs (see fig. 3.3).

The sheer strangeness of this unmotivated laughter is beautifully realized by Handl. She is one of the great performers of postwar British cinema, representing a mannered gestural style that is beyond the scope of any analysis. Her characters are vivid without being rounded and she endows every moment with an always surprising and idiosyncratic oddness. In *It's Never too Late*, her laughter is accompanied by shaking head, shoulders, and bosom, and her hand rises to cover and then caress her cheek. Her performance is all unsettled movement; she is, unlike the poised Hammonds, without stillness. The heterocentric

Figure 3.3. Laughing on the threshold in *It's Never Too Late* (Michael McCarthy, 1956). *Source:* Park Lane Films/Courtesy of STUDIOCANAL.

mirth of the married couple, which risks privileging their exclusive intimacy and creating boundaries, is met with the porous eccentricity of their neighbor, who laughs at nothing. Her laughter seems to be undirected, matched by her body as it performs its uncoordinated doorstep dance. On the threshold of their home, she delivers the laughter of the open door, neither inside nor outside, neither known nor unknown, in a state of betweenness. Even if, as some may argue, she is joining in the laughter at herself, this makes her both the laugher and the laughed-at, both of and outside the community. And anyway, Handl's performance exceeds the bounds of any one explanation. If comedy is a genre defined by the restoration of order, this gratuitous terminal sequence is needlessly disruptive; the family was already reunited. Søren Kierkegaard distinguishes between the irresolvable contradictions of tragedy and the resolvable contradictions of comedy, but Handl's performance introduces contradictions even as the film is trying to end.[66] The film abdicates its generic responsibility for constraining disordered content with reassuring form in the shape of a neat resolution; here, an appropriately settled narrative, which has rearticulated the heterocentric principles of the happy ending despite the miserable need for Laura to return to an inadequate husband, comes loose at the eleventh hour because of the explosive, liminal, boundary-shifting, carnivalesque neighbor. In other films, laughter represents the disorder that the film's conclusion settles; *It's Never Too Late* demonstrates how it is never too late for a film merrily to dislodge the impression of a stable family with the ripple of eccentric laughter, even as the closing credits roll.

As I watch this sequence, my laughter is not exactly directed at Irene Handl but at her laughing. This is despite the fact that I do not know what she is laughing at. Handl is wonderful, but her performance is so short, so incomplete that it cannot become a center around which the film's comedy takes definition. In its play, it dismantles the Us and Them logic of the domestic comedy and invites, instead, participation in a laughter that is so devoid of meaning that it accommodates everyone and perpetuates no single ideology. This is not to say that everyone will find the sequence funny. Nor is it to absolve Laura and Charles Hammond of their exclusive gesture. However, although I find Calvert and Barr unfunny through the film, they are redeemed for me even at this late stage as the camera pulls back in the final shot, not closing in on the image of their reconciled companionate marriage of conventions and boundaries but widening out to become capacious. The frame is still widening as the image fades to black, implying the possibility of a restless and ongoing continuation of this broadening of boundaries and the dilution of the home and family as stable centers. It is this formal gesture—an expanding frame to the sound of laughter—that I find *laughing forward* from this film; I glimpse, in the dying moments of *It's Never Too Late*, eccentric possibilities of the erosion of domestic boundaries and a conception of the home not as a constraining space of community and heterocentric violence (whether that be the hurling of vases, the raising of newspapers, or the censoring of mirth), but a porous threshold to a world beyond that is ready to laugh.

Ending Up with Nothing in *Laughter in Paradise*

I end this chapter with a short consideration of a film that varies the laughing-at-nothing motif. *Laughter in Paradise* (Mario Zampi, 1951) is a portmanteau film in which Henry Russell (Hugh Griffith), an old practical joker believed to have a fortune, dies. His will, another practical joke, stipulates that his relatives will only inherit if they perform various tasks that will be deeply uncomfortable to them: the upstanding Deniston Russell (Alastair Sim), who secretly writes lurid thrillers, must spend twenty-eight days in jail; the snobbish Agnes Russell (Fay Compton) must work as a servant for a month; the promiscuous Simon Russell (Guy Middleton) must marry the first woman he speaks to; and the timid Herbert Russell (George Cole) must hold up the manager of the bank where he is a clerk. The four plotlines run independently until the relatives reconvene in the office of the executor of Henry's will (Ernest Thesiger). The portmanteau structure is crucial to the film's eccentricity, denying the film both central character and central narrative. None of the narratives could carry an entire film. The nearest is Deniston's foray into criminality, as he tries to maintain his engagement to the military Elizabeth (Joyce Grenfell) while also planning his stay in prison. He attempts to commit a number of crimes, including an act of shoplifting in which he shovels an enormous mass of jewelry into his pocket only to discover, when questioned by a store detective, that *he* has been pickpocketed and has lost not only the jewelry but also his own wallet. Eventually, with calculated unsubtlety, he smashes a window with a brick and is arrested. The magistrate at his trial is Elizabeth's father (A. E. Matthews), and Deniston must be excruciatingly rude to him in order to be given the full twenty-eight-day sentence. Elizabeth, appalled, ends their engagement, but Deniston's typist (Eleanor Summerfield) steps into her place. While this plotline provides material for a number of acutely funny scenes, showcasing Sim's performance of hangdog resignation punctuated by sudden moments of electrifying energy, it is slight material; there is event but no development. Durgnat describes the film as an example of Zampi's "solid and conventional pieces" and I would not substantially disagree with the verdict.[67] The four strands run in their merry if unspectacular way toward the end.

Like *The Lavender Hill Mob* and *It's Never Too Late*, the film can be read as being about characters who learn to laugh. Deniston, Agnes, and Herbert are agelasts—constrained by embarrassment, sourness, timidity—while Simon laughs often but only in snatches of snide or sneaky sniggering, designed to impress a woman or deflate a man. The final scene remedies this when the four Russells discover the punch line of their cousin's final gag. Agnes, who has failed in her task but has discovered the rather obvious lesson that servants are human beings too, gives a pious speech: "As the one who has failed, I would like to say at once how deeply grateful I am to my brother for bringing me a measure of happiness I never dreamt of finding in this world." Compton performs against the line; never has an actor looked less happy. Her broad sentiments are repeated by Deniston and Herbert, while Simon holds out for the cash. The scene stiltedly edges toward its climax, in which the disparate strands of the portmanteau structure, which have been at risk of pulling apart, are to be united and made sense of. their forced eccentric behavior has been in exchange for the heterocentric promise of inheritance. Family meaning is dependent upon a series of inheritances, each of which makes the individuals readable as members of the family; passing on genetic, cultural, and financial elements amounts to the passing on of identity and power. As Roger Rawlings suggests, inheritance matters because "lineage is status, and status automatically confers character, quality of life, and how you are treated by the rest of society."[68] In *Laughter at Paradise*, this climax is the moment at which the most fundamental heterocentric logic will cohere the pieces of an uneven, patchy narrative structure. But this centering promise is revealed to be less than fully understood; the executor reveals that Henry died flat *broke*. The word is apposite; not only does it indicate his penury, but it also exposes the brokenness of the heterocentric contract that depends upon familial wealth surviving unto the next generation. Jack Halberstam defines queer time as, in part, "the potentiality of a life unscripted by the conventions of family, inheritance, and child rearing."[69] It is this potentiality of liberation from the constraining temporal logic of inheritance that *Laughter in Paradise* performs mirthfully. In the realization that Henry was broke, the cultural power on which the characters' sense of self and status dissipates. They have been left with—and as—*nothing*.

In response to the disorientating information that there is no fortune—they laugh. First the executor, in medium shot, is laughing so hard that he struggles to read the word "broke." After a long shot that registers their initial shock at the news, the camera turns around the group in a slow pan, registering the moment in which each relative succumbs to laughter: Agnes, concerned finger to mouth before exploding into raucous mirth; Henry, erect in his chair with furrowed brow before beginning a gurgling, crescendoing giggle; the executor, pinch-nosed and already roaring; and Deniston, resistant, his body battling as his shoulders heave and his face contorts between frown and grin, groan and chuckle. Only Simon remains unlaughing, initially slouched in his chair with screwed eyes and twitching mouth, but even he joins in when he crosses to the window and catches sight of the woman (Beatrice Campbell) who has conned him into marriage in the expectation of a fortune. In the final shot, the camera cranes up and across the table, passing above the laughing Russells and settling on the portrait of Henry (see fig. 3.4). The still-audible laughter is raucous, even dangerous; in the film's memorable opening scene, Henry dies while laughing. Eagleton records how "there have even been lethal epidemics of the stuff [laughter] in China, Africa, Siberia and elsewhere, hysterical paroxysms in which, so it is alleged, thousands of people have died."[70] The final sequence suggests that the possible expiration of his relatives is not out of the question. After all, the film announces that Henry, memorialized posthumously in the form of his portrait, is THE END. The family line potentially ends here with this clutch of laughingly, queerly, eccentrically unproductive Russells.

Figure 3.4. Inheriting laughter in *Laughter in Paradise* (Mario Zampi, 1951). *Source:* Associated British Picture Corporation/Courtesy of STUDIOCANAL.

These characters, like Holland and Pendlebury and the Hammonds' neighbor, are laughing at nothing, but this nothing is a different kind of nothing. It is a space that has previously been mistakenly imagined to signify *inheritance*, providing a center to the lives of the hopeful beneficiaries. Like all substitutes, this center is impermanent and replaceable; *inheritance* is replaced both by *no-inheritance* and the lessons learned by the four: that Deniston should not be ashamed of his crime writing and should not be engaged to a woman who could not accept it; that Agnes should reject her own attitudes to class and domestic servitude; that Simon should recognize that women may also seduce; and that Herbert should not be intimidated by his boss. In each case, these lessons represent the disturbance of a heterocentric hierarchy and a liberation into queer time. Throughout the film, a series of small carnivalesque explosions have unsettled binary structures in the comic paradoxes of law-abiding criminals, romantic misanthropists, and unruly and self-serving servants. The ending solicits the hierarchical structures of class, gender, and professional institutions and makes companionate marriage and the bourgeois home into jokes: Simon's marriage is built on deception, Deniston's fiancée has disengaged herself, Herbert's superiors did not realize that they were being menaced by him, Agnes's employer has groveled to her for a date, and the law has lied to all of them. With these cultural logics no longer reliable, there is no option but meaningless laughter because coherent, articulate speech without structure is inconceivable. Meaning becomes relative for these relatives, as their worlds move in eccentric circles and no longer orbit the myths that happiness is defined by wealth accumulation, exclusive family units, or conventional relationships. What they will say if they ever regain their power of speech cannot be known because THE END intervenes. What survives of them is their laughter, which echoes on after the film finishes and offers the possibility for rethinking the family. Walter Benjamin suggests that "spasms of the diaphragm generally offer better chances for thought than spasms of the soul," and the Russells' raucous guffawing *laughs forward* the thought of liberation from the insistence that the heterocentric family is a *something* around which we must, very seriously, orbit.[71] The punch line of Uncle Henry's last practical joke is THE END of inheritance, and the concluding—though never conclusive—joy of *Laughter in Paradise* sees the exclusive familial logic of inheritance give way to more spontaneous connections.

    Comedy in these films is an assault on the mythic scenarios by which lives are lived, blowing gales of laughter through the dignity of conventional structures. Eagleton suggests the queer unruliness of comedy when he writes that "it is as though we are all really play-actors in our conventional social roles, sticking solemnly to our meticulously scripted parts but ready at the slightest fluff or stumble to dissolve into infantile, uproariously irresponsible laughter at the sheer arbitrariness and absurdity of the whole charade."[72] The nothings laughed at in *The Lavender Hill Mob*, *It's Never Too Late*, and *Laughter in Paradise* are the arbitrarinesses and absurdities that lurk at the heart of structures that promised meaning. With iconoclastic humor, postwar British film finds the concentric arrangement of its imagined heterocentric communities—family, neighborhood, England, Britain—*funny*. Like all structures, these communities are exclusive and build their integrity only by uniting members against those outside. The comedies that I have looked at in this chapter create a network of *funny-ha-ha* gestures whose lack of clear direction or target makes them eccentrically *funny-peculiar* as they reject structurality in favor of something more porous. Boundaries between subject and object, self and other, family and stranger, inside and outside, something and nothing break down and reveal the laughter lines in hierarchical binaries. This eccentric and ex-centering laughter is what Jean-Luc Nancy refers to as the transcendental laugh:

> It is knowledge of a condition of possibility which gives nothing to know. . . . This laugh does not laugh *at* anything. It laughs at nothing, for nothing. It signifies nothing, without however being absurd. It laughs at being the peal of its laughter, we might say. Which is not to say that it is unserious or that it is painless. It is beyond all opposition of serious and nonserious, of pain and pleasure. Or rather, it is at the juncture of these oppositions, at the limit which they share and which itself is only the limit of each of these terms, the limit of their signification, the limit to which these significations, as such, are exposed.[73]

The gestures I have analyzed in this chapter may mistakenly be thought of as simple because they do not demonstrate knowledge, analysis, or clear critique in the way that satire does. They offer nothing to know because they consist of laughter at nothing. Their escape from the opposition of pain and pleasure (in the forms of the compromised Holland and Pendlebury, the mocked neighbor, and the deceived Russells) is not soft; it is the radical gesture of finding all such oppositions laughable. These films contain their share of conventional elements, but they each offer glimpses—on the steps of the Eiffel Tower, in a doorway in St. John's Wood, at the distribution of an estate—of a queer condition of possibility in which laughter is an answer to the serious and seriously constraining logics of heterocentric culture. Emerging from the limitations of centric planning, of familial exclusivity, or of the straightening logic of inheritance, each laughing character allows the discovery of alternative queer temporalities that continue to articulate their conditional-mood rejections of mythocentric structure.

Part Two

Going over the Top

4

Ruining Everything

In the opening chapters of this book, I consider how a number of elements in postwar British comedy films—which I have called explosive eccentricity, domestic drag, and laughing at nothing—unsettle the heterocentric myths that underpin social consensus. I now turn my attention to a series of visual and conceptual motifs that run through this cinema and in which these elements can be seen working. The first of these recurring icons is the ruin. As a direct result of the aerial bombardments during the war, three-quarters of a million houses in Britain had been destroyed or severely damaged.[1] When Fay Weldon arrived in the UK from New Zealand in the autumn of 1946, she made a note in her diary of her initial impression of ruination: "Here was a grey harbour and a grey hill side, shrouded in a kind of murky, badly woven cloth, which as the day grew lighter proved to be a mass of tiny, dirty houses pressed up against one another, with holes gaping where bombs had fallen, as ragged as holes in the heels of lisle stockings. I could not believe that people actually chose to live like this."[2] Three years later, when Doris Lessing arrived in the UK from South Africa, it was still the case that "buildings were stained and cracked and dull and grey; it was war-damaged, some areas all ruins."[3]

These descriptions see postwar Britain "through a register of greys: the colour of bombed ruins and rubble, the hue of fatigue and austerity, of ongoing rationing and uncertainty."[4] Even by 1960, some of the gray bombsites had not yet been cleared, let alone developed.

John Grindrod records the numbers affected by the impact of war and social indifference: "By 1951, eight million homes had been declared unfit for habitation, of which seven million had no hot water and six million no inside toilet. In 1949, a fifth of London homes were officially classed as slums. For bombed-out families crushed into sharing homes with relatives or strangers, the relief of peace was soon overshadowed by pressing problems. New homes were needed—not so much fast as instantly."[5] The regenerative building program, despite its record rate of construction in the first years of peace, could not relieve the problem instantly. Cripplegate in London, which became the Barbican, was not completed until 1976. It was from a roof garden not far from this spot that Alan Sinfield could "gasp at the bomb craters all around and watch the pageantry of the Lord Mayor's Show" in the 1950s, a bewildering image of thirteenth-century ritual (with elements of carnival and a swearing of allegiance to the monarch) playing out in the context of the gray remainders of collapsed modernity.[6] Ruins, in various states of reconstruction, came to define British urban landscapes, as in so many European cities, in the decades that followed the war.

Both banal and extraordinary, the evocative and uncanny spectacle of this dereliction proved to be exciting material for cinema. The descriptions by Weldon and Lessing, with their emphasis on grayscale images of decay, framed in murky light and the dramatic potential of dilapidation, lend themselves to the monochromatic screens of postwar cinema. Although such dramatic and unregulated sites may initially suggest themselves as more suitable for noirish thrillers—capitalizing on what Richard Hornsey identifies as their status as "a fertile breeding ground of delinquency and petty crime"—postwar comedies in Britain also made use of the iconography of ruination.[7] In chapter 1, I outline how *Passport to Pimlico*'s identity-exploding eccentricity is detonated by the bomb site and its continued dangers. Made two years earlier, *Hue and Cry* (Charles Crichton, 1947) gives an even more extensive account of life among the ruins. A gang called the Blood and Thunder Boys, whose homes stand in a state of partial collapse among the ruins of South London, play, fight, and dream on bomb sites and in the hollowed-out shells of buildings. One day, Joe (Harry Fowler), one of the leaders of the gang, recognizes a van from a crime story in the *Trump*, his favorite comic. As he investigates, he discovers that the members of a nefarious gang of crooks are using the *Trump* to communicate with each other. Joe discovers that his boss Mr. Nightingale (Jack Warner), whom he has trusted implicitly, is the criminal mastermind behind the plot. The Blood and Thunder Boys, with the grudging help of writer Felix H. Wilkinson (Alastair Sim), manipulate the next edition of the comic and lure the crooks to a final reckoning at a derelict wharf. Enlisting the help of hundreds of schoolboys via a radio broadcast, Joe is successful and vanquishes Nightingale and his villains. In 1956, Michael Balcon, the head of Ealing Studios, defined their comedies as being "about ordinary people with the stray eccentric among them—films about day-dreamers, mild anarchists, little men who long to kick the boss in the teeth."[8] This description seems to map almost perfectly onto *Hue and Cry*: Felix H. Wilkinson is the film's resident stray eccentric, the Blood and Thunder Boys provide the daydreaming, and Joe ultimately has the chance to kick his boss, more or less literally, in the teeth.

Charles Barr views this small manifesto by Balcon as "an amazing contraction of purpose," a synecdoche for a broader contraction in Britain; after the "mild revolution" of voting in a Labour government that promised a New Jerusalem of greater prosperity and egalitarianism, both Britain and Ealing Studios, according to Barr, lost their energy.[9] I, however, struggle to see a loss of energy in the image of "ordinary people" who long to kick their bosses in the teeth. I read it as an anarchic, carnivalesque image, bristling with a comic violence directed at hierarchical social structures. And, while Joe's leaping onto his boss's chest from a symbolic height in the final showdown registers as a jubilant inversion of power within an uneven binary, an even more radical instability is connoted by the bomb sites and derelict buildings that surround this Oedipal drama; these ruins, through which Joe and his friends move, are unregulated and unruly, "a place of drift and disorientation and dreams . . . a cityscape of absences, fragments and relics."[10] Although, as I make clear in the introduction to this book, my principal aim is not to produce history, I am interested in those specific aspects of postwar material culture that, when translated into screen imagery, make certain kinds of ambiguity or ambivalence visible. These material elements—including the ruins of buildings, institutions, and in certain circumstances bosses' teeth—literalize deconstruction and identify a period of flux before new norms of cultural permissiveness start to be built into the British cultural landscape of the 1960s. These ruins are a kind of manifestation of a cultural collapse of certainty, and they represent the challenges of speaking decisively on behalf of the past.[11] As Heather Love writes: "To reconstruct the past, we build on ruins; to bring it to life, we chase after the fugitive dead. Bad enough if you want to tell the story of a conquering race, but to remember history's losers is worse, for the loss that swallows the dead absorbs these others into an even more profound obscurity."[12] I agree that we build on ruins when we reconstruct the past, but the ruins of queer history are not only a matter of loss and obscurity. They also form a landscape of comic contingency. *Hue and Cry*, in sympathy with archive photographs of postwar children enjoying games on bomb sites, show ruins to be in play.[13] Sometimes, this play suggests childish anarchy; sometimes, it bears the threat of violence; always, it is unruly. In this chapter, I explore how these ruins-in-play queerly ex-center heterocentric consensus.

This heterocentric consensus, despite claiming to act on behalf of all people, remained oppressive in the years after the war. Barr suggests its conservative limits when he quotes Anthony Howard's statement that the years immediately after the war brought "the greatest restoration of traditional social values since 1660."[14] Sinfield reinforces this idea with his observation that "the consensual ideology within which party politics was conducted" was led by politicians "trapped in paternalistic Victorian assumptions."[15] Film criticism has generally shared this insistence on the period's conservatism. Sue Harper argues that "the post-war settlement in Britain entailed a return to traditional family values. . . . The liberalization in sexual behaviour, which had been widely noted during the war, did not generate a new radicalism in sexual politics."[16] Pam Cook links this feting of traditional values with big-screen images of "national identity (nostalgia for a pre-Industrial Revolution English countryside, wish for continuity and stability rather than change, espousal of traditional values of duty and service, and of qualities of stoicism, tolerance, humour and individualism) . . . [that represent a] remarkable . . . impulse to collapse all differences—of class, ethnicity, region and sexuality—into an overarching single concept of national identity, which is exactly what the consensus films attempted to do."[17] Such histories suggest that postwar British cinema was dedicated to the reactionary iteration of conventional domestic, familial, and sexual values and that it would take the shock of the swinging sixties to dislodge this commitment.

The argument throughout this book, however, seeks to complicate this image of "consensus films, which were defined in terms of realism, authenticity and ordinary people in contemporary settings."[18] Insisting on consensus can be a totalizing critical maneuver that fails to attend to the punctuating eccentric gestures that deconstruct the centric reductiveness of realism, authenticity, and ordinariness. Jacques Derrida writes that "if by community one implies, as is often the case, a harmonious group, consensus, and fundamental agreement beneath the phenomena of discord or war, then I don't believe in it very much and I sense in it as much threat as promise."[19] This threat marks the exclusion of the other; *consensus*, from the Latin for *feeling with*, always requires the expulsion of those who feel differently. Eccentricity, as I have presented it, is the undoing of consensus, the shaking of the "myth . . . that everyone submitted heroically to a common purpose" during or after the war.[20] Consensus is a mirage, a false center that hopes to constrain the play of a society by arranging its institutions and members in a series of demarcated concentric circles, with diminishing privilege and opportunity in the outer rings for those whose views are not hegemonically aligned. I do not see postwar British comedy film contributing—or, at least, contributing uncomplicatedly—to this concentric structure. Even films with streaks of conservativism contain sufficient ex-centering gestures—in performance, in design, in editing—to derange consensus and offer glimpses of queer possibilities. Their staging of the limitations of the familiar home and family and the appeal of alternative modes of being instead produce images of *dissensus*. As the sun finally set on the British Empire and debates around homosexuality and the role of women were waged in newspapers and parliamentary committees and pubs and living rooms, as the *possibility* of different understandings of status and identity began to emerge, cinema got in on the act and showed traditional social values *in ruins*.[21] Nowhere was this more suggestively presented than in the recurring images of urban rubble, a uniquely ex-centered landscape.

Ruining the City

Barr argues that *Hue and Cry* is about the daydreams-come-true of "a London community centred on a bombsite."[22] The idea of bomb site-as-center is a strange one. Geographically, it is not an accurate description of the film; the action of the film is far more widespread than in *Passport to Pimlico* and the boys roam from the derelict banks of the Thames to the leafy suburbs. And conceptually, the ruins that lend contours to the bomb sites—in the uneven undulations of rubble and the spiky peaks of gutted buildings—are too complex as signifiers to center meaning. Undiscussed, unexplained, and undefined within the film, these ruins seem to gesture in different directions. Some point backward: a boy devotes his time to producing uncannily accurate vocal impersonations of bombs and gunfire, animating sonic specters of the blitz. Others point forward: the ruins await the plans for reconstruction that began as early as 1941 and are suggested by the poster that hangs behind Joe as he is offered a job, depicting two children looking out over a shining landscape under the slogan "We've great things to do—keep on saving." The ruins gesture connotatively to both the past and the yet-to-come; they are the product of fascist bombs and the potential for rebuilding, "two sides of the same sets of issues and concerns."[23]

Italian neorealist cinema, also made in the years following conflict, offers similarly striking images of ruins haunted by a collapsed *before* and an *after* yet to come. In *Germania anno zero* (Roberto Rossellini, 1948), another film about postwar childhood, the young Edmund (Edmund Moeschke) wanders through ruined Berlin and finds himself in a derelict building in which English soldiers are playing a record of Hitler's speeches. The dead dictator's voice echoes through the shells of buildings, a ghostly reminder of a political order that laid waste to Europe and has itself come to dust. Neither the voice nor the connoted Reich has any physical substance, but they linger as intangible *not-quite* meanings in the political and social instability of Germany's year zero. Without the capacity to rely on prewar and wartime values, and without any decisive indication of what opportunities and penalties the future might bring, Edmund walks through an illegible landscape whose possibilities are ultimately so undefined that he is overwhelmed.[24] Barr is dismissive of comparisons made between postwar Italian and British cinemas, writing that *Hue and Cry* "overlaps not at all with the location aesthetic of the Italian neo-realist film-makers of the same period, being staged and acted in a perfectly conventional 'studio' manner, much of it within the studio walls."[25] This firstly overlooks the fact that large portions of *Germania anno zero* (and other neorealist films) were shot in studios. Secondly and more importantly, it dismisses the similarities in tonal and generic unevenness in these films' depictions of children wandering in urban landscapes made uncertain by the complex signification of ruins. In *Hue and Cry*, the possibilities are grasped more affirmatively and the result is comic, although the connotative range of the ruins is also open enough to threaten danger, loss, and violence.

The semiotic indeterminacy of connotation is fundamental to the way images of ruins work. Queerness has had a particular cultural relationship with connotation, as argued by D. A. Miller. Connotation allows the specter of unconventional forms of desire to be expressed in ways that always permit deniability. This same connotation has also, because it is as difficult to confirm the absence of unconventional desire as it is to confirm its presence, produced anxiety in the majority. Deniability—and its opposite—are the result of connotation's inevitable "semiotic insufficiency"; unlike the "immediate self-evidence (however on reflection deconstructible) of denotation," connotation is the ruin of meaning, a form of communication in which sense is both lacking (because deniable) and excessive (because multiple).[26] Ruins in *Hue and Cry* are queerly connotative. They do not *just* connote the blitz. The boy's imitations of the sounds of bombing are virtuosic more than frightening; there is no suggestion of trauma and the sounds of warfare are only part of his repertoire, which also includes seagull sounds. Nor do the ruins *just* connote the promised reconstruction. Regeneration is hardly in evidence in the abandoned building sites through which the kids pursue a villain (Valerie White) and in which there is no sign of work happening; the poster that hangs behind Joe has its color sucked out by the film's monochrome palette; and Joe's job offer—sign of his future—comes via a violent hoodlum disguised as a police officer (Jack Lambert). Neither Nazism nor New Jerusalem is *present*, both displaced in time, so neither can become a center to make total sense of the unruly ruins. *Hue and Cry* remains silent on the subjects of war and rebuilding; neither the origin nor the telos of the ruins—both of which would "conceive of structure on the basis of a full presence which is beyond play"—can settle them into a definite value.[27] These ruins, which become the playgrounds of errant children, represent a free play of meaning and not its constraint. Like queerness, they are eccentric possibilities "for a moment at least beyond the law and morality."[28]

This free play allows the ruins to become markers of a kind of symbolic collapse. The transitional postwar moment in Britain is constituted by coming after the thing that came before (war) and coming before the thing that came after (the rebuilding). Grindrod expresses this as the separation of the "destruction and catastrophe" on one hand and "ingenuity and humanity" on the other, with "the bombed-out, the displaced, the exhausted generation" between.[29] But this account is heavily loaded and risks homogenizing individuals who were not all experiencing the same situation. The rebuilding was not straightforward evidence of "ingenuity and humanity"; it was also, at times, the reenshrinement of exclusive structures. Filmmaker Derek Jarman finds no humanity in his recollections of life in the 1940s, writing that Britain was "an old and decadent oligarchy creaking under the weight of vacuous institutions—look at the monarchy puffed up by the stale air of the tabloids, the whole country is so awry. It is . . . Europe's madhouse, poor, derelict, and deprived; where the rulers batten on an ignorant and regressive working-class who are fed with the most tawdry material promises; so insular that no-one is able to see the shit-house this country has become."[30] There is despair in this imagery of dereliction, but also the possibility of something more affirmative. The vacuity of institutions—including the monarchy—that represent the heterocentric myths of inheritance, sex, and gender is connoted on film by the paradoxically iconoclastic icon of ruins. This British madhouse is one in which homes, institutions, and political promises lie in indistinguishable heaps of stone. Brick and mortar monuments to governmental, educational, ecclesiastical, commercial, and domestic life are severely shaken when those same bricks are disarranged—*deranged*—in piles of all but indistinguishable rubble. Authority, which has found much of its validation in the solidity of its buildings, is razed, laid low, reduced to dust beneath the feet of mischievous kids. In their amorphous state of *not-still*, *not-yet*, and *not-quite*—a heady mix of rubble, history, planning, and play—ruins become less the sites of construction or reconstruction and more spaces of *deconstruction* in which clear boundaries and meanings dissipate. Ruins in the film become eccentric as their *not-just* status as connotation expresses but never quite means anything. In her postwar account of ruins, British novelist Rose Macaulay distinguishes between old ruins, whose return to nature endows them with a significance freed from the constraints of human culture, and new ruins that "have not yet acquired the weathered patina of age, the true rust of the barons' wars, not yet put on their ivy, nor equipped themselves with the appropriate bestiary of lizards, bats, screech-owls, serpents, speckled toads and little foxes. . . . New ruins are for a time stark and bare, vegetationless and creatureless; blackened and torn, they smell of fire and mortality."[31] These new ruins are not legible according to the (rather romantic) significances of ancient ruins. Their starkness and bareness leaves them open to interpretation. In *Hue and Cry*, the ruins are caught in a state of suspension, waiting for their uncertain future, and the only force energetic enough to have begun reclaiming them is the children. These ruins are not a triumph of nature but a collapse of culture; as the boys move unpredictably and erratically through their network of tunnels and no-longer-buildings, they stage a rejection of the solid structures of society and discover a new kind of play that I call porosity.

Poring Over the City in *Hue and Cry*

Hue and Cry stages its action across a radical city in which conventional boundary markers—walls, windows, doors—are unreliable and porous. This is in sharp contrast to the image of Englishness insisted on by Roger Scruton that upholds the private–public binary. "To the English," argues Scruton, "there was no more valuable freedom than the freedom to close a door. The Englishman's home was not just a castle, but an island of 'mine' in an ocean of 'ours.'"[32] But it is this "ocean of 'ours'" that ebbs and flows through the film. The kids move freely into and out from their hideouts through architectural ruptures where walls once were (see fig. 4.1). These spaces are inclusive; they leak too comprehensively to be guardable, and ultimately the Blood and Thunder gang becomes infinitely elastic, welcoming every London kid looking for adventure. (It is the case that there is some implied exclusion of girls; but, although the call that goes out for volunteers is specifically aimed at boys, one of the regular gang members is female and she is intensely involved in the final fight.) At work, Joe moves in and out of Nightingale's shop—with or without permission—and Covent Garden is a bustling space of energy and movement. When the Blood and Thunder Boys discover that Dickie (Gerald Fox), whom they think kidnapped, is actually safe at home, they gather around the

Figure 4.1. A porous playground in *Hue and Cry* (Charles Crichton, 1947). *Source:* Ealing Studios/Courtesy of STUDIOCANAL.

gaping sash window of his parlor to chat. When they have been set up by the crooks and need to escape the police—who represent the threat of incarceration, that is, the constraint of free movement—the children's ingenuity extends to using the labyrinthine passageways of the sewers to preserve their drift. The inside–outside dichotomy is exploded and there is a dynamic flow of bodies and talk through the spaces that have burst open in the aftermath of war.

This bursting open is reminiscent of the conditions that Walter Benjamin and Asja Lacis observe in an essay on Naples in 1924. They recognize that in Naples the private is "dispersed, porous, and commingled"; "the house is far less the refuge into which people retreat than the inexhaustible reservoir from which they flood out."[33] This is the oceanic motion that Scruton so warns against but that the children of *Hue and Cry* represent, flowing across the weakened boundaries of homes and flooding the bomb site in their hundreds like a tidal wave for the final encounter with the crooks. As Dickie, Joe, and the others ignore the would-be-boundary of the sash window while they talk, "the living room reappears on the street ... [and] the street migrates into the living room."³⁴ Dickie's mother accuses Joe of being out too late; shrouded in the brooding chiaroscuro of night photography, these children, miraculously liberated from the restraints of either education or work whenever play beckons, do not observe the conventional limits of night and day. *Hue and Cry* observes the combination of youth and a landscape of ruins resulting in the "interpenetration of day and night, noise and peace, outer light and inner darkness, street and home."³⁵ Such a porous city becomes eccentric as such binary structures are exploded, and "everything joyful is mobile."³⁶

The way in which this eccentric porosity works in *Hue and Cry* can be observed in the sequence in which *Trump* writer Felix H. Wilkinson is introduced. Barr—who finds "the charm of this film very resistible"—isolates Sim's contribution as the one redeeming feature.³⁷ I, unlike Barr, find the sequence irresistible even before Sim's physical appearance. When Joe and Alec (Douglas Barr) track down Wilkinson in order to test their theory that the *Trump* is being used by the gang to communicate their plans, they enter his mansion block without restriction: no garden gate, no locked door, and no concierge stops them. As they climb the sprawling and shadowy curve of the Daliesque staircase they hear Wilkinson apparently threatening to shoot someone. The voice seeps into every corner of the stairwell, fluid and uncontained. Panicked, they dash onward and find an open door and the writer inside, framed by interior walls and doorways. It is revealed that the booming and threatening words were portions of Wilkinson's latest (and resplendently lurid) storyline recorded on a Dictaphone; Wilkinson is a recorded performance. His flat is done up in domestic drag; it is stuffed with all the items that the stage character of a kooky bachelor writer ought to have: old books on arcane subjects, a huge-belled gramophone, battered old suitcases, a fish tank, and countless stuffed fish on the walls, including the body of what looks like a puffer fish hideously reappropriated as a light fitting. It is a loaded space, and this excess of presence, which might seem to promise meaning, instead overwhelms its possibility. The objects—even the living fish—behave as props, present in order to allow Wilkinson to make gestures with them. If he were a detailed character, he might center the space and settle its clutter into sense, but the things around him pursue their own independent eccentricity.

Some have names: Wilkinson giggles as he introduces the boys to Dick the Dictaphone. The flat is a world whose limits Wilkinson is neither able to define nor defend; even though he slams the door when the boys eventually leave, he is later unable to keep out their radio broadcast, despite his futile gesture of stuffing his scarf into the bell of his gramophone (which is doubling up as a wireless receiver) to mute it.

Wilkinson as presented by Sim is a series of eccentric gestures and tics. Nineteen forty-seven had the bitterest winter on record, but the scarf that he wears is not a protection against the cold (he is, after all, in his shirtsleeves) but an object for him to play with. As he gives the boys ginger pop and admits that his "has—err—gin" in it, he pauses for the filler "err," raising a redundant deictic finger to point at the liquid, and then casts the scarf tail over his shoulder in a flamboyant and gratuitous gesture accompanied by the archaic valediction "Bung ho!" Across the scene, Sim's eccentric performance plays pride, arrogance, mirth, silliness, irritation, and fear in a quick, meandering sequence, each emotion punctuated by mannered gestures. He moves with choreographed restlessness, delivering his lines with liquid mellifluence, and hailing the boys as his "public." In "Naples," Benjamin and Lacis identify the eccentric tendency of porous buildings to "preserve the scope to become a theater of new, unforeseen constellations. The stamp of the definitive is avoided. No situation appears intended forever, no figure asserts its 'thus and not otherwise.'"[38] Sim's apartment is a fantasy space, a factory of *Trump* scenarios that stokes a sense of adventure in the boys that ex-centers the world as *thus and also otherwise*: an author hero is a coward, a trusted boss is a traitor, a policeman is a crook, and so on. Like Sim's performance, the porous Naples shows "the passion for improvisation . . . [which results in] buildings [being] used as a popular stage. They are all divided into innumerable, simultaneously animated theaters."[39] The histrionic eccentrics of postwar British comedy are often self-conscious actors in porous spaces, whose voices and bodies flow unconstrained through the cracks in the derelict edifice of their heterocentric worlds: Sim as window-smashing would-be inheritor in *Laughter in Paradise*; Margaret Rutherford as identity-rupturing interpreter of bomb-disturbed Pimlico in *Passport to Pimlico*; Joan Greenwood as incorrigible actor in a collapsing house in *Young Wives' Tale*; Kay Kendall and Peter Finch as television stars in a chaotic home-as-set in *Simon and Laura*;

Alec Guinness and Stanley Holloway as boundary-exploding friends descending an Eiffel Tower of destabilized girders and gaps; and Irene Handl as a neighbor who provokes laughter in an open doorway in *It's Never Too Late*. As Wilkinson, Sim ruptures the most robust cinematic wall of all; as he wipes his brow with his scarf and recalls the two survivors in *The Case of the Crowded Coffins*, he breaks the fourth wall and looks directly into the camera. He is both Wilkinson and Sim as he looks down the lens in the animated theater of his flat.

The porous achievement of *Hue and Cry* extends beyond *mise en scène* and performance. Douglas Smith argues that in "Naples" Benjamin and Lacis "explore porosity not only as a concept but also as a stylistic principle."[40] In *Hue and Cry*, porosity's stylistic principle can be seen as slippage between modes. Tim O'Sullivan settles the film as an example of "documentary realism" and Mark Duguid and Katy McGahan describe a "low-key naturalism" and use of "tangibly real locations."[41] But while the film has realist elements, any attempt to totalize it stylistically is to miss its complex modal and generic flow: noir shadows on the staircase as Joe and Alec approach Wilkinson's flat; expressionist chiaroscuro, angles, and shot scales as the children walk home after losing Dickie; and a carnival of violence at the end, which would be at home in a hard-boiled film about spivs, the flashily dressed criminals who traded in black market goods in postwar Britian. I find the final sequence shocking; critical accounts of the spectacle of the children's charge often overlook the horror of children repeatedly dashing a man's head against a stone and Joe's being menaced by his homicidal former boss. The bomb sites of *Hue and Cry* are playful but not cozy; they are full of both adventure and risk; the film's leaky spatial and formal boundaries allow for the unexpected irruption of both comedy and danger in a complex mixture. This generic porosity is matched by the film's use of slow dissolves, making temporal, spatial, and modal transitions visible and identifying film as a medium that both documents and *performs* realities.

Porous realism interrupts what Andrew Moor describes as realism's "claims to represent the world truthfully and [denials] that it is a style. It is saturated uncritically with its culture's common-sense, natural worldview, with its prejudices and blind spots, but the claim to Truth is maintained nevertheless."[42] Moor suggests that realism, regardless of subject matter, is not a queer mode; realism cannot embrace the real artifice of domestic drag or any other queer strategy for challenging the worldview that masquerades as Truth. In *Hue and Cry*, stylistic porosity dissolves the boundaries between realism and conditional-mood queer fantasy. Early in the film, as the *real* Joe sits on a bus, engrossed in a copy of the *Trump*, the *fantastic* hero Selwyn Pike, from the pages of the comic strip, appears in an irregularly shaped thought bubble to the right of the frame (see fig. 4.2); the mundanity of the bus is contrasted with the flash car driven by the fictional Pike. A porous dissolve transitions from bus to street, as the *real* Joe walks, still reading and imagining; his shabby ambling contrasts with the *fantastic* glamorous man of action in the thought bubble to the left of the frame. In this inventive visual gesture, Joe's fantasies become visible in the realist frame; the uneven shape of the thought bubbles gives the impression of a tear in the frame that allows glimpses of other material to seep through. And when the real world interrupts Joe's imaginings, it is in the form of two men carrying crates from a van whose number plate is identical with that of the crooks in the

Figure 4.2. A leaking frame in *Hue and Cry* (Charles Crichton, 1947). *Source:* Ealing Studios/Courtesy of STUDIOCANAL.

comic; the fantastic has now burst through to the extent that it is indistinguishable from the real. *Hue and Cry*'s form is leaky, suggesting that postwar porosity is not only architectural but cinematic and that it welcomes, in the absence of totalizingly solid structures, the conditional irruption of fantastic possibilities.

The literal ruins that dominate the film's *mise en scène* may be seen as allegories for the ex-centering of structure more generally. As I watch the film, these ruins do not lend the narrative "a jolt of reality that acts as a grounding effort."[43] Instead, their porous effect trickles out figuratively to dislodge clear boundaries between genres, modes, frames, and truths. This dynamic combination of separate parts is what Derrida calls bricolage: "If one calls *bricolage* the necessity of borrowing one's concepts from the text of a heritage which is more or less coherent or ruined, it must be said that every discourse is *bricoleur*. The engineer, whom Lévi-Strauss opposes to the *bricoleur*, should be the one to construct the totality of his language, syntax, and lexicon. In this sense the engineer is a myth."[44] *Hue and Cry* is routinely described in line with Barr's assessment of it as *just* an adventure story for kids (including grown-up kids) by a rather conservative writer, director, and producer. As I encounter the film, however, it gathers up the motifs and clichés of *Boy's Own* adventure, comic strip, film noir, spiv film, domestic drama, and neorealism—drawn from the text of a heritage that is more or less ruined—and strings them together in a bricolage of such incongruity that the result is comic indeterminacy. Derrida argues that the operation of any structure is most easily visible when it is *"methodically* threatened" in a way "somewhat like the architecture of an uninhabited or deserted city, reduced to its skeleton by some catastrophe of nature or art"; then, it is possible "to reveal not only [a structure's] supports but also that secret place in which it is neither construction nor ruin but lability."[45] *Hue and Cry*, dancing across the bomb sites and kicking up dust from the rubble, is *labile* in its eccentric resistance to totalizing logics, preferring to slip between genres and styles and to delight in the unsettled possibilities offered by a physical and cultural landscape in flux.

This image of flux is an image of defiance of postwar conventions, comparable with the defiance recalled by Jarman in his memoir of the 1940s: "Landscapes of time, place, memory, imagined landscapes. *At Your Own Risk* recalls the landscapes you were warned off: Private Property, Trespassers will be Prosecuted; the fence you jumped, the wall you scaled, fear and elation, the guard dogs and police in the shrubbery, the byways, bylaws, do's and don'ts, Keep Out, Danger, get lost, shadowland, pretty boys, pretty police who shoved their cocks in your face and arrested you in fear."[46] Such landscapes are the heterocentric landscapes of privilege and property, policed and constrained by a set of values that refuse to accommodate so many. Jarman is frank about both the delights and the dangers of such landscapes. The ruins and bomb sites of the postwar years were sites of privation and exclusion as well as play. Nead invokes a different image from Benjamin's writing when she suggests that "bombsites perhaps constitute the kind of landscape that Walter Benjamin's 'Angel of History' looks back at as it is propelled onwards by the energy of progress whilst being forced to look at the devastation that is accumulating behind."[47] The realities of lives lived among ruins were always also devastating. *Hue and Cry*, with its violence and fear, does not sentimentalize the landscape or the moment. But it does offer a queer glimpse of an alternative 1940s, of a postwar porosity that warns no one off, which has no Keep Outs or Get Losts, and in which walls give way and let you through. Far more than a *Boy's Own* adventure, the film is a *laughing forward* of extraordinary postwar possibilities for the illicit adventures of kids together in unruly urban spaces, possibilities that in a twenty-first century still defined by heavily regulated city structures remain subversive.

The porous ruins of *Hue and Cry* reveal an absurd comic beauty in a monochrome postwar London in which suddenly fluid boundaries mark a partial suspension of the private–public binary. The kids fashion their own routes through the mapless spaces of their transformed city. Even geography becomes wonky, as the children move between distant parts of London between shots; this topographical trick is not merely a type of magic offered by cinema, but also what Smith refers to as "a congenial alternative to the modernist orthodoxy of functional zoning."[48] Such zoning was a logic dear to the postwar urban planners in Britain who determined that every area should be clearly identifiable according to function: commercial, financial, residential, recreational, and so on. Zoning is particularly committed to defining discrete families, facilitating businesses, constraining leisure so that it does not become unruly, and censoring unconventional sexual behavior. *Hue and Cry* gives a glimpse, instead, of unzoned social structures that leak, and bleed, and ebb, and flow; of tidal motions that unsettle the authority of parents, police, and even geography; of an eccentric city given over to the anarchic play of children. Unlike the comedies that I discussed in chapter 3 and most other Ealing comedies, *Hue and Cry* is indifferent to the family as a structure; fleeting domestic scenes with Joe and Dicky are all the focus that family life gets and it seems constraining and unsupportive, encouraging dull responsibility over productive play. Family is displaced not by community but by a torrent of adventuring people discovering the legal and ethical freedoms of their open city.

Triangulating Ruins in *Genevieve*

Genevieve (Henry Cornelius, 1953) is one of the most fondly remembered of all postwar British comedy films and a substantial amount has been written about this story of the London to Brighton vintage car rally. When the drive to Brighton for Alan and Wendy McKim (John Gregson and Dinah Sheridan) is delayed by several problems with their vintage car, they miss both the celebratory parade and official dinner. They arrive in time to spend a somewhat tipsy evening with their friend Ambrose Claverhouse (Kenneth More) and his new girlfriend Rosalind (Kay Kendall). Rosalind wows the assembled crowd with a remarkable jazz trumpet performance, but her turn is not enough to distract from the resentments developing between the two men. Alan suspects that Ambrose has designs on Wendy and the two drivers fall out. They decide to race each other home. The film takes its name from Alan's prized 1904 Darracq, which he will forfeit if he loses the race. The return to London is beset by various calamities for both cars. Rivalries are heightened by the men's relentless attempts to sabotage each other, involving engine tampering, setting the police on each other, and issuing false reports of fatal accidents. When, at the last moment, the tires of Claverhouse's 1905 Spyker become caught in a tram track and the car is steered off course, Genevieve is left to limp—amusingly, but somewhat ingloriously—over the finishing line on Westminster Bridge.

Criticism has generally agreed that the film is, in one way or another, about the postwar British ideal of companionate marriage that presented matrimony as the coupling of two equal individuals rather than a constraining institution built on reproduction and private property. Durgnat sees *Genevieve* as the originating film of what he calls "the 'affluence cycle' of the fifties," defined by "lower-upper-middle-class cosiness . . . [and an] air of gay, youthful, relatively modest contentment and sauciness."[49] He emphasizes the relatively egalitarian relationships between Alan and Wendy (a "nice young couple" with the admirable postwar qualities of being "spruce, smart, and cosily prosperous") and Ambrose and Rosalind (who enjoy "a spicey frankness").[50] Geraghty, on the other hand, reads the film as a series of ritualized humiliations of the female characters; "male enthusiasm" is celebrated for its "greater feeling for tradition, which is, in the end, justified . . . [while] the women pay for their aloofness by being made to look childish and immature."[51] In this interpretation, the rosy picture of the companionate marriage is tarred by the pressure on women to "move into a more sympathetic position with their men."[52] Bell-Williams synthesizes the two positions by building on Conekin, Mort, and Waters's depiction of British modernity as "a balancing act between innovation and tradition"; she argues that the film offers "a degree of ambiguity [that] was necessary to provide spectators, stratified by age, class and gender, with a choice across different, even contradictory, meanings."[53]

Whether regarding the film as spicily sexy, mildly misogynistic, or both, criticism has agreed that the film's narrative teleology is toward bringing the men and women "back into alignment . . . on the basis of heterosexual companionship."[54] This is what leads Medhurst to describe it as a film "which captured the centre of British film comedy for a whole squadron of bright young middle-class couples."[55] I am suspicious of such talk of centers and middles. I am also suspicious of the claim that teleological heterocentric narratives are straightforward. Instead, I see *Genevieve* (as I did the domestic drag comedies in chapter 2) as a sending-up of married bliss. I disagree with Geraghty that Wendy and Rosalind—despite their "dishevelled hair and wet clothes"—are peculiarly subject to scorn; Alan and Ambrose are made to look just as ridiculous in their increasingly deranged rivalry.[56] Whatever victory is enjoyed in this race, it is not a victory for harmonious monogamy or masterful masculinity, which are both made a laughingstock.

I want to suggest that *Genevieve* is as much about ruins as *Hue and Cry* is. Bell-Williams, echoing Geraghty, argues that the cars "signify, symbolically, the importance of tradition."[57] If this is the case, it is a tradition that is in ruins. Alan recalls at one point how his father salvaged Genevieve from a rubbish dump and it is as a loosely cohering pile of car parts that Genevieve finally arrives on Westminster Bridge: a wing lost, a tire split, an engine hemorrhaging oil and unable to start. As Alan and Wendy, who are filthy from pushing the car, laugh at the spectacle of Ambrose losing control of his Spyker, Genevieve's brakes *fail* and she rolls her own way onto the bridge. During the race, both Alan and Ambrose have to stop repeatedly to tinker with and patch up and replace parts of their engines. Recalling the Ship of Theseus thought experiment that asks whether a ship remains the same ship after its constituent parts have been replaced, it is questionable whether Genevieve even remains Genevieve. The slow ruination of the cars gestures to the absurd failings of marriage (as Alan and Wendy squabble), of conservative 1950s sexual morality (as Ambrose plans to have unmarried sex with Rosalind), and of masculine competence (as neither driver is in control of his car as they approach the finish line).

The broader ruination made visible in *Genevieve* is the razing of certain binary systems of knowledge that underpinned British social life before the war. The most commonly identified binary at play in the film concerns the expression of gender in a porous moment of shifting opportunities for women and expectations for men. *Genevieve* performs (that is, both *stages* and *constitutes*) alternative possibilities. In this new contingency, domestic porousness—which sees Wendy leaving her front door open and allows Ambrose to come and go from the McKims' home—reflects a resistance to enclosed domestic life by both men and women. This is the legacy of a conflict in whose "topsy-turvydom," as Ethel Alec-Tweedie phrases it, "every man is a soldier, and every woman is a man."[58] British women's active roles during the war, in the absence of men, had necessitated a level of independence that *remained a possibility* in peacetime. This is not to underestimate the challenges faced by women; William Beveridge, in the 1942 report that formed the basis of the welfare state, argues that women's principal role was to "ensure the continuation of the British race" as stay-at-home mothers, and subsequent social security legislation presumed the financial dependence of wives on husbands.[59] Even though this meant that "many women may have returned to the home after the war, with the birth rate soaring and attitudes towards working wives largely hostile," it was no longer credible to dismiss the *possibility* for women to discover a life beyond the domestic.[60] Chris

Waters records how "the sociologist, Mark Abrams, addressing this issue in 1945 suggested that the family, as an institution for 'biological continuity,' was failing—often because new opportunities for leisure and personal fulfilment were eroding the desire for children."[61] An increased focus on the egalitarian companionate marriage, extradomestic leisure pursuits for women, greater responsibilities at home for men, the possibility of careers for wives, and the increased availability of divorce left solid faith in a fixed gender binary in ruins.

The growing flexibility and porosity of social and sexual binaries also informed the shifting cultural position of gay men and women in Britain in the postwar years. The suggestion that the heterocentric home and family were not natural but only conventional produced an ideological cacophony in which multiple views were expressed and hope for moral consensus was ruined. Douglas Warth amplified the cacophony with his run of weekly pieces in the *Sunday Pictorial* in May and June 1952, denouncing homosexuals as "Evil Men." Warth's articles work hard to reinforce heterocentric standards against which homosexual men can be defined as deviant and dangerous. He positions homosexuality as "something that threatens our own children," constructing an exclusive community through his use of the possessive adjective *our*.[62] Outrageously, he even trawls through the ruins of the Third Reich to resurrect the British reader's well-remembered and centering hatred of fascism, attributing "the horrors of Hitlerite corruption" to homosexuality and advocating a "final solution" for the problem.[63] But alongside Warth's virulent heterosexism ran a growing swell of voices arguing for reform: in 1955, psychiatrist D. J. West published his book on *Homosexuality* that found developmental explanations for homosexuality and advocated compassion and legal reform; in the same year, Peter Wildeblood published *Against the Law*, an account of his own homosexuality and trial for homosexual acts; and in 1957 the government-assembled Wolfenden Committee published their report on homosexuality and prostitution and recommended the decriminalization of the former.

These calls for reform, it should be understood, were less than radical. Wildeblood, uncomfortably echoing Warth's invective almost exactly, dismisses "the pathetically flamboyant pansy with the flapping wrists, the common butt of music hall jokes and public-house stories," championing tolerance only for the discreet homosexual.[64] He explicitly endorses society's heterocentric mythology: "It is up to me to come to terms, first with my own condition, and secondly with other people whose lives quite rightly centre upon the relationship between a man and a woman."[65] The Wolfenden Report pursues a similarly tepid radicalism when it recommends decriminalization but only for men over the age of twenty-one acting with total discretion. But in the din of postwar attitudes and counterattitudes, sexual *possibilities* in Britain were proliferating and could not be constrained by a centric binary model. The best-selling articulation of this was the reports by the American zoologist Alfred Kinsey and his collaborators, published as *Sexual Behavior in the Human Male* (1948) and *Sexual Behavior in the Human Female* (1953), which argued that sexuality operated on a spectrum and that homosexual behavior was commonplace. The postwar British comedies in this book are allies of Kinsey, reflecting as they do a process of slow breakdown in sexual pieties. Heather Love advocates an approach to telling the past that values "the importance of clinging to ruined identities and to histories of injury. Resisting the call of gay normalization means refusing to write off the most vulnerable, the least presentable, and all the dead."[66] Postwar eccentric comedy suggests that this litany of ruined identities includes *heterocentric* identities and replaces Warth's bile with a comic spirit that laughs at the myths that underpin all normalization and plays in possibility.

Genevieve's comic assault on sexual epistemology is more extensive and more eccentric than its reputation as a marriage comedy suggests. The *Oxford English Dictionary* defines the verb *to queer* as *to put out of order* or *spoil*, a fitting term for a film that so wittily ruins the smooth operation of both vintage cars and sexual conventions. With their myriad detours, breakdowns, and collisions, the characters prove themselves incapable of staying on the straight and narrow. In particular, I see the film ruining heterocentric systems of knowledge—which depend on the sanctity of the couple—with proliferating and binary-exploding triangles of desire. The sexual geometry of the triangle is familiar to queer theory. Developing the theories of René Girard, Sedgwick explores the complex homosociality and eroticism at work in "the relation of rivalry between the two active members of an erotic triangle."[67] In such triangles, "the bond that links the two rivals is as intense and potent as the bond that links either of the rivals to the beloved . . . [and] within the male-centered novelistic tradition of European high culture, the triangles . . . are most often those in which two males are rivals for a female."[68] In *Genevieve*, the bet and climactic race are the results of the intense and intimate rivalry between Alan and Ambrose; there are repeated reminders that Ambrose knew Wendy before Alan did and that one year Wendy accompanied Ambrose on the London to Brighton rally. Ambrose and Wendy are physically close and Ambrose's ultimate provocation—that Wendy is excited when Ambrose visits—is borne out by the film's opening sequences in which she clearly enjoys his company and confides in him about her dislike of the rally.

The intensity of this male–male rivalry may explain why Ambrose, after so many years of trying, has not succeeded in finding his "really beautiful emotional experience" with a woman. But this is, ultimately, a limited and limiting approach to the film's eccentric patterns. Even if the two men's rivalry does contain an erotic component, it can offer nothing more than an entrenchment of binary structures in which the homosocial, homoerotic, and heteroerotic are neatly delineated. The film is disturbing not because of one triangle but, rather, the interactions and intersections of many triangles. The first triangle is both balanced and deranged by a second homosocial triangle, this time with two female rivals, consisting of Wendy, Ambrose, and Rosalind; in Brighton, Ambrose describes his desire for Rosalind as he dances with and kisses Wendy. This triangle is, in turn, one of a potentially infinite series involving the other women whom Ambrose will bring on the rally in the future; although Geraghty suggests that the "work of the narrative is to get this couple [Ambrose and Rosalind] into a position where they might begin to be the kind of couple that Wendy and Alan are"—that is, married—I see no evidence for this.[69] There is no rushed proposal in the film's dying minutes, no symbolic wedding bells, and no indication that Rosalind necessarily even wants to see Ambrose again. Ambrose has brought a different woman on the race every year and there is no reason to suppose that this will not continue in an endless series in which they are always rivals with Wendy. The triangles become more surprising aboard the Spyker, where Rosalind is the object of desire for rivals Ambrose and Suzi (Rosalind's pet Saint Bernard whom she found wandering in rubble having been blitzed and left traumatized). Suzi emphatically growls when Ambrose tries to seduce Rosalind, at which Rosalind smiles. Even the trumpet later forms a kind of rival for Ambrose; Rosalind exhausts herself in her virtuoso display of lip action and is subsequently so worn out that she is unable to sleep with Ambrose.

There remain at least two further triangles, which I find especially arresting. The first positions Wendy and Genevieve as rivals for Alan's affection and attention. The second positions Genevieve as the beloved object for Alan and Ambrose. Both depend on Genevieve being more than a symbol for tradition. The car is the object of a love that is both heterocentric (because directed at an object inherited by Alan from his father) and queer (because directed at a machine). Genevieve may very well prove the terminal unsettling of the McKims' marriage, implausibly playing the part of the other woman who receives at least as much attention as Wendy. One of the funniest and queerest moments in the film comes early, before they begin the journey to Brighton. Alan and Wendy have fallen out over the race, which really means that they have fallen out over Genevieve. Downstairs, Wendy finds a driving bonnet he has bought her. She tries it on and admires herself in a convenient mirror; she seems to be delighted, even turned on, by what she sees and hurries upstairs. In long shot, she appears in the bedroom doorway, wearing the bonnet; Alan lies in bed in the foreground, reading a car magazine. The frame is defined by a triangle: Wendy in the background, Alan and Genevieve (in magazine form) in the fore. Wendy is both elegant and absurdly everyday, combining the new hat with face cream and pajamas. Alan turns away from her and carries on reading. There is a cut to Wendy in medium long shot, isolated from Alan and expelled from the triangle; she breathes Alan's name seductively. In long shot again, the triangle reinstated, he turns to her. In close-up, she moves her lips to speak but makes no sound. In a symmetrical close-up, he smiles at her, the magazine expelled from the frame as he gazes at his wife. In long shot again, she joins him in bed and he leans over her and away from the camera in order to kiss her (see fig. 4.3). The camera tracks in toward the couple. She whispers "I've got grease on my face" (connoting also the engine grease that Genevieve figuratively wears) and the camera—apparently with admirable discretion—pulls to the right and settles on the discarded magazine and a full-page picture of a vintage car. Wendy's voice is heard uttering the euphemistic line, "Oh, darling—mind my bonnet"; having a bonnet that may be dislodged by passion is another quality that she shares with Genevieve. The car picture, shown in close-up as the couple hold each other off-screen, acquires a comically erotic dimension, compounded by a J-cut in which a voiceover, seemingly from nowhere, says "What is taking place here is by now an old

Figure 4.3. Illicitly triangular carryings-on in *Genevieve* (Henry Cornelius, 1953). *Source:* Sirius Productions/Courtesy of ITV Studios.

story—but surprising as it may seem, it was quite illegal until 1896." The sequence ends with a dissolve to the start of the rally; the voice is revealed to belong to a commentator who is describing the history of driving in the UK. Nevertheless, the gag—and it is a very funny one—leaves the impression that there is something illicit, only just legal, about the McKims' threesome.

This moment *laughs forward* an image of the erotics of a form of polyamory that proliferates in irregular triangular patterns, porously shifting and reforming in unstructured and deconstructed eccentricity. The binary model of the companionate marriage—despite its greater emphasis on equality—is ruined as desire, affection, and attention play freely. *Genevieve* suggests that it is the attempt to constrain and curtail such erotic triangulations that results in tension. The film bestows a sensitivity to Alan's relationship with his car that is touching. Poignancy—coming from the Latin for *to prick*, that is, to make pores in, to be open to an affective relationship with the world—is most acutely felt in a sequence in which Alan sacrifices his competitive position just minutes from the finish line in order to talk to an old man reminiscing about proposing to his wife in a Darracq. They are able to talk because Genevieve, even without the ruptures and breaks that threaten to ruin her, is *porous*: open-top, without doors and windows even. In a nod to prewar etiquette, the old man coyly acknowledges that he has spoken to the McKims without a formal introduction; even for the elderly, such niceties are becoming redundant in the porous spaces of the film. The punch line of the sequence, played sweetly and not sardonically, is that the old man, conjuring up another triangle, suspects that his wife accepted his proposal because of the car. The poignancy of the sequence, which could feel cloying, is undercut by the comic absurdity of Genevieve's flapping rear wing as she drives on. *Genevieve* ends on Westminster Bridge, a space between, a porous space that is neither north nor south of the river Thames. Such an unstable position is appropriate for a film that giggles its way through a series of triangles that queer all efforts to cling firmly to binary ways of understanding the world. Moments before their arrival on the bridge, Genevieve, in her marriage-complicating eccentricity, explodes; great belches of black smoke pour from her near-ruined form. It is a fitting prelude to the final spectacle: as THE END is pronounced, the two couples merrily exchange embraces beside the ruined, porous, beloved, uncentered and uncentering Genevieve. As the film's final image fades, in a reminder of the countless triangles that have replaced heterocentric exclusivity with porous desire, it is Ambrose and Wendy who are embracing.

Ruining the Suburbs: *The Green Man*

Porous desire becomes explosive in *The Green Man* (Robert Day, 1956), in which Alastair Sim plays Harry Hawkins, an assassin for hire whose preferred technique for dispatching his targets is the bomb. Sim's performance offers a very funny demonstration of the explosivity of his brand of eccentricity. Hawkins, who is neither validated nor condemned by the film, in his acceptance of only those offers of work that allow him to bring down "the so-called great, those overblown balloons who just cry out to be popped" echoes Orwell's postwar definition of the funny.[70] Hawkins extends the metaphor and refers to himself as "a humble pin." *The Green Man* is the story of his assignment to assassinate businessman Sir Gregory Upshott (Raymond Huntley) who is involving himself in the postwar sensitivities of the Middle East. Hawkins has planned to explode Sir Gregory while he is enjoying a dirty weekend with nervy typist Joan (Eileen Moore) at a seaside inn called the Green Man. This plan has been formulated with the unwitting assistance of Sir Gregory's secretary Marigold (Avril Angers) whom Hawkins has seduced. She becomes suspicious and goes to visit Hawkins at his suburban home. Wanting to avoid a confrontation, Hawkins sends his confederate McKechnie (John Chandos) to switch the name sign of his house with the unoccupied house next door. Marigold is lured into the empty house and set upon. No sooner has McKechnie deposited Marigold's body in the grand piano than he is interrupted by vacuum cleaner salesman William Blake (George Cole), who has an appointment with Hawkins's housekeeper and has been misled by the swapped signs. The salesman sets up his wares while McKechnie runs away. Ann Vincent (Jill Adams), who is due to be moving into the house imminently, arrives. William finds the body and he and Ann are cowering together in a compromising position when Ann's fiancé Reginald (Colin Gordon), a radio announcer, arrives home from work. After much confusion, he leaves, refusing to believe in the existence of the corpse that has been retrieved by McKechnie. The not-quite dead Marigold, however, deposited in the boot of McKechnie's car for disposal later, wakes and staggers to Ann's house. She tells Ann and William about the assassination plan and they hurry off to save the day.

In its second half, the film's action transfers to the coastal hotel where Hawkins's plan is foiled. The need for this failure is not born of sympathy for Sir Gregory, who is ghastly, taking advantage of his clearly uncomfortable young companion and loving the sound of his own voice (a fact that Hawkins makes use of by concealing the bomb in a radio and timing it to go off during the broadcast of a speech by Sir Gregory himself). Rather, Hawkins's plan must fail, not for some pious moralistic reason but in order to detonate the film's ex-centering and playful energy. As with *Passport to Pimlico* (see chapter 1) and *The Lavender Hill Mob* (see chapter 3), a plan in ruins opens up a space for improvisation in which the certainties of *what will be* are traded for the more slippery, more porous possibilities of *what might happen now*. This emphasis on improvisation and play defines

Hawkins's early career, as recalled in an extended series of flashbacks with voiceover in the film's opening minutes; the assassin more or less spontaneously blows up his headmaster (the dictatorial center of his school) and develops a taste for the anarchic removal of pompous political leaders. The relentless, indiscriminate, repetitive machinery of war, however, encourages him to take temporary retirement between 1939 and 1945 because, as he says, in a macabre piece of humor, "the competition was too fierce." He cannot be spontaneously spectacular while violent death is ubiquitous and predictable.

When he returns to business after the war, his technique seems to have changed; in line with the political habits of the day, he is now committed to (and constrained by) intricate planning. The clockwork precision of a timer in a radio, set to explode at a precise moment, is so fixed that it becomes a limiting center; such regulation causes Hawkins no end of bother. Each time the plan is ex-centered by the unforeseen, Hawkins embraces play. Things begin to go wrong in the hotel when Hawkins is faced with the challenge of what to do about three musicians in the hotel lounge whose performance will make it impossible for Sir Gregory to listen to the radio. As the trio plays (the actors miming entirely unconvincingly), Sim pulses and throbs along to the music in ecstatic collapse, sliding down in his chair and grinning manically. When there is a pause in the music, Hawkins histrionically applauds (Sim giving a peerless performance of comic eccentricity), in order to seduce the women into joining him for a drink at the bar during the critical period of the radio broadcast. Hawkins slides contingently between affective states, between frustration and rage and ecstasy, never settling long enough to give any indication of essential identity. He rewrites and unwrites his own plan in a series of gestures, colored by Sim's ability to produce angularly awkward physical expressions of woe, of mirth, of irritation, and of cynicism. Hawkins is a sliding between plan and play, structure and spontaneity.

In the contingent moment of British postwar possibility, the rhetoric of planning that constrained play did so by imposing orientation and teleology. This planning had a utopian dimension; J. B. Priestley characterized the period by saying that "instead of guessing and grabbing, we plan. Instead of competing, we co-operate."[71] The degree, however, to which Priestley's *we* is genuinely inclusive is unclear. Family planning, for example, which became both a popular phrase and a widespread concern in the 1950s having been popularized by the US eugenicist Margaret Sanger in the 1930s, extended only as far as heterocentric standards of mixed-gender marriage and biological reproduction. Alternative kinship structures were considered, by definition, to be unplanned, shapeless, and unnatural, and not a constructive contribution to a collaborative cooperative *we*. Pat Thane details the challenges faced by planners:

> One face of modernity was the tendency towards uniformity—in the mass production of goods, for example, in expanding strategies of mass control (through radio, advertising, propaganda), and in the apparent capacity for centralised large-scale planning. The other face of modernity, however, was a growing emphasis on individual autonomy and the desire to assert it, the general realisation of a selfhood that was resistant to tidy planning. . . . The experience of controlling birth numbers stimulated women's imaginings of wider possibilities for themselves, shaping the aspirations of their own, as well as later, generations.[72]

Thane explicitly links planning with the constraint of play within a centrist political structure. Conversely, she also presents play—and particularly the play of liberated women—as potential relief from this centrist planning. In Britain, postwar planning found its apotheosis in the form of a suite of plans—ranging from the drably functional to the utopian—for housing programs, given top priority by governments in the postwar years. The ruins and slums of 1945 were to be swept away and replaced. As early as 1943, by which time the devastation of the blitz was already clear, the catalog for an exhibition entitled *Rebuilding Britain* stated that "the very first thing to win is the Battle of Planning. We shall need to have planning on a national scale, boldly overstepping the traditional boundaries of urban council, rural council, County Council."[73] In this "overstepping" can be glimpsed precisely the kind of centrist power grab that Priestley says is the opposite of planning. A significant thrust of the planners' work was a desire to revitalize the suburbs and build garden cities. Ernö Goldfinger, an architect who was critical of this approach, summarized the task for the planners as the need *"to create a frame for human life,"* acknowledging the risk of plans stopping—by structuring—play.[74]

This frame for human life is the principal casualty of farcical play in *The Green Man*. While Hawkins may be unsuccessful in planning the explosion of Sir Gregory, his improvisations do succeed in ex-centering—and blowing up—the planned heterocentric logic of leafy suburbia. Ann and Reginald are an incarnation of the planned suburban family. They are to be married; they are then to move in together (cohabitation in advance would be unthinkable); they are then to have children, which she will look after. But Ann also represents the constrained second face of modernity, as described by Thane. She has been enjoying trying on new and rather sexy underwear when she is caught by Reginald rolling on the floor with William. In a disobedient dismissal of her fiancé's efforts to manage her back into order, she asserts "individual autonomy" and realizes some of the "wider possibilities" for herself by discovering adventure, and quite possibly adventurous sex, with William.[75] The best-laid plans of BBC radio announcers gang aft agley, however, and Ann ex-centers the suburban consensus by spending the night with another man in a seaside hotel (uncovering a plot to create a very big bang). The film laughs merrily at the reminder that a young woman can leave a Reginald—bowler-hatted, conventional face of planned respectability—for a William—silly and chaotic dreamer with no particular prospects. Hawkins, in voiceover, contemplating his bête noire in lugubriously elongated vowels, states that "when fate takes a hand she sometimes chooses the meanest instruments for her purpose," in this case "a stray nonentity called William Blake." William may ultimately help to scupper Hawkins's plan, but it is as true and more important that Hawkins explodes William's heterocentric attitudes and encourages him to play.

Just as Holland in *The Lavender Hill Mob*, another "nonentity," is liberated by his ex-centering involvement in crime, so William is transformed. When he first meets Ann, he says that it is refreshing to hear that she and Reginald will not be moving in with each other until after marriage. He is prudish and conventional. This bastion of suburban values, however, is transformed as those values are undone by the merrily subversive energy of farce. William's pleasure at hearing that Ann and Reginald are not cohabiting is comically undermined as the farcical aspects of the film subvert the suburbs and make the proposed marriage look like the laughable union between bowler-hatted stuffiness and coiffured vivacity. They are not really engaged romantically; they are engaged in a series of unfortunately timed entrances and exits. As the action moves to the Green Man—a hotel where suburban husbands take their mistresses for dirty weekends—William abandons his performance of faith in heterocentric respectability. The detonation of the bomb becomes a visual metaphor for this explosive ex-centering. Despite being thrown by William from a ground-floor balcony, the radio is shown spinning and falling through a three-second shot (see fig. 4.4). Against an abstract, blurred background, this magical object falls and falls before disappearing in an ethereal blast of light. When the radio explodes, it cracks the veneer of respectability behind which the hotel has hidden its moral hypocrisy. The blast of light from an impossibly falling radio has illuminated the death of suburban niceties and left shattered windows, wonky walls, and a traumatized trio of musicians playing with manic fervor. Amid this evidence of exploded convention, William's conventional moral compass falls apart and he encourages Sir Gregory to make a run for it in order to avoid the awkwardness of exposure as an adulterer in the *Daily Mirror*. This is a seismic shift from suburban salesman who

Figure 4.4. Moral compasses spin in *The Green Man* (Robert Day, 1956). *Source:* Grenadier Productions/Courtesy of StudioCanal.

disapproves of cohabitation to seaside derring-doer who is happy to let an adulterer get away with his peccadilloes.

A second radio explodes still more of William's suburban attitudes as he and Ann despondently drive away together. She recalls how angry Reginald was. The potential for a downbeat ending hangs in the air. The car radio, with timing so perfect that it seems planned, begins to broadcast Reginald reading a series of modernist poems called "Vicious Cycle." The first describes a binary-busting woman whose beauty is also ugliness and who is called—predictably?—Ann. As the free verse continues, William fights to suppress a laugh. Just ahead of the repetition of the name, the film cuts to a shot of a distressed Reginald pulling a handkerchief from his pocket as the camera tracks in quickly and shakily; this pillar of respectability comes undone in medium close-up. Another cut: Ann and William sit silent and somewhat inscrutable in the car. On the radio, Reginald begins to intone the name—"Ann, Ann, Ann"—the repetitive chant becoming as stripped of meaning as an indefinitely reiterated indefinite article in search of a noun. Suddenly, his voice rises in a strangulated cry—"Ann!" A cut back to the studio, and Reginald buries his face in the microphone; his words—"Listen to me wherever you are; you can go to your blasted vacuum cleaner; I'm through, through, through, through, through!"—are indistinguishable from the parodic free verse. The camera tracks out as another radio announcer (Terence Alexander) steps into the frame and pushes Reginald's swivel chair out of frame left. "We must," he says, restoring central control, "apologize to listeners for a slight technical hitch." The hitch is that Ann and Reginald will not be hitched; marriage is abandoned; another radio has exploded, this time metaphorically, leaving the suburban plans for nice home, professional husband, glamorous wife, and secure future in ruins. Instead, William Blake—with some of the iconoclastic eccentricity of his namesake—puts his arms around Ann and turns the radio off.

Although Hawkins plans to blow up the elite, he succeeds in blowing up a heterocentric suburban couple. In his diary of 1954, Richard Rumbold describes "an age in which the greatest crime is to do or speak differently from one's neighbour in the new garden suburb or housing estate; an age which extols petit-bourgeois values of stupidity, respectability, and moral hypocrisy."[76] A year later, Ian Nairn edited an issue of *Architectural Review* in which he expressed fear that this kind of homogeneity would make itself felt throughout society;

he condemned what he called the "subtopia" of "cosy plots and bungalows" that was "making an ideal of suburbia. Visually speaking, the universalization and idealization of our town fringes. Philosophically, the idealization of the Little Man who lives there. . . . What is not to be borne [is that its] ethos [should] drift like a gaseous pink marshmallow over the whole social scene, over the mind of man, over the land surface, over the philosophy ideals and objectives of the human race."[77] The suburbs of *The Green Man* are home to assassins who play chess with police constables; they are disturbed by zombie-like almost-corpses who crawl out of car boots and wander abroad; and they are visited by vacuum cleaner salesmen who do not sleep with other men's fiancées but, nevertheless, ruin marriage plans. This is a suburbia of stronger stuff than marshmallow. The film was written (and unofficially part-directed) by Frank Launder and Sidney Gilliat, to whose work I return in chapter 5. Durgnat writes about this most puckish of writing teams that: "their consistent freshness and mischief, their cheerful lightly-and-slightly anarchism, their relaxed romping in and out of the system's little loopholes and bye-ways, is always a welcome break from the rigid ideological routines and closures which characterize so many films. And they give great scope to the weariness, the cynical drollery, the dour eccentricity, of Alastair Sim."[78] I agree with Durgnat that byways are more scenic (and queerer) routes than the main roads that lead straight to the planned heart of officialdom. I also agree that Launder and Gilliat's anarchism is light, but I am not convinced that it is slight. I think that what is left in ruins in *The Green Man* is the center of the postwar plan for British regeneration, which remains a political focus today: the reproduction of acres of identical houses structured around an imagined ideal of heterocentric familial bliss.

In the film's lightly-but-mighty anarchism, there is on offer, instead, a queer glimpse of possibilities of unplanned lives of improvised moments of erotic pleasure and adventure rather than the heterocentric schedule of engagement-marriage-children. Ann and William, cuddling on their unmarried night away, ex-center the predictable life she had planned. The queerness of this postwar moment lies in an investment in proliferating, overlapping, contradictory, and unorthodox futures. It was not limited by the scope of its utopian plans but was abandoned in its reckless capacity for imagination. Whether it is in the rough-and-ready landscapes that find physical articulation in the bomb sites on which children play, the collapse of order in triangulated unconventional desire, or the disorientation of suburbanite propriety, these films, with the logic of comedy, *laugh forward* possibilities of something else. This *els*eness does not demand the forgetting of past ruins in order to imagine a brighter future. Possibilities lie in the ruins themselves, in the temporal moment before reconstruction sought to reintroduce order, when institutions, attitudes, and values were in eccentric play. As Britain built back, despite the very best efforts of the *Sunday Pictorial*, it could not forget what it had glimpsed of homosocial camaraderie, female independence, and porous cities. And those intimations of something besides the constrained domestic logic of twenty-first-century neoliberal Britain remain visible in the films.

5

Being Beside Yourself

In this chapter, I shall look at a motif that, like the iconoclastically iconic ruins explored in chapter 4, produces eccentrically proliferating meanings. The split-screen effect that permits the same actor to give multiple performances within a single frame is a recurring trope in postwar British comedy. It is thanks to this comic device that the inimitable Alastair Sim, star of *The Green Man*, comes face-to-face with himself early in *The Belles of St. Trinian's* (Frank Launder, 1954). Sim plays both Millicent Fritton, headmistress of St. Trinian's, and her bookmaker brother Clarence. Clarence, up to no good, wishes his expelled daughter Bella (Vivienne Martin) to be reinstated at the school in order to secure him inside knowledge about a racehorse owned by the father of another pupil. This plot—which is slackly handled through the film—is largely irrelevant. The emphasis is predominantly on narratively gratuitous spectacle. Much criticism on the film focuses its attention on the violence and disruption caused by the pupils, who, with unrivaled postwar high spirits, blow up the conventions of how they should behave; the film begins with a pre-credits shot of a hand-painted sign for ST. TRINIANS SCHOOL FOR YOUNG LADIES being machine-gunned into ruination. Other criticism discusses Sim's drag performance. But very little attention has been paid to the striking visual impact of putting Millicent and Clarence—Sim and Sim—together in the same frame.

The sequence in which they are seen together for the first time begins with a conventional shot–reverse shot pattern; there is a frisson created by Sim's duplication, but it is dampened by the isolation of his personae in separate shots. Clarence is oily, creepy, dressed in the checked sports jacket and tweed hat that pass for a uniform among the racetrack fraternity; he carries a binoculars case that is later revealed to contain only his sandwiches and a bottle of milk. He has a kind of sardonic rich-voiced mirth that borders on the sinister. He is a fake, but a fake so familiar from British film that he acquires a kind of credibility. Millicent, who returns his gaze through pince-nez and across a cluttered desk, is a creature of a different world and time; she is draped in a voluminous frilled blouse and coils of beads and pearls but, in the muteness of the black-and-white photography, her clothes lack color and her jewelry luster. It becomes clear quickly that she is no more a respectable headmistress than he a legitimate racing enthusiast; her accessories are fakes and ultimately as devoid of meaningful content as Clarence's binoculars case. The room is swamped with redundant bric-a-brac: vases that hold no flowers, candlesticks that give no light, a metronome that does not keep order. Millicent is a fraud, the pantomime performance of a vanished respectability associated with the kinds of private school that St. Trinian's can only dream of being.

The sequence becomes more arresting as shot–reverse shot is abandoned and Clarence steps into the same frame as his sister, an impossible doubleness made possible by the split-screen effect (see fig. 5.1). Millicent—with twisting hips, air-swiping hand, and dipping head—performs agitation. The serene figure who was seen working at her desk at the beginning of the sequence is seemingly disturbed by Clarence, although that earlier stiff-backed display of studiousness looked so unnatural that it, too, seemed staged rather than spontaneous. As the sequence continues (with some return to shot–reverse shot) Millicent articulates the differences between the siblings: "When poor Frieda and I started this school during the General Strike of 1926, we vowed to make it the happiest, most carefree establishment in the whole of Britain. And what a gay arcadia of happy girlhood it was then, until the war broke out and such things as good manners and good taste were replaced by your black market values." On the face of it, she is female, altruistic, generous, respectable, and dreams of utopia, while he is male, selfish, greedy, criminal, and indulges in underworld fantasies. The casting of Sim in both roles, however, renders the siblings opposite *and yet the same*; they each bear the visually inscribed trace of the other, which, in the film's own spirit

Figure 5.1. Family Sim-ilarities in *The Belles of St. Trinian's* (Frank Launder, 1954). *Source:* London Films/Courtesy of STUDIOCANAL.

of bad punning, I might call their Sim-ilarity. Sim the actor becomes more visible as he faces off with himself and both characters amount to a series of performed gestures; Clarence is no more meaningfully full than his binoculars case and Millicent no more convincing than her hairpiece. St. Trinian's is not the last bastion of prewar propriety but a site of gambling, bathtub gin, free(ish) love, and all manner of fakery and fraud.

This Sim-ilarity in difference continues as Millicent and Clarence share a frame to trade insults and gestures. Differently histrionic, both siblings flail and pose, self-indulgently performing for each other. He, louche and seedy, slouches in his chair and drawls his words; she, alert and mobile, sits forward and sings her lines *moderato*. They are off-kilter reflections of each other. As his underhand plan to secure valuable racing information comes into focus, she performs outrage: standing, pushing her heavy chair back sharply, extending then retracting her arms. As she sings that "this is a *school*" she positively shrieks the final word, extending the double *o* into a histrionic diphthong that incorporates several discrete vowel sounds and a high-pitched rattle in the throat. She begins to pace, heaving her shoulders in a gestural show of offendedness. Clarence, lips set in a slight curl and eyes hooded, leaves the frame as he draws out the name "Milly" with such weight that it uncovers quantities of menace in the sound. The gloves slowly come off revealing the knuckles beneath as Clarence proceeds to blackmail his sister, threatening to tell their mother that she has mortgaged the family home. The threats are issued as Clarence stands beneath a painting of Mrs. Fritton, another likeness of Sim, this time dressed in a sleeveless evening gown with low front and ornate floral corsage (see fig. 5.2). Returning to a shared frame, the blackmail having worked its magic, Millicent and Clarence come to terms; Bella may return if Clarence pays ten pounds on account against her outstanding school fees. When Millicent demands more and Clarence threatens to reclaim his tenner, she demonstrates her savvy and snaps her outstretched fingers back into a fist with the light-

Figure 5.2. A boy's best friend is his mother in *The Belles of St. Trinian's* (Frank Launder, 1954). *Source:* London Films/Courtesy of STUDIOCANAL.

ning rapidity of a predator and then, for security's sake, deposits the banknotes into the depths of her bosom. With an irony wonderfully at odds with both the snap and strength of her own physical gestures and the silently stuffed barn owl that haunts the frame behind her, she chants the plaintive line, "Oh, I suppose I'm just a foolish, weak woman, and you're an unscrupulous rogue, Clarence."

I find the laughter in this sequence in the fact that this *I* and *you* do not behave as polite company might expect them to. The neat binary distinctions between I–you, female–male, respectable–roguish, foolish–crafty, weak–strong, honest–unscrupulous are no more secure than the bullet-marked school sign. This is in part because of the doubleness created by irony, in which, as Paul de Man puts it, "words have a way of saying things which are not at all what you want them to say . . . [creating] a total arbitrariness . . . which inhabits words on the level of the play of the signifier. . . ."[1] This play, in which language abandons the myth of centered meaning, allows Millicent to say that she is a foolish, weak woman without (only) meaning it. Bruce Babington argues that Launder and Gilliat "cultivated actors' skills of irony, understatement and allusiveness, particularly in comic modes," creating a special rapport with Sim "whose range of meanings within the parameters of middleclass paternalism (both good and bad), as a comic actor who could shade to a sinister, almost vampiric inflection of his benign eccentricity, proved particularly fitting for their purposes."[2] The collapse of concentric binary structures in *The Belles of St. Trinian's* acquires its force from the casting of Sim, both benign and vampiric, in two roles. The *I* that speaks in this sequence speaks to a *you* that is both its other and itself. Millicent and Clarence are distinct characters, and yet not as distinct as they would have been were they played by two actors. The comparison is an easy one to make; *The Happiest Days of Your Life* is a 1950 school-based farce by the same writing-directing team, starring Alastair Sim and Margaret Rutherford as warring head teachers whose schools are combined as the result of an error in the Ministry of Education. The repartee between Sim and Rutherford is exhilarating and the collision of their respective eccentricities is spectacular, but it does not have the comic, disorientating strangeness that accompanies the encounter of Sim and Sim in the study at St. Trinian's. In this chapter, I shall consider filmic multiroling as a strategy for ex-centering characters, narratives, and frames by putting figures *beside themselves*.

Being Beside Themselves in *The Belles of St. Trinian's*

The English language enjoys a number of felicitous phrases that describe states of instability by linguistically complicating the self–other boundary. Examples include "You are not yourself," "You are out of your mind," and "You are not all there." Such phrases might be called on to describe the boundary-busting descent down the Eiffel Tower in *The Lavender Hill Mob* (see chapter 3) or the spilling over of P. C. Spiller into the paradox of being both English and foreign in *Passport to Pimlico* (see chapter 1). In *Sailor Beware!* (see chapter 2), Emma Hornett accuses her sister-in law Edie of "trailing around the place as though [she] wasn't all there." Each phrase registers a moment of lostness in which an individual behaves outside their usual and predictable parameters, momentarily unanchored by a clearly defined center. The collapse of self–other, in–out, and here–there suggests a *both/and, not-just* state of indeterminacy in which the self is momentarily suspended and a freer, less convention-constrained play can occur. Being *beside yourself* is another common euphemism, which slides imprecisely across a range of meanings, gesturing toward any experience of madness, grief, or joy that disturbs the smooth operation of the structured self and reveals a parallel alternative at work.[3] This suggestion of structural disturbance and the embracing of otherness is reminiscent of the ways in which *eccentricity* is understood in this book. The phrasing, however, marks the continued hegemony of centric myths of identity. To be *beside yourself* is an aberrant state (in sensation, behavior, desire) measured against the authentic *self* that one is *beside*. The phrase implies that in a state of being *beside yourself*, there remains a clear original self, a definable center. If you lose track of this center you need, according to the stuff-and-nonsense bluster of traditional British advice, to *pull yourself together*.

Queer theory has critiqued the idea of a self that must or should or even can be pulled together. Jasbir Puar writes that "there is no entity, no identity, no queer subject to queer, rather queerness coming forth at us from all directions, screaming its defiance, suggesting a move from intersectionality to assemblage, an affective conglomeration that recognizes other contingencies of belonging (melding, fusing, viscosity, bouncing) that might not fall so easily into what is sometimes denoted as reactive community formations—identity politics—by control theorists."[4] Puar abandons the centric structurality of identity, with its absolute distinctions and categories, in favor of the eccentric assemblage, an idea borrowed from Gilles Deleuze and Félix Guattari that suggests the contingent, shifting, transformational connections between elements, objects, and bodies.[5] Assemblage theory challenges confidence in seamless and organic structures and embraces, instead, more unsettled states of changeability and unexpected comings together. Although the basic idiom seems to reinforce the idea that *yourself* is not permanently threatened or lost when you are *beside yourself*, *The Belles of St. Trinian's*, I think, offers an alternative image of assemblage. The spectacular siblings, in their Sim-ilarity, are duplications with no original, elements drawn together within a shared frame as parts of a cinematic assemblage. Queerness—in the fidgeting–slouching, drawling–singing, female–male bodies of Alastair Sim's performances—comes forth from all directions, creating a contingent coming together that laughs its rejection of a settled politics of identity. These Sim-ilar figures are not anchored to a self, but are parts of an assemblage in which each is in a state of *beside*ness. Sim himself cannot settle this structure into meaning by introducing a sense of original self, as there are too many Sims onscreen to offer reassurance. There is no way of knowing which came first, the Sim or the Sim.

Unhierarchical plurality, then, is key to the effect of this visual sharing of the frame by versions of the same performer *beside themselves*. *Beside* may be productively contrasted with other prepositions; as Eve Kosofsky Sedgwick expresses the point, *beneath* and *beyond* both suggest "depth or hiddenness, typically followed by a drama of exposure" in which they "turn from spatial descriptors into implicit narratives of, respectively, origin and telos."[6] "Origin" and "telos" are two of the names that Derrida offers for the center.[7] *Beneath* and *beyond* have an unshakable faith in concealed cores where meaning resides. But there is nothing stable *beneath* or *beyond* the fake studio sets of domestic drag, or the undisciplined laughter at nothing, or the rubble of ruined buildings and institutions. Postwar British comedy does not trade in depth. *Beside*, by contrast, is a preposition of flatness; its arrangements suggest simultaneity, and proximity, and even intimacy—but not the excavated forms of meaning implied by metaphors of depth. This flatness should not be mistaken for simplistic inertness or dullness; the dynamic between elements can comprise what Sedgwick describes as "a wide range of desiring, identifying, representing, repelling, paralleling, differentiating, rivaling, leaning, twisting, mimicking, withdrawing, attracting, aggressing, warping, and other relations."[8] Contrasting with the excavation of depth-fixated identity, the logic of *beside*ness champions the collisions and constellations of assemblage—as elements, defined as often by difference as by similarity, encounter each other in constantly shifting formations and produce new ideas without ever cohering around a definable stable center. Eccentric comedies of *beside*ness are in the conditional mood, asking *what if* two different, incongruous, oppositional, even irreconcilable elements were combined.

The eccentric speculation concerning *what if* an actor could be in more than one point in the frame—could stand *beside themselves*—is one of the recurring interests of postwar comedy screens. The most celebrated example is Alec Guinness's turn as almost the entire D'Ascoyne family in *Kind Hearts and Coronets* (Robert Hamer, 1949), that fantasia on serial killing. In a celebrated matte shot, which depicts six members of the family, Guinness—who "*was* the ensemble"—sits beside himself, and in one guise (Lady Agatha) silences the snoring of another (the general) (see fig. 5.3).[9] Michael Newton argues that

Figure 5.3. A family beside itself in *Kind Hearts and Coronets* (Robert Hamer, 1949). Ealing Studios/Courtesy of STUDIOCANAL.

this casting is about heterocentric family *identity*: "The film bears witness to the biological principle that underlies the aristocratic system."[10] This reading retains a sense of depth; according to Newton's schema, familial figures are effectively arranged *behind* each other in an unconquerable series that, with each death, reveals yet another D'Ascoyne. This suggests the *behind*ness and *beyond*ness of family inheritance. The simultaneity of Sims in *The Belles of St. Trinian's* could be explained according to a similar (if less homicidal) familial logic: the simple assumption that parents and their offspring might bear a great family likeness. It is this logic that leads Newton to suggest that "the multiplying of Guinness into all the D'Ascoynes . . . [gives] the nightmarish sense that each murder is the same murder; that there is a series of the same person."[11] This not only cements an idea of self and identity ("the same person"), but it also insists on "series," namely a linear temporal development that, in the words of Lee Edelman, offers "the promise of sequence as the royal road to *co*nsequence."[12] This consequence—which combines causation, meaning, and impact—is pegged firmly on the explanatory function of the natural likeness of family members.

Edelman, skeptical of this royal road, suggests that the promise of sequence "displaces the epistemological impasse, the aporia of relationality, the nonidentity of things."[13] I am unconvinced by Newton's reading and see the proliferation of Guinnesses (and Sims) not as images of a genealogical *behind* but a deranged *beside* in which the relationality of relations is in the grip of aporia (the logical disjunction in a frame that screens impossible duplications) and nonidentity. Sedgwick points out that *beside*ness can disturb "several of the linear logics that enforce dualistic thinking: noncontradiction or the law of the excluded middle, cause versus effect, subject versus object."[14] Family inheritance is the linear logic disturbed by this *beside-themselves*ness; these families, iconically represented by the simultaneity (and not the sequence) of performances, are *flat*. Earlier generations are reduced to the two-dimensionality of portraits. In the assemblage of the matte shot, performances filmed at different times are made uncannily concurrent. In the aesthetic of *beside*ness, the boundaries between subjects and objects become murky when they are all played by the same actor. This flatness of character encourages a shift in focus to the technical gestures of virtuosic actors (as well as skillful cinematographers). Newton points out that *Kind Hearts and Coronets* is "most famous for Alec Guinness's *tour de force* of playing eight roles," but Guinness the performer remains visible as he distinguishes characters by broad vocal and physical gestures.[15] Similarly, Sim characterizes Millicent and Clarence through histrionic mannerisms. The Frittons are, like the D'Ascoynes before them, *flat*. *Beneath* their clothes and *beyond* their gestures, they are hollow.

In this double-dealing world, in which meaning does not lie beneath surfaces, authority collapses. It cannot express itself sincerely in a language that becomes two-faced in its incorrigible ironies: the double entendre of "I can no longer afford to have continual arson about in my school"; the parapraxis of Millicent's claim that the school cups "have gone to be pawnished—I mean, polished"; the ironic use of the words *belles* and *young ladies*, showing up some of the gendered double standards that continue to haunt postwar Britain. Perhaps the most anarchic feature of the depiction of school life is not that the girls behave with homicidal wildness but that the teachers—a troupe of "vamps, gin-addicts and mistresses who merely keep a nervous eye out for a police Wolseley clanging up the driveway"—have no authority to stop them.[16] Millicent approaches the girls' relentless laying of potentially deadly booby traps for her as test of her mettle and not of her authority; she does not chastise or discipline. Landy argues that Sim's female "impersonation also divests power and authority of its solemn aura."[17] This divesting is amplified by the fact that Millicent and Clarence are *beside themselves*, splintering authority, robbing it of a center as the bifurcated star gives two star performances. A world that is *beside itself* is too unruly to locate authority in a decisive, single figure. In this way, the film connotes a general disorder in postwar Britain. As the veneer of wartime consensus gives way to partisanship, disappointment, disputed enemies, and conflicting images of the future, St. Trinian's produces a competitive arena in which survival is everything and specific moral and legal schemata are an irrelevance. The film's radical gesture is to present this world not as horrifying but as comic, delightfully presented in the images of Millicent chuckling as a riot upstairs deposits plaster dust all over her, of Old Girls at a reunion enthusiastically arming themselves and charging into battle with cut-price hoodlums, and of blissed-out members of the Ministry of Education (the "Lotus Eaters") in the pavilion. Landy describes the film as having a "carnival atmosphere in which morality, sexuality, and all social conventions are turned on their head. From the portrayal of the headmistress, Miss Fritton, played by Alastair Sim, to that of the schoolboys [sic], the films not only satirize the myths of British educational institutions but also turn their attack on the family, the police, government bureaucrats, journalists, and economic exploitation."[18] While this reading recognizes the film's mischievous disruptions, including of sexuality, it articulates them in a centric rhetoric: the turning of convention on its head is a simple inversion that preserves binary divisions and satire depends on a clearly delineated target in opposition to which the speaker defines themselves. As I watch it, *The Belles of St. Trinian's* is more ambivalent than Landy's comments suggest—with chaos both unproductive and enjoyable, both dangerous and invigorating, both futile and emancipatory—and this holds the film back from being just satire. The private school system is both mocked as dysfunctional and celebrated as a utopia populated by independent, intelligent, and resourceful pupils. In particular, satire requires a cleaner sense of the I–you divide than the film's leading actor allows; such clear-cut statuses as hero and villain are exploded with the same vigor as poor little Bessie who does not heed Millicent's warnings about nitroglycerine. The eccentric Frittons ex-center each other as they vie for the film's principal role. Babington argues that this ambivalence ultimately diminishes the film because it is "as stripped of tendentiousness as possible, but the very suppression of tendentiousness, which probably guaranteed the films' success, leaves them tame for later viewers."[19] I disagree; the *laughing forward* of the film, which has me giggling, lies in its destabilizing of perspective. Tendentiousness is inconceivable in a world so disarrayed that I–you ceases to be a reliable binary and everything is *beside itself*.

Upsetting Family Values

The queer effect of this *beside themselves*ness is predicated on two elements of Sim's twin performance: *gender difference* and *family likeness*. As a statement on gender, *The Belles of St. Trinian's* has been read in very different ways. Babington argues that "the comic problematics of the release of the postwar 'monstrous regiment of women' are not able to be satisfactorily registered in plots as oldfashionedly centered on 'gees,' illicit stills, smoking fags, big girls in little gym slips."[20]

Such an interpretation is constrained by an assumption that these elements (including the MacGuffin of the gee, or racehorse, who is almost entirely incidental) *center* the film. I argue that such elements are constantly being displaced as they collide with disparate elements *beside* which they are eccentrically arranged. The sixth formers in their gym slips, for example (who play a far more uncomfortably prurient role in the later St. Trinian's films), routinely collide with their dysfunctional teachers or the hooligan fourth formers who rob them of any chance of centering anything. Melanie Williams takes a more affirmative view, suggesting that girls in 1950s cinema, including the pupils of St. Trinian's, hopefully "hint at a future where twilight and night might finally yield to day."[21] While I am more sympathetic to Williams's belief in the political impact of the film, her neat binaries (past–future, night–day, despair–hope) are at odds with a film that complicates binaries throughout. Twilight, rather than something that must yield, represents a queer state of *between*ness, of unsettled possibility; flickery postwar monochrome suggests just this crepuscular half-light. The bright day dreamed of by Williams represents a settlement, a new consensus that will favor some and exclude others. The hopefulness that I see in *The Belles of St. Trinian's* is twilit, an unsettled world in which differences—played by Alastair Sim and Alastair Sim—can look themselves in the eye and marvel at possibilities.

Landy represents some of this indeterminacy in her description of Sim's drag: "Sim's female impersonation casts the films in another light, signaling the reversal of all roles and therefore all behavioral expectations about males and females."[22] The drag that Landy describes is a primarily theatrical technique that highlights gender's performativity. Judith Butler argues that "performativity is not a single act, but a repetition and a ritual, which achieves its effect through the naturalization in the context of a body, understood, in part, as a culturally sustained temporal duration."[23] The complex socially prescribed gestures that form gender occur sequentially through time. Beneath a theatrical drag performance is a history of repetition, countless stylized gestures from the past that, performed and reperformed, constitute gender. Although this theatrical drag upsets the gender-centric myth of essential identity and shows gender in play (despite the emphasis by some twenty-first-century commentators on authentic self-expression), its effect is limited. Sedgwick, in her exploration of *beside*ness, critiques Butler's single focus on time and suggests that "with the loss of its spatiality . . . the internally complex field of drag performance suffers a seemingly unavoidable simplification and reification."[24] She substitutes a focus on *spatial proximity* and recommends "an extra alertness to the multisided interactions among people 'beside' each other in a room."[25] This *beside*ness of performers, musicians, managers, audiences, and so on suggests "that drag is less a single kind of act than a heterogeneous system, an ecological field whose intensive and defining relationality is internal as much as it is directed toward the norms it may challenge."[26] This assemblage of elements together in space adds a useful dimension to Butler's model of drag as an assemblage of gestures through time, but it remains theatrical. *The Belles of St. Trinian's* explodes the constraints of theatrical drag and the emphasis on either *temporal repetition* or *spatial proximity*. It institutes a peculiarly *filmic* drag that identifies an alternative form of *beside*ness through *spatial repetition* (in which Sim is repeated in the space of the frame) and *temporal proximity* (in which the two distinct times at which Sim was recorded are laid alongside each other in the same moment). Both spatial repetition and temporal proximity use dynamics of *beside*ness to derange logic. This logic is, in part, the heterocentric logic of gender. Sim's performance as Millicent reveals the stylized gestures that signify femininity. In addition, as Millicent asks her brother why he is in "that dreadful get-up," Sim's performance as Clarence reveals the stylized gestures that signify masculinity. Inscribed in the frame as both female and male, both feminine and masculine *at the same time*, Sim's filmic drag, queerly *beside itself*, regards its own bead-swinging, tweed-wearing, wig-fiddling, chair-slouching, girl-educating, girl-fancying artifice and destabilizes every gender.

Given this complication of gender, it is surprising that Geraghty should argue that:

> Women are generally relegated to the sidelines in fifties war films, and although comedies such as the Doctor series, films by the Boulting brothers and the St. Trinian's series certainly satirised old-fashioned attitudes, they also mocked contemporary attitudes towards, for example, marriage and women's modes of consumption. . . . Fifties British cinema . . . provides evidence of a strong resistance to the notion of the new woman and an inability to imagine her as any kind of modern heroine.[27]

Geraghty here seems to be advocating a cinematic depiction of the postwar evolution of heterocentric myths in the shape of updated (though still constraining) attitudes. If checked for positive images of contemporary marriage and women's modes of consumption, *The Belles of St. Trinian's* will probably disappoint. Its mature women are both unheroic and unmarried and its girls show no excitement at the prospect of wedlock, companionate or otherwise. Clarence has a daughter, but her mother is never referenced; dramatically, Bella is a miraculous aberration who exists simply in order to give Clarence a reason to visit the school and become involved in the plot. The film makes me laugh not so much because it says something about marriage in the 1950s but because it is a marriageless world in which all gender is arranged *beside itself* and heterocentric structures that dare to signpost themselves are machine-gunned.

Millicent, who fails as a modern heroine but may succeed as a postmodern antiheroine, stands *beside* her brother, ex-centering not only gender but also family. Millicent identifies a "frustrated mother instinct" in herself and imagines her school as "one big, happy family. . . . Perhaps just a teeny weeny bit unorthodox, but, there, that's better than being old fashioned, isn't it? You see, in other schools, girls are sent out quite unprepared into a merciless world. But when our girls leave here, it is the merciless world which has to be prepared." In the world of the film, the modern family is charged not with merely teaching its young how to turn the conventions of an indifferent world to their own advantage, but how to trample those conventions and terrorize the world's structures. This strange and disruptive kinship finds one of its preeminent expressions in the frame-deranging *beside*ness of Millicent and Clarence. The dominant cultural metaphor for family is the tree, with its reassuringly linear and centered structure from roots (origins) to buds (future). This is a model of family predicated on inheritance, on what is *behind* and *beneath* the present, and all ideas of inheritance are structured according to hierarchies in which *through time* the earlier bestows power on the later. The family tree is a structure that Deleuze and Guattari critique as "a sad image of thought that is forever imitating the multiple on the basis of a centered or segmented higher unity."[28] Such "arborescent systems are hierarchical systems with centers of significance and subjectification."[29] Deleuze and Guattari contrast "acentered systems, finite networks of automata in which communication runs from any neighbor to any other, the stems or channels do not preexist, and all individuals are interchangeable, defined only by their *state* at a given moment—such that the local operations are coordinated and the final, global result synchronized without a central agency."[30] Their name for such an acentered—or eccentric—system is the *rhizome*.

It is not my contention that *The Belles of St. Trinian's* is a rhizomatic text. I do, however, want to suggest that it does offer glimpses of a family that does not operate according to a linear *inheritance through time* but as an *encounter* or even *collision in space* of different and non-linear *times*. The slippery values and vices represented by the gestures of the two Frittons/Sims—ingenuity, resilience, pluck, guile, outrage, ire, masculinity, femininity, and so on—are "interchangeable" and the characters are "defined only by their *state* [or performance] at a given moment." Neither is superior to the other; neither is dependent on the other. Mother is nothing but an image placed *beside* her children, painted at a moment in which she was the same age as they are now. The logic of inheritance is exploded as the content of any possible bequest—the family home—is mortgaged "up to the hilt." The Fritton family stands "in contrast to centered (even polycentric) systems with hierarchical modes of communication and preestablished paths, [and is more like] the rhizome [, which] is an acentered, nonhierarchical, non-signifying system."[31] Family, in this image of nonreproductive, simultaneous *beside-it-self*ness has no hierarchy, no consistent flow of power, no past and no future based on inheritance. Clarence has a daughter, but neither she nor the troops of other St. Trinian's girls mothered by Millicent could possibly be mistaken for the Symbolic Child whom Edelman associates with a heterocentric ambition to "*affirm* a structure, to *authenticate* a social order."[32] Geraghty's frustration lies in the film's failure to offer an image of the remodeled postwar family; my delight, by contrast, lies in the film's exorcism of the image of "gender conformist, married, hetero couple and their obviously well-planned child, immersed in and surrounded by what one might think of as 1950s-style white picket fence values."[33] Any white picket fences in the world of St. Trinian's would be torn down, knocked over, or blown up.

The film's image, then, is of a flat and futureless family, arranged according to horizontal combination rather than vertical succession. This simultaneity, however, does not diminish the comedy's potential for *laughing forward*. This process is helped by the *funny-ha-ha, funny-peculiar* film strategy of multiplying an actor across a frame in a kind of condensation that makes visible the typically camouflaged operation of all film. Film performs the pretense of seamless presentness, arranging its temporally and spatially discontinuous elements into a semblance of the smooth and uninterrupted unfolding of time and space. The continuity effects of editing in most narrative cinema encourage the suppression of knowledge that shots filmed at different times and in different places have been edited together. The paradoxical simultaneity of Sims (or Guinnesses) laughs at such mythic continuity. Cause and effect are thrown into disarray; Millicent and Clarence react to each other, but it is impossible to know which of them was filmed first, which of them is the cause and which the effect. As neither accepts the mantle of origin or telos, there is no clear center to either the frame or the family. Seamlessness is comically threatened as the film risks giving away the trick behind its magic with this eccentric superfluity of Sim, this *too-much-to-believe*ness. The duration of the shots of Millicent and Clarence and the settledness of the camera (in order to allow the split-screen exposure) give time to notice the clues to how the shot was achieved: the *not-quite* accurate eyelines, the careful choreography in separate zones of the frame, the slight differences in focus on the characters, and so on. As formal continuity withers and seamlessness buckles, the Fritton frame does what Sedgwick sets as a mission: "to *dis*articulate them one from another, to *dis*engage them—the bonds of blood, of law, of habitation, of privacy, of companionship and succor—from the lockstep of their unanimity in the system called 'family.'"[34] The film *laughs forward*, for me, an image that replaces the centered seamless biological family—upheld by its heterocentric bonds—with an anarchic, deranged form of kinship whose elements collide and shatter and that is always *beside itself*, an eccentric family rhizome of tics, mannerisms, and stereotypes.

Dragging Up the Nazis in *The Square Peg*

The eccentric effect of the doubling in *The Belles of St. Trinian's* is amplified by the eccentric acting technique of Alastair Sim. His style generally consists of such overt physical and vocal gestures (the stuffing of the scarf into the gramophone bell in *Hue and Cry*, the heaving shoulder laugh in *Laughter in Paradise*, and the squeal of the word "school" in *The Belles of St. Trinian's*) that the notion of a character *beneath* the performance is always under interrogation. Norman Wisdom, although a very different type of performer, shares some of this commitment to histrionic gesture. Wisdom, the most popular British cinematic clown of the 1950s, is most famous for playing variations on a character usually called Norman and referred to as the Gump. The Gump is a childish little man, capable of both ingenuousness and mischief. His clothes are typically too small, giving him a scruffy, unkempt look. Never particularly bright, he delights in bad jokes and laughs with such abandon that his laughter looks to require a dislocated jaw. He is not cynical and is generally optimistic, but his sense of injustice is sometimes great. He fears, respects, and mocks authority. He sings romantic songs in a series of outrageous lip syncs, typically dedicated to the pretty girl who ultimately finds him irresistible. He is violently clumsy; his life is a series of falls, until the moment comes for his ultimate, spectacular rise into the arms of the girl he loves, just in time for the final fade.

Medhurst attributes Wisdom's success to his adroit combination of "the two fundamentals of popular comedy, slapstick and sentiment."[35] The excessive, mannered gestures of his slapstick and tumbles are often eccentric, making strange the familiar worlds (a department store, a gentlemen's club, a dry cleaner's, and so on) through which he passes. These pratfalls are typically counteracted by pathos, and his films can "rely too heavily on the 'lovable idiot' persona, and topple over into sheer sentiment."[36] Often a balance is struck, and sentimental resolutions coincide with what looks like the coming-good of the slapstick through the *restabilizing* of structure in the narrative worlds. As Landy writes, "through his blundering he manages to expose trouble and to act ethically in destroying the enemies of order."[37] Such enemies might include the ex-centering menagerie of characters who help to queer the corners of Norman's world and who are ultimately disciplined: Jerry Desmonde who, despite his straight-man status, slaps Norman's arse and watches him bathe in *Follow a Star* (Robert Asher, 1959); Fenella Fielding who vamps her way through a party in the same film and ultimately runs from Norman, screaming "You're not normal!"; and the peerless Margaret Rutherford on eccentric form as a genteel shoplifter in *Trouble in Store* (John Paddy Carstairs, 1953). Heterocentricity, thrown into temporary disarray by the anarchy of such messing about, is restored as the Gump (usually clumsily) gets the girl, defeats the baddy, humiliates the pompous prig, and hails a charmless future of schmaltz.

Although Wisdom's comedy films of the 1950s and 1960s are formulaic to an extent, the description above remains an unfair reduction. One complication of the Norman-as-lovable-scamp motif can be seen in a series of films—*Just My Luck* (John Paddy Carstairs, 1957), *The Square Peg* (John Paddy Carstairs, 1959), *On the Beat* (Robert Asher, 1962), and *Press for Time* (Robert Asher, 1966)—in which Wisdom is *beside himself* in double roles. The first of these is an unexceptional story about Norman's desire to make enough money from betting on a six-horse accumulator to buy the object of his affection a pendant. The miracle happens, of course, aided by Mrs. Dooley (Margaret Rutherford), who lives with an elephant and a chimpanzee and excessively pronounces the young couple to be "reckless, foolish, mad, crazy, adorable." When the gamble has paid off and paid out, there are three signs of Norman's triumph: Anne (Jill Dixon) accepts his proposal; his stern mother (Marjorie Rhodes) smiles and drops her belligerent insistence that he is "subnormal"; and his father returns, having abandoned his wife and son years earlier. The family is reunited in a sentimental performance of heterocentric bliss. The girl is caught; the mother is tamed; the father is domesticated. At their center is Norman, who has magicked up this happy resolution through the miracle of money. This *happy ever after* bubble, however, is pricked by the casting of Wisdom as his own father. Dressed in an absurd combination of checked suit, checked waistcoat, and polka-dot cravat, Wisdom-as-father stumbles in from a different decade. He is padded and wears a bald cap, neither wholly convincing. His face is not aged, and he resembles nothing more than the childish Gump fresh from a rummage in the dressing-up box. He suggests to his wife that they should "forget the past and start all over again"; the past is obliterated in this image of Norman facing his father across the frame, the laughter arising from a family *beside itself*, rearranging the temporal logic of inheritance into a spatial logic of proximity. Norman has not simply inherited his looks from his father; the joke is that his father, who arrives only in the final seconds of the film, has also inherited his looks from the film's main character. In a final gesture, as grotesque as it is sentimental, Norman winks at his father with his left eye and his father, as though in a mirror, returns the wink with his right. This is a comparable—if slighter—disturbance of familial structure to that seen in *Kind Hearts and Coronets* and *The Belles of St. Trinian's*.

The next film in which Wisdom plays double is *The Square Peg*, a foray back into wartime adventure in which the Gump's lookalike is General Schreiber of the Third Reich. This similarity is not presented as family likeness, but as a coincidence that can be transformed into wartime strategy. The narrative idea borrows from *The Goose Steps Out* (Basil Dearden, 1942), in which Will Hay plays both the bumbling William Potts and the German spy Muller. Whereas *The Goose Steps Out* is comic propaganda made during the conflict, mocking the ineptitude of the Nazis who are taken in by the idiot Potts, *The Square Peg* is a harking back, a resurrection of an iconography—the uniforms, props, and gestures of European fascism—that is neither obviously pertinent nor obviously funny in 1959. Richard Dacre points out that Wisdom had to fight for the opportunity to play Schreiber as director "John Paddy Carstairs, the man so crucial in Wisdom's cinematic development, was against the star taking both roles and mixing comic styles."[38] A different actor in the part of Schreiber would have eroded the film's eccentric effects considerably.

Unlike *The Goose Steps Out*, in which the likeness between Potts and Muller is identified almost immediately and becomes the comic and dramatic driver for the whole narrative, the likeness between Norman and Schreiber is not recognized until just over halfway through the film. Before this, the film follows the misadventures of council worker Norman Pitkin who, in his somewhat officious determination to mend roads regardless of the impact that this has on the war effort, routinely falls out with serving soldiers at a local training camp. Eventually, in order to get the Gump under their control, the local military top brass arrange to have him and his boss Mr. Grimsdale called up. The first half of the film, which is fun but unexceptional, operates as a series of loosely connected set pieces and strongly resembles the run of 1950s comedy films about national service including *Carry on Sergeant* (Gerald Thomas, 1958) and *Idol on Parade* (John Gilling, 1959) and the ITV sitcom *The Army Game* (1957–61). There is a shift in the second half when Norman falls for Lesley (Honor Blackman), an officer who is about to parachute into France as a spy. As the result of a mistake, Norman is parachuted into the same region as Lesley, where his likeness to the local commandant is noted. When Lesley, Mr. Grimsdale, and members of the Resistance are captured, Norman dresses as Schreiber and effects a daring rescue. He returns to England where his reward is to be made mayor of the borough of St. Godric's in the town of Durham.

Although "Wisdom's films are built around his persona"—silly, childish, accident prone, prudish, both deferential and puckishly disobedient—the Gump is not so unyielding a structure that it entirely constrains the play of Wisdom's performances.[39] The father in *Just My Luck* gives a glimpse of this play, but *The Square Peg*'s double motif gives it freer rein. Postwar diarist Anthony Heap notes in January 1959 that the film offers Wisdom a "gratifying—and well seized—opportunity to get away from his customary cloth capped 'little man' character."[40] This getting away from custom could hardly be more pronounced, and Wisdom's performance as Schreiber is wholly differentiated from the Gump. He is violently cruel, a tendency measured in the sharp precision of his gestures, each slap, each salute, each brandish with his swagger stick a sharply delivered piece of choreography. It is worlds apart from the bumbling, fumbling gestures of Norman. This contrast is revealed deliriously in the moment in which the likeness between Norman and the general becomes apparent. Not realizing that he is in German-occupied territory, Norman strolls into the French town of Fleury. On the wall, behind some beer-swilling Nazi soldiers, hangs a poster declaring in French and German that the town and its environs are under the command of General Schreiber who will use his powers to maintain order in the region. The photograph of Schreiber, barring the dueling scar, is the perfect likeness of Norman. Unaware of the poster, Norman strides into the town with a knotted handkerchief on his head and swinging a shopping bag. As the soldiers, mistaking Norman for their leader, stand to attention and raise their hands sharply in Nazi salutes, Norman obliviously travesties the gesture by returning a high-armed, limp-wristed wave. The chilling salute finds its comically distorting mirror image in the silly wave.

Literal mirrors become important when Norman and Schreiber finally meet. This event is deferred substantially, and it is more than two-thirds of the way through the film before Wisdom is seen *beside himself*. Having entered the chateau occupied by the Nazi forces, Norman has decided to knock the general out and rescue his friends. Schreiber has been performing lieder (and various parodic courting rituals) with his lover Gretchen (Hattie Jacques). When Schreiber retires to his bathroom in order to gargle, Norman waits outside the door with a raised candlestick. The anticipation of the moment in which the two men will share the frame is played as comic suspense. Gretchen intervenes and summons Norman, whom she mistakes for Schreiber, to sing with her. He locks Schreiber in the bathroom and goes to duet (tunelessly) with Gretchen, who fails, for incomprehensible reasons, to notice that he speaks a bizarre combination of accented English and amusingly unconvincing German. Finally, after further complications, Norman and Schreiber share a frame. Seen momentarily *beside themselves* by Gretchen—who passes out—they then stage a reworking of the mirror sequence from *Duck Soup* (Leo McCarey, 1933). Using the specifically filmic solution of a process shot (rather than a profilmic double as the Marx Brothers did) Wisdom faces himself (see fig. 5.4). Norman's imitation follows just a beat after Schreiber's; the logic seems to be that this *beside-themselves*ness is arborescent, with Schreiber marked as the clear root of the gestures, the clearly original and originary figure. But the sequence climaxes in the disruption of this logic. Schreiber realizes that something is afoot when he notices that his uniform is unbuttoned while his reflection's (that is, Norman's) is not. Schreiber lifts his clenched fist to punch his doppelgänger. Norman, in contravention of the hierarchy that has established that Schreiber moves first, swings, his fist erupting from

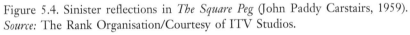

Figure 5.4. Sinister reflections in *The Square Peg* (John Paddy Carstairs, 1959). *Source:* The Rank Organisation/Courtesy of ITV Studios.

the mirror frame and knocking out the general. This carnivalesque gesture is an explosive, frame-shattering complication of hierarchy, in which causal energy flows in every direction within a momentarily rhizomatic image.

Norman's rescue of his friends is conducted as a farcical hurly-burly of running, chasing, and confused identities. Lesley—as part of a remarkably dull performance by Honor Blackman—thanks Norman for his courage and kisses his cheek. Despite the coldness of the gesture, it succeeds in smudging the painted scar without which he is distinguishable from Schreiber. A guard spots the smudge and the game is up. While his friends get away, Norman is condemned to death by firing squad and the film teeters on the brink of melodramatic catastrophe. A crane shot, which brilliantly conceals a cut, descends from a balcony, on which Schreiber is dressed in a silk dressing gown and brandishing a cigarette holder à la Noël Coward, to a doorway below, through which the condemned Norman is led. Hierarchies are reinstated. Even here, with Schreiber back on top, the traveling shot performs their *beside-themselves*ness. And when Norman, blindfolded and helpless, falls into the very tunnel that he dug to get into the chateau grounds and escapes, he carries forward the trace of his double, the Nazi general.

The hierarchy-complicating *beside-themselves* logic of Wisdom's performances in *The Square Peg* plays with high stakes as it engages the gesturality of the Third Reich. At first glance, the film appears to be, as might be expected in the postwar years, a defense of individuality over the totalitarian nightmare of the Nazi state. The titular square peg in a round hole could be taken as an idiomatic description of eccentric individualism. The fascist totalitarian vision is of a state structure that accommodates no square pegs; uniformity—in the form of racial, political, and sexual homogeneity—is privileged absolutely. But Norman is not a straightforward representation of antitotalitarian idiosyncrasy. He is introduced, as the film opens, by a set of title cards: "The Second World War saw many remarkable adventures on sea, on land, and in the air. Strangest of all perhaps was the story of Norman Pitkin, indomitable fighter, rugged individualist—and faithful employee of the St. Godric's Borough Council." The joke is predicated on the bathos of the final phrase. The line's irony extends beyond mere implausibility. The Norman who works for St. Godric's Borough Council is not an individualist; he is a petty stickler for the rules. He lives by the book, and the book in question is so tedious a piece of text that the world for Norman is a largely prosaic set of regulations. Even heterocentric romance looks dull in this world; Lesley (thanks to the limp performance by Blackman) offers no color at all and is not seen again after Norman's escape. Norman's monochromatic fate as the film ends is not romance but to end up as mayor, barking a barrage of impotent ire down the phone at the War Office. The fanfare of the title music interrupts his puerile diatribe, and for twenty seconds the frame is devoted to a muted Norman railing inaudibly before the frame announces that this is THE END. Such anti-individualist by-the-bookery suggests that this square peg has found himself a square hole in the world of British bureaucracy. This bureaucracy, whose dreams of ruled-and-regulated homogeneity were certainly less chilling but no more eccentric than fascism's nightmares of sameness, expressed itself in certain trends in postwar planning; housing plans, for example, resulted in estates that, in the words of government adviser Cleeve Barr, consisted of "two hundred standardised houses on a flat site [that] look like a shop full of shoe-boxes."[41] Any false equivalence between the savage anti-individualism of Nazi Germany and the quest for consensus in postwar Britain would be offensive. But for queer eccentrics, the climate of 1950s Britain remained hostile—as it still does today. The casting of Wisdom *beside himself* as German general and British bureaucrat throbs the frame with glimpses of these parallels. The reflection is inexact, but for some moments Schreiber fancies he sees his own reflection in Norman's eagerly book-bound face. A more eccentric outcome of the out-of-the-mirror punch might have been that their twin fists make simultaneous contact with their twin faces and knock each other out, leaving space for alternative possibilities not represented by either of these Wisdoms. The film's unfunny *beside-themselves*ness (whose slapstick potential in the film is hardly capitalized on, the mirror sequence less baroque, less amusing, and more violent than its precursor in *Duck Soup*) has a flattening effect whose totalizing duplications mark the erasure of depth and history in an uncanny image of sameness.

In such a pessimistic reading, which sees the little man *beside himself* only in his exercise of violence and impotent rage against an enemy disarmingly like himself, there is no obvious space for *laughing forward*. The spectacle of petty British bureaucracy looking silly in the performance of its own intolerance is funny, but also disheartening. But the brilliance of the film lies in its ex-centering of totalizing gestures. By showing the clothes, voices, mannerisms, and even faces of political groups to be repeatable, the film reveals them to be draggable. This—still edgy today—is Nazi drag. And it does not stop there. Norman in his mayor's getup is also in drag; he draws attention to this costumed performance as his hand gets caught in his chain of office, his cocked hat topples from his head, and he is forced to hide his polished shovel under his desk. The film gives a glimpse of politics as a kind of—sometimes deadly—drag, constituted by performance more than principle or essential fact. Freedom does not exist within the constraint of a consistent role, but in the free play that comes when identity slips between turns. Norman is not a petty councilman; he is a drag artist, allowing for the fact that drag is a question not merely of gender but of any identity constituted through the performance of learned acts and not deriving from essence. When he parachutes into France, Norman slips into French national drag and kisses Mr. Grimsdale (whose conventionally British sensibility is appalled) on both cheeks; he seems to be launching a kiss aimed at his mouth when Grimsdale stops him. Later, he drags up as a French road digger in order to get access to the chateau grounds; in an exquisite piece of silliness, he persuades an initially reluctant Nazi officer to let him dig by slipping into pantomime sobbing, to which the officer with gentle effeteness says, "You are a nice boy. You dig that hole." Earlier, while still in Britain and before he is enlisted, he is locked up by an irate sergeant and escapes by borrowing the uniform of an officer from the Auxiliary Territorial Service (ATS), the women's branch of the British Army during the Second World War. Now in female drag, he bumps into the sergeant who is clearly smitten by Norman and invites him to a fancy-dress ball:

SERGEANT: You could go as—err—Lady Godiva.

NORMAN (*giggling coyly*): Oh, no.

SERGEANT: Why not?

NORMAN: I've just had my hair cut.

SERGEANT: Well, that wouldn't matter.

Norman looks up at him with an expression of horror.

NORMAN: How dare you.

SERGEANT: Oh, no—don't be angry. I'm not the kind of man you think I am.

NORMAN: Oh, well, that's good—because I'm not the sort of girl you think I am either.

The Square Peg's drag is funny because Norman is never the sort of general, private, lord mayor, road digger, Frenchman, lover, or girl that anyone thinks he is. Whatever might be expected *beneath* each uniform would never be found upon inspection. Wisdom's *beside-himself*ness in the frame—as general and Gump-as-general—is a filmic declaration of a multiroling that is quietly going on through the entire film. Flattened by the emphasis on *beside* rather than *beneath* or *beyond*, even the iconic figure of the Gump becomes drag: he is an outfit and a manner. The critically derided sentimentality—which *The Square Peg* abandons altogether—is only ever a series of gestures (the schmaltzy songs, the put-upon looks and puppy-dog eyes, the tokens of affection). Identity—including the heterocentric identities of gender and sexuality—is fluid. It is worth noting that Norman does not deny to the sergeant that he is a girl, only that he is a particular *sort* of girl. For the period in which he is in the ATS outfit, he *is* a girl, just one of an unusual type. I find the sequence funny, not because it mocks women or even because it mocks the sergeant, but because it opens Norman up to further possibilities for self-expression. There is even a delicious further hint of taboo as Norman's trusty spade seems to fall out from under his short skirt while he walks away, begging the question of where its long handle has been concealed. This comic queering of the niceties of both manly behavior and heterosexual romance is a long way from the "asexual gormlessness [stupidity]" credited to Wisdom by David Kynaston.[42] Avoiding the starker and more obvious double entendres of Benny Hill or the *Carry On* team, Wisdom's films were nonetheless queering postwar expectations about the performance expected of a male lead.

The *laughing forward* of *The Square Peg*, then, lies not simply in positioning a Nazi general beside a petty British bureaucrat, both of whom believe in centric structures that favor order and homogeneity. It lies, rather, in the fact that a drag star, who is potentially everything because he is not anything, is positioned *beside himself* in a series of turns. In this *beside*ness lie glimpses of disordered gender, slippery national identity, and taboo desire. Salvation from the evils of fascism and the suffocating strictures of bureaucracy lies in play, which rings out as a decisive rejoinder to Douglas Warth's scandalous linking in the *Sunday Pictorial* of sexual and gender nonconformity to "the horrors of Hitlerite corruption."[43] Conformity is incredible in a frame in which the star does not even conform with themselves; in *The Belles of St. Trinian's*, *Kind Hearts and Coronets*, and *The Square Peg* the laughter of *beside-themselves*ness erupts from an excess that sees *one proliferating actor* performing *more than one* gesture in the same moment and in the same space. No center is possible when Sim, Guinness, and Wisdom paint the screen with the incorrigible multiplicity of their filmic drag. The repetition in the frame never becomes totalitarian because it is always in play, predicated on a difference that solicits the structures and institutions that seem to define the characters. The films have been—quite reasonably—described as satires, of the school system, the aristocracy, and local council and fascist politics respectively. But to find in them only such satirical statements, laudable though they may be, is to narrow the films. I prefer to widen them, following the logic of a *beside*ness that broadens the performer across the entire width of the frame, and to see them instead as the utterance of proliferating possibilities. Being *beside yourself* in postwar British comedy is not about identity but idiosyncratic variation. These queer gestures refuse the structure of identity as a constraint on play and revel, instead, in the mercurial magic of film.

6

Going Wild

IN THIS CHAPTER, I TURN TO two instances of queering postwar motifs that play with the concept of the natural: the *animal* and the *wild landscape*. Earlier chapters have explored how the family—the dominant heterocentric structure in British culture—is made laughable in postwar comedies by domestic drag, porous ruins, and *beside itself* drag. In their study of *The Anti-Social Family*, Michèle Barrett and Mary McIntosh argue that:

> The realms of the "natural" and the socio-moral are nowhere so constantly merged and confused as in our feelings and thoughts about the family. . . . The moral and hence socio-political claims of the family rest in large part on its being seen as a biological unit rather than as a social arrangement. Considerable effort is put into defining the boundaries of the "natural" and in decrying things that fall outside them—be it incest, celibacy or homosexuality—as unnatural. . . . It is in the realms of gender, sexuality, marriage and the family that we are collectively most seduced by appeals to the natural. The prevailing form of family is seen as inevitable, as naturally given and biologically determined.[1]

These "appeals to the natural" are fundamental to the efficacy of heterocentric structures whose concentric hierarchies are justified by the claim that the centered term—whether that be heterosexuality, monogamy, marriage, procreation, inheritance—is a synonym for *nature*. Throughout this book, the queer has marked an intellectual and political disturbance of the "boundaries of the 'natural,'" not in order to make a structure's center more accommodating but to ex-center the structure altogether. This process requires the interrogation of the system of knowledge that is generally known as *nature*. I have explored how the queer and the eccentric have often found an ally in the category of the *artificial*; the artifice of mannered performance, multiroling, and domestic drag denaturalizes ideas of identity and home. My aim has been to undermine the argument that postwar British comedy films—with their concentrations on family and romance—are parts of a naturalization process in which repeated images of heterocentric socio-moral conventions produce an impression of inevitability and naturalness. This outstandingly *artificial* cinema is the undoing of the cultural category of the *natural*.

In this chapter, images of more-than-human animals and wild landscapes, despite being intimately connected with conceptions of the natural, become parts of this queerly artificial world.[2] They do this, I argue, in part by not remaining as natural as they at first appear. Considering the more-than-human animal first, it can be noted that a startling assortment of species charges, careers, and canters through this book. A trio of canine cameos is offered by Suzi, the Saint Bernard who accompanies Rosalind and Ambrose in *Genevieve* (see chapter 4), the neighbor's Alsatian who steals the Sunday roast as *Young Wives' Tale* ends (see chapter 2), and the neighbor's dog in *It's Never Too Late* who runs uninvited through the Hammonds' house (see chapter 3). The feline Otto wanders and prowls through the mansion block of writer Felix H. Wilkinson in *Hue and Cry* (see chapter 4). In *Sailor Beware!* a business of ferrets lives in Henry Hornett's shed (see chapter 2). And in *The Belles of St. Trinian's* the racehorse Arab Boy wins, but only after a certain amount of confusion with the milkman's horse (see chapter 5). Typically, human structures intervene to constrain the animal's free play; Suzi is put on a lead, Otto is picked up and brought inside, the ferrets are caged, and Arab Boy is saddled and bitted. In addition to these constraints within the diegetic world, the more-than-human performers are trained to act within the limits of a narrative and a film frame. As Mel Y. Chen writes in their theory of queer animacies, in which they explore how language and politics generate hierarchies of power predicated on problematic assessments of agency, "objects, animals, substances, and spaces are assigned constrained zones of possibility and agency by extant grammars of animacy."[3] These grammars—which permit full subject status only to certain human modes of being—might be seen to include a film grammar that situates the *animal* as a *narrative function* rather than a personality, a *spectacle* rather than a performance, often unindividuated and sometimes nameless.

Nevertheless, despite these diegetic and extradiegetic constraints, each of these roles interrupts some element of heterocentric logic: Suzi growls as Ambrose makes a pass at Rosalind; the roast-stealing Alsatian drags Sabina out of the secure interior of domestic drag; the invading dog is the harbinger of the neighbor who provokes the Hammonds into eccentric laughter; Otto is the explanation given for the open door that renders Wilkinson's home porous as the boys approach; the ferrets' prolific reproduction encourages more interest and paternal pride from Henry than he shows toward his biological daughter; and after Arab Boy's success only courtesy forbids Millicent Fritton from telling the assembled and irate parents "exactly where [they] can send [their] daughters." These canine, feline, musteline, and equine actors—just a sample of the many more-than-human performers who populate postwar British comedy—may appear in cameo only, but their effect is a disruptive one as they test the boundaries and limits of human convention and even the category of the human itself. The first part of this chapter explores how far this boundary disruption goes and to what extent the heterocentric human is deconstructed.

No mere cameo, the eusuchian titular character of *An Alligator Named Daisy* (J. Lee Thompson, 1955) dominates the film. On a boat traveling between Ireland and Britain, Daisy is abandoned by her doting owner (Wilfrid Lawson) because his wife has put her foot down over sharing her home with a kipper-stealing crocodilian. He leaves her with his sleeping cabinmate Peter Weston (Donald Sinden), who is the bearer of a "kind face." Peter is keen to get rid of Daisy, but he changes his tune when she excites the interest of attractive fellow traveler and animal-lover Moira O'Shannon (Jeannie Carson). When they arrive back in Britain, Peter faces an uncomfortable choice. He is drawn to Moira who values Daisy highly, but his family and fiancée Vanessa (Diana Dors) are less sure. Eventually, after a number of mishaps including losing his job in a department store when he hides Daisy in an upright piano, Peter threatens his engagement by taking Daisy to a weekend party at the house of his prospective father-in-law, Sir James Colbrooke (James Robertson Justice). The alligator's presence predictably causes panic. Despite this setback, Sir James lays on an alligator rally to please his daughter, which ends in pandemonium and, somewhat incredibly, the romantic unions of Peter and Moira, Vanessa and Moira's brother (Stephen Boyd), and Daisy and a male alligator named Nelson. The film ends neatly, if predictably; the heterocentric logic of the happy-ever-after climax of canoodling couples and imminent matrimony seems unassailable.

Nevertheless, Daisy—who has, it should be remembered, the title role, just as Genevieve does—represents a persistent destabilizing of the boundaries of human convention. Peter's relationship with Daisy is presented throughout as quasi-romantic: he describes her looks at him as "loving" and she is at one point referred to as his "very odd girlfriend." The instability that Daisy represents is suggested in a short but significant sequence in the film. Peter, charged by his family to get rid of Daisy, takes her to the police. They have no interest in helping him and direct him to a nearby pet shop. There he meets the eccentric owner (Margaret Rutherford) who speaks to more-than-human animals, including Brazilian alligators, by breathing down their noses. She is rhapsodic about Daisy but insists that Peter must keep her because Daisy finds him "very attractive." The sequence is gratuitous; it introduces no narrative developments. It does, however, help to establish the film's notion of animality and to ex-center systems of knowledge that insist on or derive from the human–animal binary. Without it, the film would be a series of often objectionable jokes at the expense of Daisy; with it, the film allows glimpses of a more deranged world in which the reductive human–animal binary itself is laughed at. My argument is that this eusuchian laughter is both eccentric and queer.

Denaturalizing Natural Tendencies

It could be argued that Daisy's suggestions of unconventional behavior are the result of her status as an ambassador for the natural world. She is excused from *total* interpellation in the structures of human society because she is inevitably in a *tangential* relationship with that society. The *animal* in comedy cinema is often the figure of a kind of naughtiness that would be inexcusable—and may even be unthinkable—in a human being. At the same time as her naturalness affords her some freedom to play (she is not expected to observe social niceties), Daisy is, in other ways, excluded from access to systems designed to protect liberty: she is at various points confined in a bag, a drawer, and a piano. The natural, it seems, can be forgiven its anarchy *up to a point*, but it must also be contained and controlled in order to limit its effects. Despite this domestication, the *animal* remains an Other against which humanity can define itself within an anthropocentric structure.

Anthropocentrism is a concentric hierarchy at the center of which sits the human being, mastering nature (including other animal species) by categorizing, labeling, narrativizing, and disciplining it. This centric attitude finds one of its key expressions in the Cartesian tradition in which "non-human creatures have routinely been consigned to the lower, mechanical order of the body as opposed to that of the mind and spirit."[4] For Descartes, and much of the Western thought that has followed, the human is that which is other than and superior to the animal. This is what Lori Gruen describes as "*arrogant* anthropocentrism . . . a type of human chauvinism that not only locates humans at the center of everything, but elevates the human perspective above all others."[5] Like all the concentric hierarchies looked at in this book, this structure purports to *describe* conditions but, in fact, *constitutes* systems of knowledge that produce realities. Fiona Probyn-Rapsey writes that this anthropocentrism "is expressed by individuals in particular acts or statements that indicate a chauvinist attitude to animals, such as 'animals are mindless,' but it also informs our epistemologies or what we think we know about animal 'mindlessness,' for example."[6] Daisy—who is named and categorized and manipulated and spoken for—is *known* and *understood* by people who never question the legitimacy of bagging her up and transforming her into spectacle.[7] At one point, in a preeminent display of human arrogance posing as comedy, she is described as a potentially "good pair of shoes." Seen as an irrational, unspiritual body only, Daisy is an object and not a subject.

Alongside this anthropocentric tendency to define the human as that which is not animal, an understanding of natural animal behavior is also contradictorily used as a metric by which normative human standards are legitimized. Jack Halberstam writes that "scientists and humanists invented and explored the natural world in order to challenge or validate various man-made systems of morality and to create, by the end of [the nineteenth] century, a new system of norms."[8] The *animal* is, therefore, simultaneously *both* the defining opposite to the human, unruly and in need of constraint, *and* an original state of uncorrupted ethical and physical purity; in both cases, it has been used as the rhetorical justification for structures of power according to which some behaviors and identities are celebrated and others condemned.[9] This *both/and* dual role performed by the symbolic *animal* suggests that it is so embedded in cultural conditions (which define what is both unruly and ethical) that it exists less as nature than as discourse. Cinema's contribution to this discourse has been profound; fictional film worlds have been populated by natural agents (including more-than-human animals) that have been constrained by and understood within the various structures of narrative, symbolism, human trainers, and the limits of the frame, while documentaries have produced systems of knowledge through voice-of-God narrations that explain more than they explore. The *natural animal*—including the cinematic naturalness of Daisy—is not something that exists before, outside, and despite culture but something that is constituted by the culture that names, describes, and films it. This is part of the sense of Donna Haraway's neologism *natureculture*, which marks the inextricable entanglements of nature and culture, the biophysical and the social.[10]

This double function of the *animal*—as disparaged Other and legitimizing ideal—has specific implications for understandings of the queer. A violent heterocentric rhetoric of condemnation has stemmed from both uses of the duplicitously malleable term *nature*. On one hand, the eccentric behavior of sexual nonconformists has been condemned as *too natural*, as the abundance of animal energy that compromises the reasonable restraint demanded by heterocentric human civilization. This animal energy is typically characterized as an excessive lust that results in promiscuity and the failure of monogamy. In this way, the queer is a form of the natural that requires constraint. At the same time, the natural is called on to justify the privileging of heterosexuality. Carla Freccero writes that "animals have been enlisted, for centuries, to represent the 'naturalness' of reproductive heterosexuality" and Matthew Calarco describes the "frequent objection raised against individuals who manifest queer behaviors or identities . . . that their actions are 'unnatural,' which is to say, they run against the grain of supposedly universal biological sexual structures found throughout the human and animal worlds."[11] With *nature* as their ally, mixed-gender monogamy and the biological family structure have masqueraded as universal, precultural truths. The supreme legitimacy of heterocentric structures has appeared so natural that it is naturally self-evident and in no need of sustained argument. Douglas Warth in 1952 offers no evidence to support his claim that homosexuality consists of "unnatural ways," and the Thatcher government legislates against "the acceptability of homosexuality as a pretended [that is, unnatural] family relationship" in the 1988 Local Government Act.[12] Even as evidence increasingly presents itself of the extensive incidents of same-sex, nonprocreative sex within—and between—other species, it is regularly ignored by heterocentric discourse or dismissed as anomalous.

The effects of such heterocentric views extend beyond other species; arrogant anthropocentric structures have permitted the relegation of individuals and groups considered unnatural or too-natural to concentric rings outside full humanity through processes of "sexism, racism, and similar kinds of dehumanization."[13] These individuals and groups—who have routinely included the sexually unconventional as well as the gender nonconformist, the minority ethnic, and the disabled—are dislodged from their seat at the structure's center and forced into satellite positions, in which their play is constrained by the central figure of the *natural*/conventional human being against which they are always found wanting. Daisy is put into flexible symbolic service on behalf of these groups: she is pitched as the queerly interspecies lover of Peter; she is emphatically presented as female and both managed and protected by her male owner; she is an immigrant from Brazil, whose movement is routinely accompanied by a Latin American musical theme; and she is characterized by a set of physical impairments and needs, requiring bathing, carrying, and wheeling in a cart. Like the dehumanized Others who are excluded from the power that comes with centricity, Daisy is defined by her *not-quite*ness; named, clothed (in a pink ribbon), enculturated, she is nevertheless the mark of both an excess and a lack of the *natural* qualities possessed by the heterocentric, androcentric, Eurocentric, ablecentric figure privileged at the center of the anthropocentric structure. The film questions heteronormativity by giving glimpses of the queer artifice of *nature* and the artificial naturalness of the normal. The binaries natural–artificial and real–fake are confused. And just as the real homes of domestic drag are also artificial, the stable institutions of blitzed cities are also ruins, and *beside-themselves* characters are both self and other, the *nature* that *naturally* underpins *natural* heterocentrism is also a made-up myth. If the natural were not already mythic, it could not get away with performing such contradictory conceptual functions. When allowed to play, both the *queer* and the *animal* are names for potentially ex-centering forces that can expose and unsettle these myths. As I watch it, the little pet shop in *An Alligator Named Daisy* sells, alongside its grimly caged birds, an image of the risibly ex-centered human, and laughs at the idea of naturalness.

Making a Joke of Anthropocentrism in *An Alligator Named Daisy*

Margaret Rutherford's cameo in *An Alligator Named Daisy* is one of the shortest in her career. It occurs within a single sequence that is less than two minutes long. She is first seen gripping a bulldog's head as she uses a unique communication technique to tell him that he has been a "naughty boy." The frame is riotously cluttered; dog leads hang, boxes of cat food are piled high, and the vertical and horizontal metal strands of birdcages unevenly slice the image. Rutherford's marvelously jowly profile hangs beside that of the jowly bulldog, her head tilted down almost far enough to meet his upturned face. As she puffs and snuffles the panting exhalations with which she claims to communicate with more-than-human animals, both her head and Winston's twitch; there is a sense of exchange, of reciprocity. There is, however, a sense of constraint also: Winston's head is held and the edges of the frame pulse with the colored movement of caged birds' flight.

These images of nature recontextualized and denaturalized—that is, caged and transformed into a kind of cultural ornament—complement the sequence's foregrounding of its own artificiality. Rutherford is histrionically ex-centering, the pitch of her gestures declaring this as *performance*; as she first sees Daisy, she totters backward before raising her splayed-fingered hands and slapping them to the cheeks of her slack-mouthed face. This eccentric style is both so mannered and so erratic that—as was observed in *Passport to Pimlico* in chapter

1—continuity editing is rendered all but impossible; her wholebody performance sees her, at one point, bending down beneath the counter and then—across a cut—instantaneously upright again. Such discontinuity in editing makes the cut visible and marks the unnaturalness of film movement; the full complexity of Rutherford's movement is absent and what is presented is a mosaic in which its parts are arranged in a montage that only almost creates the illusion of continuity. The artificiality of this form subtly hints that *nature* (in the form of alligators, dogs, birds, and pet shop owners) has been *culturally* constructed by the human apparatuses of cage and film.

This construction of nature—through dramatic performance and film form—translates these bodies into forms that can be understood and consumed. Derrida describes such mediated spaces of consumption as the products of *carnophallogocentrism*, a neologism that articulates the ways in which anthropocentric structures establish a centric idea of the human and exclude both the *queer* and the *animal*; the carnophallogocentric human being is legitimized through their logocentric privileging of (human) reason, phallocentric favoring of heterosexual masculinity, and carnocentric sacrificing and consuming of other animal species. Such a structure prizes a "carnivorous virility" and particularly the heterocentric "virile strength of the adult male, the father, husband . . . [who] does not just want to master and possess nature actively . . . [so] he accepts sacrifice and eats flesh."[14] The privileged subject in this schema—privileged, that is, within the institutions and logics of Western cultures—is a rational, self-aware, speaking, conventionally masculine, human subject. In demonstration of these claims, Derrida questions whether a national leader who declares themselves a "vegetarian . . . to say nothing of celibacy, of homosexuality, and even of femininity" would be imaginable.[15] Derrida's work is a self-declared assault on the structures that police the exclusion of the *queer* and the *animal* through the political and philosophical operation of binary systems of knowledge (heterosexual–homosexual, normal–deviant, reproductive–sterile, profamily–antifamily, human–animal, and so on) that name them, disadvantage them, mediate them, and render them knowable. Such structures fail to recognize the complex interaction of selves with others across boundaries of species, gender, and sexual difference. The reduction of complexity to the binary systems that underpin heterosexism, misogyny, racism, and speciesism can be presented in an eminently consumable form in popular cultural media such as film. But, by confusing boundaries and celebrating porous indeterminacy, the comedies in this book have all, in their different ways, laughed heartily at the nonsense of carnophallogocentrism and the indigestible binary systems it relies on.

None seems to do this more heartily than *An Alligator Named Daisy* in its little pet shop scene. Rutherford performs a conversation with Daisy that uses every possibility for comic strangeness afforded by her remarkable face; she inflates her cheeks and jowls so completely that her head appears to expand and her mouth is displaced forward, giving a startling sense of rearrangement. She uses a pipe and stethoscope to aid communication with the seemingly rational, thoughtful, intelligent, and individual alligator who (according to her human translator) expresses the somewhat unorthodox views that Peter is "very attractive to the female sex" and that she "does not want to be sold." Akira Mizuta Lippit records the ways in which philosophical and cultural thought has typically denied more-than-human animals a relation to language: "Animals are linked to humanity through mythic, fabulous, allegorical, and symbolic associations, but not through the shared possession of language as such. Without language one cannot participate in the world of human beings."[16] The reciprocal gestures of the shop owner and Daisy—their shared breathing in what the owner refers to as "a secret language in the animal world"—is, in this sense, apparently, the admission of the alligator into "the world of human beings," that is, into a logocentric structure of power.

And yet—this reading remains unsatisfactory. It preserves precisely the logocentric agenda—that is, the privileging of reason and meaning—that has previously been used to exclude both the more-than-human animal and the irrational queer. Daisy's legitimacy in such a reading rests on her ability to resemble a human being. Indeed, although the shop owner refers to animals' "secret language" she also worries that Daisy may only speak Spanish (presumably because she comes from Brazil, although this would make her more likely to speak Portuguese) and is relieved to discover that "she speaks English after all." Derrida dismisses the anthropocentrism of insisting on human behaviors in other species. He is clear that the object should not be to insist on linguistic capacity in other species but to ex-center the insistence that human beings' linguistic capabilities allow them to manage their own meanings with certainty:

> It is *not just* a matter of asking whether one has the right to refuse the animal such and such a power (speech, reason, experience of death, mourning, culture, institutions, technics, clothing, lying, pretense of pretense, covering of tracks, gift, laughter, crying, respect, etc.—the list is necessarily without limit, and the most powerful philosophical tradition in which we live has refused the "animal" *all of that*). It *also* means asking whether what calls itself human has the right rigorously to attribute to man, which means therefore to attribute to himself, what he refuses the animal, and whether he can ever possess the *pure, rigorous, indivisible* concept, as such, of that attribution.[17]

If the achievement of the pet shop sequence were only to suggest that Daisy is capable of language—a claim seemingly supported by the "loving looks" and other meaningful gestures that she gives throughout the film—it amounts to nothing more than a logocentric red herring. But, as I watch it, this is precisely *not* what the sequence is doing. The owner is *not* talking to Daisy. The comedy of the sequence, at least as I laugh along with it, does not lie in the comic incongruity of a woman and an alligator conversing, but in the funny spectacle of a woman who performs an ever more extravagant social ritual that *poses as meaningful conversation*. The human is spectacularly implicated in a speech that is unstable, ambiguous, uncertain—no more in touch with "the *pure, rigorous, indivisible* concept" than Daisy's occasional groans and growls. The shop owner makes an elaborate use of instruments that connote a kind of scientificity, but the science is bogus, suggested not only by the artificiality of Rutherford's histrionics but also the comically bathetic placement of a marketing gimmick for SPRATTS BONIO dog biscuits directly beside the operation. The sequence does not posit a fantasy world in which human beings can talk to reptiles; it laughs at a world in which human beings pretend to talk meaningfully to anyone. When the idea of *nature* can mean ideally good or primitively wicked, can justify compulsory heterosexuality and condemn homosexuality, can mean so many things that it ends up signifying its own opposite and being exposed as a cultural concept, language looks less than secure in its meanings. In the film, this effect is compounded by the fact that the Daisy who shares the frame with Rutherford for the conversation—after a dash of verisimilitude in two brief shots of her roaming around the counter earlier in the sequence—is a rubber stand-in. The uncanny stillness of the alligator as Rutherford puffs and wheezes onto her face is both disquieting and funny. The eccentric shop owner and the rubber alligator are involved in a dummy conversation.

The "secret language in the animal world" in which this dummy conversation is conducted draws on the generic figure of the *animal*, which is, in Derrida's terms, an "*asinanity*."[18] Derrida argues that human beings "have given themselves the word ['animal'] in order to corral a large number of living beings within a single concept."[19] This mythical category is the result of coercive homogenization and underpins one of the fundamental structures by which human beings understand themselves and justify their power. Derrida troubles the assumptions at work in this logic by devising, instead, the term *animot*. A homophone for *animaux* (the French plural of *animal*), this allows "the plural *animals* [to be] heard in the singular. There is no Animal in the general singular, separated from man by a single, indivisible limit. We have to envisage the existence of 'living creatures,' whose plurality cannot be assembled within the single figure of an animality that is simply opposed to humanity."[20] The *animot* exposes a rhetoric that imposes a false general singular, a mythic homogeneity. Like all terms locked in reductive binaries, the effect of this is to efface both the myriad differences that exist *within groups* and the porosity of the boundaries that exist *between groups*. The heterocentric binaries of heterosexual–homosexual, male–female, cisgender–transgender, and so on perform the same homogenizing coercion by both denying the differences within each category and the points of intersection and convergence between the categories. Freccero acknowledges the link between the anthropocentric and the heterocentric when she argues that "sexual difference and animal difference are co-constitutive and that, rather than 'difference'—which institutes a binary that easily becomes an opposition and usually results in the hierarchical valuation of one over the other—there are instead differences, both sexual and animal."[21] An insistence on a singular difference between two monolithic blocks results in hierarchized binaries; a recognition of plural differences within and between flexible groups, forming and reforming in shifting assemblages, ex-centers all structures and asserts a kind of porous reciprocity. In this way, the queerness of the films explored in this book complicates heterocentric boundaries not by insisting on a reductive assimilationist model that presents heterosexuals and homosexuals as meaningfully equal, but by playing with a disruptive model that argues that clean-cut categories do not exist at all. This same queerness, this same anarchic delight in boundary disputes, also troubles the seemingly self-evident divides between culture–nature and human–animal.

An Alligator Named Daisy is about an *animal*. It is not about an *alligator* named Daisy, because Daisy is not an alligator. Dressed in a pink ribbon and forced to perform for human pleasure, Daisy is a generic *animal* constructed for comedy. She could as easily have been a lion, a viper, or a Komodo dragon. Sir James plans to make alligators as popular a pet as dogs and cats, not inspired by any particular eusuchian qualities but in a belief that alligators, dogs, and cats are simply interchangeable. Detractors who argue that the film fails because of an overuse of obviously rubber stand-ins for Daisy miss the point that the alligator is *always* a fake, even when being played by a living alligator, and is therefore most transparently herself when made of rubber. The nearest thing to an alligator gesture comes in the final scene when, responding to what one female witness describes as "the call of the wild," one of the apex predators gives so superficial a nibble to a human character that it does not even tear his trousers.

If Daisy is never really an alligator, the question becomes: What is she? This question is less easily answered than it may appear. Daisy, for all the cutesy bows and anthropomorphic explanations for her behavior, evades the best efforts of human reason to understand her. It is because of this epistemological slipperiness that she can slide, during the course of the film, between states of variously abjected Otherness: the animal; the criminal (who steals kippers and whom Peter takes to the police station); the immigrant (who is at moments a samba-loving Brazilian and at others branded a dangerous "mugger" by Peter's grandfather [Stanley Holloway], a general late of the Indian army); the overly sexualized female (who apparently gives lascivious looks at Peter); and the queer (who imperils the domestic calm of Peter's family home). At the same time, she and Nelson are called on to represent the myth of heterocentric *nature* and both mirror and legitimize the romance between Moira and Peter; despite Peter's being something of a cad, breaking his engagement with Vanessa after starting to court Moira, the new couple is presented as naturally meant to be together. Never understood as alligator, Daisy is caged into all sorts of anthropocentric and anthropomorphic structures, including gender, sexuality, kinship, race, beauty, and so on. Ultimately, she is only ever allowed to be the cultural idea of an *animal* who is called on to represent whatever requires representation—and never her own "unsubstitutable singularity."[22]

It is this semiotic abundance that allows Daisy to work her queer magic in the film. As she lies on the pet shop counter, inert to the point of vulcanization, she has nothing to say (or even breathe) about being an alligator, but she has much to suggest about the human beings who surround her. In her static nonparticipation, Daisy disengages from the conversation, rendering the huff-and-puff display by the shop owner less about communication and more about social ritual. The ex-centering effect of this spills over into the conversation between the shop owner and Peter, where logocentrism is fatally flawed by confusion, ambiguity, and *double entendre*. Throughout, there is a parody of seduction that sits in comic discomfort with what Bruce Babington describes as "Rutherford's absolute sexless, celibate status."[23] When she announces that she will talk to Daisy in Spanish, the shop owner winks naughtily at Peter, but the wink is broad, stagy. She accompanies Daisy's assessment of Peter's attractiveness to the female sex with a suggestively tipped head and a slight, just slight, protrusion of her tongue; the gesture implies an unstable combination of the flirtatious, the childlike, and the lewd and is shot (uniquely in the sequence) from a low angle that effectively offers a perspective from Peter's crotch (see fig. 6.1). As she describes her own pet alligator (who, she provocatively not to say erotically claims, nibbles her toes while she is dressing), she becomes an image of eye-screwed, chin-thrust, mouth-set indeterminacy, as much grimace as smile. And as the sequence ends, and the camera tracks over the counter to position itself with the shop owner and Winston, she utters the incomprehensible line: "Quiet, quiet, Winston. Don't be so impatient. It's good to keep the ladies waiting." The silent, recumbent dog is hardly in need of such censure and nothing leads to the conclusion that any "lady" is waiting for him. As she utters the line, almost lost in a dissolve to the next sequence in which Peter's fiancée makes her first appearance, the pet shop owner half looks over her shoulder toward the departing Peter. Is she speaking to Winston or Peter? Is the lady of whom she is speaking Vanessa, Daisy, or herself? Certainty is impossible in a conversation

Figure 6.1. Dummy conversations in *An Alligator Named Daisy* (J. Lee Thompson, 1955). *Source:* Raymond Stross Productions/Courtesy of ITV Studios.

that has the form of a social ritual (complete with phatic speech) and the slippery meanings of ambiguous gesture. In her unnatural little shop of cages and Spratts Bonio, she openly performs the fact that she does not possess "the *pure, rigorous, indivisible* concept" any more than an *animal*.[24]

The shopkeeper's eccentricity—which is the focus of the sequence far more than Daisy—is a joke at the expense of arrogant anthropocentrism. Surrounded by the bars of cages and gesturing in ways that are so errant, so strange, so outside convention that they are no more meaningful (and quite possibly less meaningful) than the calls of birds, she throws sense into disarray. And—just as eccentricity is always contagious, always ex-centering—the ritualistic, mediated world of her pet shop rubs off on the human world of the film more generally. When Peter arrives in the pet shop, he has to push apart a curtain of hanging birdcages whose swinging vertical and horizontal bars frame him. This human being—who carries his alligator friend in a cricket bag—seems suddenly confined, and his pressed suit, bowler hat, and furled umbrella look more like encasement than self-expression. The literal images of constraint—cages, bags, boxes, and fences—that fill the film draw comparisons with the metaphorical constraints by which the human characters are held back. Such parallels between the confinement of more-than-human animals and the ideological pressures brought to bear on human beings anthropocentrically neglect the full brutality of the former. Nevertheless, the film is queerly subversive in its performance of clichéd and constraining heterocentric scripts, in the run-up to the final, bathetically predictable mass betrothals. The clichés reach their zenith in the song-and-dance numbers performed by Jeannie Carson, awkwardly gratuitous in a film that is not quite musical enough to be a musical. Unexplained diegetically, these songs erupt from nowhere and are poorly staged. The first of them is a seemingly endless variation on the theme of her love for Peter, but this is wholly at odds with the fact that they have only just met and that the principal thing she knows about him is that he wishes to get rid of Daisy. Carson performs the choreography with perfunctory indifference. The song's words are a derivative list of heterocentric platitudes more than lyrics: "Beat the drum, bang the gong, let the golden wedding bells chime! My heart's a flutter, I'm walking on air—I'm in love for the very first time." Characters helplessly express themselves in unoriginal movement and language and the film becomes what the domestic comedies are without acknowledging it: a zoo, in which the human exhibits are caged by heterocentric conventions, clichéd scripts, and the myth of their own freedom.[25]

Ultimately, the film ex-centers arrogant anthropocentrism by blurring the boundaries between human beings and other species and exploding the idea of human exceptionalism. In the final moments of the film, as Peter and Moira drive away together, freshly engaged, she reprises her earlier banal song. On the back seat, Daisy and Nelson snuggle (see fig. 6.2). As the car departs, the two couples are *beside themselves*. Moira asserts that the alligators mirror her heterocentric union with Peter, insisting that "Nelson has obviously fallen for [Daisy] completely." But the alligators are not so easily readable and do not provide evidence of the naturalness of the human couple's exclusive heterosexuality. On the contrary, the film's final glimpse of heterocentric human monogamy is of a woman singing out that "I'm in Love for the

Figure 6.2. Aping heterocentric happy endings in *An Alligator Named Daisy* (J. Lee Thompson, 1955). *Source:* Raymond Stross Productions/Courtesy of ITV Studios.

Very First Time" for the second time, positioned beside a constrained man and two constrained *animals*—sometimes rubber, often locked up, and *never really alligators*. With such unconvincing ambassadors as Daisy and Nelson, "the so-called natural world is neither the backdrop for human romance nor the guarantor of normativity."[26] The eccentric human gestures that punctuate this film—the blowing of pipes, the singing of songs, the carrying of umbrellas, the choosing of frocks, the caging of birds, the planning of weddings—are not naturalized because nature is shown to be endlessly mediated; without nature as the naturally centering term to constrain the play of the structure, this romance begins to look less inevitable. The gestures do not mark the exceptional species at the center of anthropocentric structure but are a demonstration that "as much feminist, queer, and post-Foucauldian scholarship has emphasized, there is nothing especially 'natural' about the ways Euro-western societies generally understand sex."[27] The film's happy ending, in its abundance of clichés, makes the systems of knowledge through which heterocentric cultures understand sex visible and they are as unconvincing as Carson's lip-synching.

Freccero argues that "animal theory is (always already) queer, insofar as it crosses and deconstructs the boundary-making projects of humanism's taxonomic categorizing" and makes use of "queer's most productive indeterminacy as that which is perverse, but also odd, strange, askew and open."[28] Radiating out from the odd, strange, askew little world of the pet shop, where the anthropocentric taxonomies that insist on clear-cut distinctions collapse in a gale of meaningless huffing and puffing, the film makes a joke out of the kind of fraudulent categorization that generates binary prejudices. The heterocentric human—in one way or another laughed at in all the films explored in this book—is an unstable category and one of the effects of both eccentricity and comedy is to make visible postwar Britain's contingencies, conventions, and constructions, too contradictory and too scripted to be explained by the term *nature*. To this end, Freccero suggests that "the encounter between queer and animal ultimately reinforces the notion . . . that identity and subjectivity are originarily social and relational."[29] With its dummy alligators (faked in rubber and by the ideological meanings imposed on them as *animals*) in dummy conversations with dummy human beings, *An Alligator Named Daisy laughs forward* queer possibilities of anthropo-eccentric connection with forms of alterity that, by remaining unknowably Other, illuminate the limits—and not the superiority—of human understanding. These possibilities encourage a humility that may provide the best path forward in dismantling anthropocentric structures and liberating the play of difference—of species, of race, of sexuality.

Bewildering Structure in *Alive and Kicking*

The eccentricity that I have explored so far in this book has largely queered heterocentric systems of knowledge through its play with artifice. By querying the natural status of mixed-sex monogamous marriage, the biologically defined family, the conventional home, and the temporal logics of reproduction and inheritance, this artifice has laughed at the insistence that the postwar period was straightforwardly the preserve of antiqueer moralities. In the remaining part of this chapter, I explore whether postwar British comedy film also offers glimpses of spaces that are outside artifice. By this, I do not mean spaces that are simply outside the studio; the streets of St. John's Wood in *It's Never Too Late* and the Brighton promenade in *Genevieve* are locations beyond the studio but they are rendered artificial by scenario, performance, film form, and urban planning. Even the ruins discussed in chapter 4—whose unrestrained and broken forms are the collapsed remnants of regulated and regulating institutions—are always-already in a process of domestication, categorized and conditioned by the plans for reconstruction. The spaces that I am interested in now are not just outside, but *wild*.

The wild, as I shall use the term, is a space that is always-already before or outside artifice. It is a name for the potential that marks the limit of artifice. It is, in Derrida's term, the *limitrophy* of the artificial: "what sprouts or grows at the limit, around the limit, by maintaining the limit, but also what *feeds the limit*, generates it, raises it, and complicates it."[30] This list articulates some of the difficulty in both identifying and analyzing the wild. It is simultaneously derivative from ("sprouts," "grows"), constitutive of ("maintains," "feeds," "generates," "raises"), and threatening to ("complicates") the edges of artifice. It is required as a concept against which the artificial, the human-made, the cultural, the organized, the *structural* can be understood—but it is, itself, so without structure that it resists all attempts to pin it down. It is what Halberstam calls "the outside of categorization, unrestrained forms of embodiment, the refusal to submit to social regulation, loss of control, the unpredictable."[31] The *wild* and the *eccentric*, then, both complicate the stately order of conventional structures of knowledge and even threaten the possibility of knowledge altogether.

This section asks whether postwar British comic cinema, so committed to and defined by an aesthetic of artifice, is able to trace this wild limit of understanding. *An Alligator Named Daisy* represents the subsuming of the wild by a system of knowledge; it reemerges as the *natural*—homogenized, categorized, and mediated into submission and ready to be packed up into a cricket bag. Daisy—even, perhaps *especially*, in the form of a rubber stand-in—is an alligator whose nature is understood (and routinely explained by Moira) and whose wildness is eroded. The wild is what exists outside the anthropocentric and the heterocentric, outside all structure, uninhibited by the considerations of common sense or social nicety. André Bazin suggests that such a space may be fleetingly accessible through cinema: "The human being is all-important in the theater. The drama on the screen can exist without actors. A banging door, a leaf in the wind, waves beating on the shore can heighten the dramatic effect. Some film masterpieces use man only as an accessory, like an extra, or in counterpoint to nature which is the true leading character. . . . The camera puts at the disposal of the director all the resources of the telescope and the microscope."[32] This quotation and the wider essay from which it comes mark what Calarco, in a very different context, calls "the deep entanglement of the human and more-than-human worlds."[33] The leaf in the wind, the beating waves, and even the human-made-but-abandoned banging door are all filmed in a moment in which they are unconstrained by human involvement. They are precisely at the limit of human understanding; they can be recognized and identified, but they exceed any attempt at decisive *meaning*. Leaves do not blow and waves do not crash and doors do not bang because such gestures mean something. They are eccentric gestures because their significance is without origin or telos, without author or intended audience, without structure or system to constrain the play of their proliferating possible meanings. A film may coerce such images into a meaningful relationship by combining them with other images, edited to mean the experience of a human character. But in and of themselves, these Bazinian images of photographic realism eschew all the artifice of anthropocentric narrative and wildly evade systematic understanding.

By comparison with more location-focused films from later decades, most comedies of the postwar years retain at least a sizable foot in the studio. *Alive and Kicking* (Cyril Frankel, 1958) boasts more location shooting than many comedies of the same era and the locations in question are wilder. Set largely on the Irish island of Inishfada, the film's many location sequences were shot on the Scottish islands of Seil and Easdale. The film tells the story of three women—Dora (Sybil Thorndike), Rosie (Kathleen Harrison), and Mabel (Estelle Winwood)—who have lived together in a retirement home. Having been told that they are to be separated and sent to different homes, they run away to the seaside. When they see some policemen and fear capture, they hide on a motorboat. They accidentally start the engine and the boat heads out to sea, eventually ending up out of fuel and drifting far from land. They are picked up by some good-natured Russian sailors with whom, despite not having a shared language, they discuss Tolstoy and ballet. Rather than sail on with the Russians, the three women elect to go ashore on a rugged island. There they make themselves comfortable in three abandoned cottages. No sooner are they beginning to plan for the future than MacDonagh (Stanley Holloway), the owner of the houses, arrives from America. He reminisces about his youth in Ireland and demonstrates his skills as a singer, even though he has a bad heart and has been warned not to exert himself. Shortly after, he has a heart attack and falls off a cliff into the sea below.

The three women decide to pose as his nieces and pretend that he is still alive in order to keep the cottages. The islanders, who initially mistake them for the polygamous wives of MacDonagh, threaten violence, but when they discover that the newcomers are not a "harem" and that they have a substantial supply of whiskey, relations become friendly. Dora, whose cousin owns a boutique in London, becomes interested in the local women's unique style of knitwear and quickly engages the entire island in a profitable business. Things become tricky when MacDonagh's solicitor (John Salew) arrives, demanding to see the old man. Disaster is averted, however, when MacDonagh turns up having survived his fall and spent two weeks on an uninhabited island. He proves happy to play along with the ruse. The three women discover that they have been reported dead in the newspapers and the islanders throw a lively wake for them.

Given that the cast includes Thorndike, Harrison, Winwood, and Holloway, the performances are rich in eccentricities, but I am more interested in exploring how the film presents the wild spaces of Inishfada. There are five strategies at work in this presentation. The first, which is continuous with the various forms of artifice that have populated this book, involves the (re)creation of the island in a London studio. The aesthetic is distinctive and the transitions between studio and location are jarring. The high-key studio lighting (which is flatter than the dynamic sunlight on location), the studio backdrops (which create views whose distances do not convince), and the sets and decor (whose decrepitude lacks convincing age and whose grime lacks filthiness) collectively articulate the artifice at work. It is in this Inishfada that the women fabricate their family (as the three nieces of MacDonagh), negotiate the islanders' rage at their suspected sexual impropriety, and begin a capitalist venture. It is, in other words, in the artificial Inishfada that the women engage in heterocentric life, translating the eccentricity of their friendships and histories (which includes a criminal past for Rosie) into a performance of respectable convention. This Inishfada operates as a form of domestic drag and, despite its wonderful drunken singing and dancing, is not wild.

The other strategies for presenting Inishfada in the film all make use of footage filmed on location. Two of them use this footage in ways that make an anthropocentric emphasis clear, and I shall address these (interesting though they are) fairly briefly. As is commonplace in British cinema of the period, there is an extensive use of rear projection in *Alive and Kicking*. The challenges of filming on location—especially so craggy and windswept a location as this—are considerable, and in this case the comfort of the actors and the quality of the sound recording both favor the filming of sequences in a studio in front of a screen on which location footage is projected. The effect is a particular kind of unreality, transforming such sequences as the women's being lost at sea (in which the waves projected behind them are far more violent than their motion in the foreground suggests) with a degree of fantasy. Laura Mulvey compares rear projection with the effects of certain Renaissance painting in which "the figure or figures occupy the surface of the picture, celebrated, as it were, in 'close-up,' and 'superimposed' on a far-away landscape that stretches into the distance."[34] This effect, according to Mulvey, "'regresses' and breaks with realist expectations of seamless and integrated representation of space" and produces an "opposition between the flattened foreground occupied by the figure . . . and the distant landscape background."[35] Mulvey links this opposition to the privileged position of the film star, presented as separate from and superior to their context. With rear projection, the foregrounded human figure can never be *beside* their (wild) background, and only ever *before* it. This privilege is visible as MacDonagh sings to the beauty of the sea, shortly before he falls from the cliff and miraculously survives. He and Rosie are filmed against a backdrop of craggy rocks and rippling sea that they are never part of; the aesthetic implies the projection of his fantasy and memory. This is the landscape that he recalls from childhood, that he associates with family, and that underpins his heterocentric sense of personal identity. Surviving a fall from a *real* cliff would be highly unlikely; surviving a fall from this *projected* cliff is believable because the space is already the product of a human-centered set of fantasies. The wild, as a space *before* and *outside* knowledge, cannot be rear projected, because such a projection is always conditioned by the naturalized structures of anthropocentric dramatic convention and the star system.

A form of fantasy is also at work in the third strategy for presenting the location. This strategy uses expressionism to translate the physical space into an expression of human emotion. When the rumor spreads that MacDonagh has moved in with his three wives, the islander referred to in the credits archetypally as Old Man (Liam Redmond) whips the small but fierce population into a frenzy of heterocentric outrage at the specter of polyamory. The villagers, carrying pitchforks no less, head to the cottages to confront the three women. As the islanders begin their slow jog toward the confrontation, a series of shots use chiaroscuro, camera angle, and shot scale to produce an expressionist rendition of the emotion gripping the crowd. A garden fork is monumentalized in a ground-level shot through its enlarged prongs as it is ripped from the ground by an irate man; another ground-level shot follows, in which a woman emerging from a ramshackle cottage in the background is dwarfed by a foregrounded thistle that stands massive and silhouetted against a threatening sky (see fig. 6.3); black rocks shot from the ground abut the sky as the running

Figure 6.3. Thistly expressionism in *Alive and Kicking* (Cyril Frankel, 1958). *Source:* Associated British Picture Corporation/Courtesy of STUDIOCANAL.

feet of a broom-wielding woman pass. The high-contrast black-and-white images play with size, and the grasses, the thistles, and the rocks of the landscape are made the monstrous markers of social rage. In her defense of Bazinian realism, Anat Pick invokes the philosophy of Simone Weil and, in particular, her call for realism as a "bulwark against the seductions of the imagination."[36] This means "surpassing a certain kind of romanticism that views the world as a reflection of one's mental state."[37] Such a view is inevitably anthropocentric, and the wild—those portions of the world that exceed the knowledge or control of human society—are tamed through an elaborate pathetic fallacy. Just as the projected cliffs are always eclipsed by the MacDonagh who dreams them and sings them, so these thistles and rocks are pressed into service as the articulations of heterocentric human anger at the possibility of sexual nonconformity.

With the remaining two approaches to landscape, however, glimpses of a wildness independent of human systems of knowledge do break through. Both are shot on location and in neither case is the wild made submissive to anthropocentric meaning. The first presents characters—and the three principal characters especially—moving through the landscape *while being played by different performers*. There are practical explanations for this; for time and money reasons, it is often advantageous to have a second film unit recording such sequences while the stars are filming more intricate dialogue sequences elsewhere. In addition, Thorndike, Harrison, and Winwood may well have preferred to avoid clambering over rocky terrain. But these practical reasons do not constrain the shots' effects. The three women, believing they are to be undone by the arrival of MacDonagh's lawyer, make a run for it. They head to the quay in an attempt to catch the steamer to the mainland. A studio sequence presents Thorndike, Harrison, and Winwood throwing some belongings into bags and leaving the cottages. These filmed-in-the-studio cottages are ordered, tamed, flat-floored, and comfortable. Still on a sound stage, the three women move through the frame from back right to front left. A cut, and three women enter the frame from front right heading back left. The angle of their travel seems to have changed, but the discontinuity is announced more emphatically by the fact that they are suddenly in a location space with its sense of distance, and age, and menace. Running between the high rocks, the women are played by doubles. Their movement and dimensions are clearly different from those of the three stars.

To dismiss this as a convention of location filming misses the opportunity to read these panicked, retreating women as suddenly *not quite themselves*. Halberstam, in his exploration of *Wild Things*, describes bewilderment as the condition of being outside of constraint and order. It is "a form of lostness and unknowing, . . . the space rendered by the absence of meaning and direction."[38] As the women run, their homes and new ways of life are lost to them and the future unknown. They are bewildered, "becoming wild by shedding knowledge (as opposed to becoming civilized by acquiring it), [which] offers both escape and madness, desire and disorder."[39] Having surrendered first the comforts of their care home and then the idyllic order of the cottages, they escape through a dangerous space (they could fall or be arrested at any moment) on an unpredictable errand (they miss the steamer). Their island identities—their heterocentric cover story that they are three relatives of MacDonagh—are exploded and, in the resultant scramble, they totter and topple, their faces averted from the scrutiny of the camera, their legibility predicated on only a few clothes and bags. This strikes me as a matter less of artifice and more of transformation. Every time, it makes me laugh—as I laugh also at the double who rappels down a cliff in Thorndike's place to collect gull eggs, or the double who rides a donkey for Harrison as she herds sheep—and I think that I am laughing with delight as three stars become unrecognizable and nameless *beside* and *within* the wild spaces that make them unknowable. This suggests what Calarco refers to as nonhumanist theories that, "in opposition to the traditional notion that an individual human being serves as his or her own foundation or center, . . . prefer to characterize individuals as being 'decentered,' 'dispossessed,' or 'ex-posed' (in the sense of being posed outward toward others)."[40] The three women ex-pose themselves to the ex-centering landscape and become labile and porous as they are transformed by the wild spaces around them.

The last—and I think most poignant—of the strategies for presenting the wild is the occasional punctuation of the film by fleeting glimpses of the *unpopulated* spaces of Inishfada. It is in these shots that the film most clearly demonstrates cinema's potential as set out by Bazin. In these sequences, human beings, if they are represented at all, are merely "an accessory."[41] These examples of unmanned wildness could be considered elements of what Pick, echoing Derrida's suspicion of the carnocentric, refers to as "vegan cinema." In such cinema, which has nothing to do with the political or ethical *content* of a narrative, "the reality of the cinematic object is the measure of its resistance to appropriation by the observer-voyeur. Qualifying our approach, objects affirm their reality as something we witness without consuming. Instead of looking-as-devouring, gathering the world into our private sphere, looking consents to the being of objects as external to us, persisting beyond our grasp."[42] In these moments, the beauty of the island is wild because it is not knowable. It is not easily appropriated or devoured or straightforwardly positioned within heterocentric systems of knowledge. It is remote to an extent that Daisy, in her placid rubberiness, never is. It escapes the artificial drag of the studio, the star-centered *in-front*ness of rear projection, and the emotional constraints of expressionism, and exists as something *outside* the characters and even *outside* the possibility of or need for laughter. It is not nature—which would be incorporated into human systems of thought and have meaning—but a space that exceeds human structure altogether. It cannot be heterocentric, because it has no center.

Such images are, nevertheless, mediated; they are framed and edited into a narrative, aesthetic, and political context. Even the word *wild* bears down on the images with a disciplining set of meanings, to constrain their play within the systematic structures of language. A film's landscapes are the product of a complex interaction between the world, the film apparatus, and the "habits, belief systems, personal histories and so on" of those who produce and view the images.[43] But for me, moments of unpopulated wildness escape mediation for just a moment and *laugh forward* a glimpse of the unconstrained, uncontrolled, undisciplined spaces outside a set of beliefs whose logic straightens out the eccentric, the *funny-peculiar*, and the queer. To mark this fleeting escape, it is better, perhaps, to think of the wild *sous rature*, as a term that is needed but whose inadequacy is always-already acknowledged; these glimpses in the film, which are unknowable for a moment, are ~~wild~~ and resist some of the insistences of language.

Just before they first glimpse the island, the three women, still aboard the Russian ship, have a delirious conversation:

DORA: Oh, it's daylight now.

MABEL: Is it today or tomorrow?

ROSIE: Or yesterday?

DORA: There's land over there.

MABEL: Yes, but what land?

The women's temporal disorder (with Harrison's high-pitched cockney croak and deranged grin making her line especially good) ex-centers knowledge as the land comes into sight. A reverse shot drags the image out of the studio ship with its laughable rear projection and into a moment of visual splendor (see fig. 6.4). The rocky outcrop, a dark mirror of the billowing cumulus clouds above, is both austere and enticing. In this sudden irruption of distance, the island is too far away to offer any details. It is a spot of something solid and solidly unknown across a sea whose waters ignore the demands of design and ripple in and out of the frame, unenclosed and unconstrained, in the crazy nongeometry of waves. The horizon pitches and rolls with the camera, and the inconstant but harmonious lines of rocks, clouds, and water rob the screen of any neat horizontals or verticals. This is a glimpse of an unstraight world, which exists only as possibility. It is ~~wild~~ because it resists any attempt to constrain its play. As the women arrive on the island, they express their uncertainty primarily

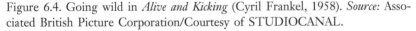

Figure 6.4. Going wild in *Alive and Kicking* (Cyril Frankel, 1958). *Source:* Associated British Picture Corporation/Courtesy of STUDIOCANAL.

as a concern about whether it is Christian. Even when they are later assured that it is, their proof comes in the disorientating sight of a monk tearing off his habit and diving into the sea in his underpants. The island is a space that, in this first glimpse, free of anthropocentric structures, cannot be made tame with reference to Christianity or any other system of knowledge. This remote place—before rear projection, and studio sets, and expressionist photography have their way with it—is *not-yet, not-quite, not-just* anything. The ~~wild~~ is what I glimpse in moments when the routines and regulations of human structures are not just shaken but *absent*; it is an intimation of possibilities that *laughs forward* the most radical eccentricity, in the case of this shot borrowing comedy from the conversation that precedes it and existing momentarily outside the centric logics of then–now, here–there, and every other binary system of thought.

Writing about a shot of leaves blowing in the wind in an early film by the Lumières, Pick describes how "the beauty of the fluttering leaves made visible the operation of natural forces, undirected by human hands, to which the cinema is witness. Pleasure in this and other Lumière actualities that feature staged or semi-staged human action alongside the display of natural phenomena like the motion of waves or the gust of wind derives from the gesture of 'letting be': the manifestation of necessity as the mechanism of the world."[44] Pick, following Weil, suggests that beauty can be conceived of as "the thing we let be" without wishing to devour it, either literally by eating it or metaphorically by understanding it within human systems of knowledge. She suggests that "the leaves in the wind are literally useless. Their function is purely revelatory: they affirm the world as extrinsic to human intentions, and are all the more beautiful for it."[45] It should be stressed that this uselessness is, itself, defined according to an anthropocentric arrogance; the leaves are useful to the tree and to other species who live lives entangled with the tree's. Nevertheless, I want to suggest that the anthropocentrically *useless* lump of rock, the *useless* waves, and the *useless* clouds—and all the other *useless* images that punctuate this film—are also affirmations of the world as extrinsic to human intentions. More than this, I want to suggest a definition of *queer* as precisely *that which lets the world be*. Uninterested in reducing the wildness of our devices and desires to systems of knowledge that encourage assimilation, give structure, and constrain play, the queer *lets the world be* in all its restless state of possibility. As they glimpse the island across the waters—before they understand it through the familiar systems of family and capitalism—the women face a queer possibility in which they, three gender-unconventional old women on the run, might lose themselves. This is an eccentricity marked not by artifice, nor by ruination, but by the simple acknowledgment of a world beyond the heterocentric structures that stifle queerness. All these years later, the possibility of that eccentricity still delights me.

Conclusion

Concluding Nothing

WHEN *VICTIM* (BASIL DEARDEN) was released in August 1961, it was in a cultural moment that has been described by Robin Griffiths as the "most progressive . . . in terms of its exploration of gender and sexuality."[1] The progressiveness that was on display as the 1950s gave way to the 1960s was driven by "a desire to question, if not overturn, traditional political ideologies."[2] British screens began to thrum with the sexual outspokenness of the "New Wave cycle, [in which] the key institutions of 'heteronormativity' (i.e., marriage and family) are hardly the attractive or idealised prospect that one would come to expect from such seemingly 'straight' social narratives."[3] Although *Victim* is not part of this New Wave, it shares the movement's politics of speaking out. Its story of a blackmailer who targets gay men—including barrister Melville Farr (Dirk Bogarde)—earns its place in the annals of British cinema for being the first film to speak about homosexuality openly. The relative openness of *Victim*'s dialogue, which according to Medhurst "advocates coming out," is startling, but it does not mean that British cinema after this point gave up its eccentric play with double entendre, irony, euphemism, and indeterminately proliferating meaning.[4] The 1960s continued to produce amiable (and sometimes less than amiable) sex comedies in which openness was eschewed in favor of the kind of queer suggestiveness that I have been preoccupied with throughout this book. Nevertheless, it is difficult to disagree with Stella Bruzzi's argument that *Victim* "was a turning point."[5]

The achievements of *Victim* are considerable and it contributed to a shifting cultural debate around homosexuality that culminated, eventually, in the partial decriminalization of sex between men in England and Wales in 1967. I am interested, in these final few pages, to reflect on how these enormous gains nevertheless came at a cost. In his defense of *Victim* as a "social object," Medhurst describes it as "the first British film to centre its narrative around male homosexuality."[6] This sense of *centeredness* transforms the cinematically unspeakable topic of male–male desire into explicit statement and (relatively) sympathetic characterization. This explicitness is, for many, refreshing after the silences and indeterminacies of earlier films. As Medhurst goes on to state: "*Victim* is not a film that makes us dig very deep to unearth an ideological project; it is a film with a specific social intention," which is to campaign for a change in the law.[7]

I do not disagree with Medhurst about *Victim*'s credentials as an important film. It has, however, been my ambition in this book to critique the dominance of *centeredness* in aesthetic and political discussions of queerness. Eccentricity—that is, the subversive solicitation of centered structures—produces a playfulness that, among other things, makes heterocentric mythologies around the naturalness and unique legitimacy of mixed-gender marriage, the conventional home, and familial inheritance laughable. It also, more importantly, invites a resistance to regimes of identity that insist that the curious and complex flux of desire must be reducible to a socially endorsed ontological category. Medhurst celebrates the moment in which, through Bogarde-as-Farr, "irresistible sexual desire finds, literally, its voice"; it is, Medhurst argues, a "desire that British cinema fought so long to suppress, and here it becomes unanswerable, the text's project irreparable."[8] By contributing so openly to the debates on decriminalization, *Victim* made an enormous contribution to the slow evolution of the possibility for gay men to come out. But coming out in "unanswerable" terms is more explicit, more direct than the unstable gestures that I have explored in this book. It is an action monolithic enough to obscure other, more eccentric possibilities. Vito Russo praises *Victim* because it "made gays real" by not being one of those films full of "amorphous sissies."[9] "Real" here suggests grounded, legible, centered. Not only does Russo's account imply a rather distasteful prejudice against "sissies," but it also overlooks the political efficacy of amorphousness. An amorphous individual, with the suggestion of flux and unpredictability, ex-centers the systems of knowledge on which both prejudice and progress rest.

Without ever dismissing *Victim*'s many impressive qualities, I want to disrupt the relentlessly linear—that is, *straight*—insistence that it marks "significant progress."[10] Accounts of progress run the risk of reinforcing the straightforward idea that, to borrow a phrase of Harold Macmillan (who was UK prime minister from 1957 to 1963), *we've never had it so good*. Its implications of relentless, continuous improvement do not encourage the idea that things as they are could be different. Alan Burton describes approvingly the rising wave of identifiable gay characters who followed in *Victim*'s wake through the 1960s and 1970s.[11] Throughout my analyses in this book, I have attempted to query the logic that the representation of stable identity is necessarily the appropriate aim for a *queer* cinema, and that perhaps, instead, a critique of this structure is more advantageous. Ideas of identity, expressed through metaphors of depth, are limiting. They offer certain—very useful—political arguments around which a rights agenda can be built, but they also constrain imaginative play. This play unsettles fixed meanings and expectations for individuals, texts, and institutions. *Queer*, as I understand it, is not an identity but the restless play of possibilities that always outdoes and undoes the limited set of options presented by conventional understanding of desire. Medhurst argues that "suppression, this clamping down of desire . . . [is a] major structuring force . . . across the whole range of post–World War II British film production."[12] He credits *Victim* with ending this by allowing one man to declare his desire for another. But *Victim* is a clamping down of another kind, a settling into an orthodox idea of identity. What I see in the "whole range of post–World War II" comedy film, by contrast, is the queering of structure—by showing its artifice, its ruination, or its absence—and the subsequent *release* of unquantifiable desire. The sheer unsuppressed, proliferating, indefinable explosion of possibilities in these films is so unstructured that it blurs boundaries between self–other, family–world, masculinity–femininity, monogamy–polyamory, human being–machine, human being–animal, something–nothing.

At least, this is how I see the films. I have never pretended that these readings are definitive. Such totalizing claims would sit very uncomfortably with my ideas of eccentricity as the complication—the solicitation—of totalizing structures. I suspect that some might find my readings too wishy-washy, defective in their failure to lock each film securely into its historical moment. My response would be twofold. Firstly, I have attempted to give some sense of the postwar moment in Britain—and especially the ways in which these years were a between time, a moment of (forced) national self-evaluation, when old structures (with their certainties about sexual morality, gender roles, imperial power) were fading and their replacements were not yet settled. It was, in some ways, an unstructured moment in which "the redefinition of meanings and boundaries was . . . powerfully at work within political culture."[13] The debates that sprang up around questions of sexuality, gender, and the family—and that continued in the post-*Victim* 1960s—were only possible because people perceived a broader proliferation of possibilities than they had prewar. Secondly, and more importantly, I have been determined not to allow capital-h History to become a center to the texts and to shut down their play. Medhurst defines a film as a "social object" only insofar as it reflects the "historical specificities of the moment of production."[14] He offers this without any real means of supporting the claim. As a result of this ideology, any producer or director can be quoted as transparent evidence of the meaning of a text. I do not understand this willingness to submit a text's capacity for different readings to the constraining, structuring straitjacket of such an understanding of context. I agree that films should be social objects, but I do not agree that the only society that matters is the one that existed as the immediate context of the film's production. The interest in the twin centers of origin (the history of production) and telos (the anticipated trajectory of social and political progress) risks omitting the *now* of actual viewing. The films that I have written about may not have been queer by any standard or definition or understanding that existed when they were made (although I stress the *may* here; it is not by any means impossible that they discovered a queer, queering, or queerable audience in the 1940s and 1950s), but that should not—must not—prevent them from being queer now. As I have argued throughout this book: these films do not hark back dully to Thatcher's image of the British postwar years as a last golden age of sexual propriety but, more excitingly, *laugh forward* glimpses of eccentric social possibilities that we could, even now, seize.

Victim is worth studying not only for its declarations but also for its eccentricities. Medhurst believes that the critic should "snatch moments of radicalism from the text, moments which could still be of particular use to gay spectators."[15] We disagree, however, about the moments to be snatched. While he chooses moments in which identity most emphatically *comes out*, I prefer the moments in which identity most emphatically *blows up*. In *Victim*, I am less interested in the identity-declaring Farr and more interested in the presentation of the young man (Derren Nesbit) who assists the blackmailer. He spends his time dressed in leathers, cruising around parks on his motorbike, picking up gay men (in order to blackmail them). This (not very subtle) description of the character suggests the eccentric complication of this gay-coded blackmailer, straddling the abyss between both sides of this moral discussion. As he is leaving his realistic little bedsit to go and offer a "salutatory warning" to Farr, Sandy Youth (as he is credited) swings at a punchball. This gratuitous show of masculine strength is ex-centered by its positioning directly in front of a print of Michelangelo's *David* on the wall beyond. As Sandy Youth leaves, the camera rather ostentatiously sidles over to *David* and gazes at the naked image. This boundary-busting gesture (which both does and does not prove the young man to be gay) is, to me, a more suggestive moment than Farr's coming-out scene, which (fan of Bogarde though I am) seems rather uninterestingly direct. The Sandy Youth is *beside himself*—both boxer and aesthete, both bearer and admirer of the idealized male form—which throws up the more subversive possibility that heterosexuality does not exclude homosexuality, and vice versa. But according to the emancipatory logic of *Victim*, such eccentric instability of identity is villainous. The indeterminate Sandy Youth who cruises and blackmails, who condemns and commits, is a *baddy*.

I realize as I write this that I do so from a position of historical comfort. I have lived, despite Thatcher's best efforts, in a Britain that has generally accommodated my sexuality. My interest in Sandy Youth is not glib nostalgia for predecriminalization days. I am not arguing that there was something exciting about concealment and hiding and fear. I am not arguing that there has been no political progress. What I am arguing, in fact, is quite the reverse of any of these things. One of the reasons for my nervousness about steeping my argument in too detailed a historical account is precisely because I do not want this book to be a statement about the past at all, but rather about what is yet possible. The glimpses of polyamory, shared parenting, wild unconstraint, gender play, domestic artifice, silly inheritance, male intimacy, and ruined convention are precisely more available to us now because of our twenty-first-century political climate. Proud identity and cultural assimilation do not need to be the extent of queer ambition. Available to us—and visible in the eccentric gestures of many postwar comedy films—are other possibilities, and British culture today is belatedly growing into these postwar films. Mill, whose hymn to eccentricity I quoted from extensively in chapter 1, writes that "as it is useful that while mankind are imperfect there should be different opinions, so is it that there should be different experiments of living . . . when any one thinks fit to try them."[16] The experiments of living *laughed forward* to me by postwar comedies are not modes easily assimilable by the structured conventions that still exist. Their laughter, as I have suggested, ex-centers these structures, making such assimilation impossible. They are not experiments to be conducted *within* existing structures, but *beside* other modes of living, none of which is privileged over others. I am not convinced that *Victim* seeks to dispense with a notion of *normal*; it understandably wants to expand it to permit middle-class white gay men to huddle with their middle-class white heterosexual counterparts at the center of the social structure. *Victim* makes the *existence of homosexuality* cinematically visible, which is a terrific stride forward in all sorts of ways, but it should not overshadow the queer achievements of cinema from the previous fifteen years that makes the *contrived mythologies of heterocentrism* cinematically visible. When I laugh with postwar comedies, it is a laughter that is able to believe, for a moment, in the end of myths of normality and centricity, and to think fit to try experiments in living differently.

My attempts to articulate these possibilities have drawn heavily on the eccentric poststructuralist theories of Jacques Derrida. It is a well-rehearsed complaint about poststructuralism that it critiques without offering a political program for concrete change. Richard Rorty, refusing poststructuralism's potential to have an appreciable impact on the politics of sexual difference, writes that "nothing politically useful happens until people begin saying things never said before—thereby permitting us to visualize new practices, as opposed to analyzing old ones."[17] *Victim* is a film in which people begin saying things for the first time. Such a claim cannot be made for the films that I have championed in this book. But such outspokenness is the medium of planning and not of play. When Rorty insists that "the most efficient way to expose or demystify an existing practice would seem to be by suggesting an alternative practice, rather than criticizing the current one" he lets slip his attitude that all campaigns for change should be on behalf of a singular alternative and not the free play of indeterminacy.[18] Thatcher's campaign to create a 1980s in the image of an imagined 1950s was the suggestion of an alternative practice. As I have argued throughout this book, even benevolent attempts to restructure concentric hierarchies must inevitably exclude someone; the idea of structure cannot accommodate a center so capacious that it includes everyone. *Victim*, like Peter Wildeblood's *Against the Law*, speaks out to restructure sexual politics, but only in order to allow the *good homosexual*, a fantasy object who is so assimilated and so constrained that he becomes entirely invisible, a degree of discreet comfort at the edges of the center.

Rorty concludes his critique of poststructuralist politics by writing that "neither pragmatists nor deconstructionists can do more for feminism than help rebut attempts to ground [present patriarchal and heterocentric] practices on something deeper than a contingent historical fact."[19] Rorty may think that a negligible achievement. But when political structures "attempt to make present practices seem inevitable," to find a vocabulary for resistance is crucial.[20] When Thatcherism hijacked the postwar period and reinvented it as a justification for its program of attacks on the sexually unconventional, these films resisted, showing the nonsense of the argument. They did not do this by suggesting an alternative and differently exclusive practice, but by deconstructing contingent structures so wittily that unconstrained possibilities flooded out. They made Britain seem eccentric, porous, and wild. They may be less outspoken than *Victim*, but in their unspokenness lies the silent sound of a desire resisting structure and articulation altogether, shrugging off the baggage of set patterns for family, and inheritance, and reproduction, and identity. What *is*, the films suggest, only *is* contingently; what *might be* need not be constrained by a country that is also somewhere else, a politics that is in ruins, a way of living that collapses in a pile of artifice, or an identity that can be *beside itself*. The wrestling of these films from a conservative rhetoric—a rhetoric that would make them evidence of a heterocentric utopia—*is* political, because it is the beginning of a challenge to the whole edifice of conservative fantasy. It is the beginning of dismantling the knowledge that underpins prejudice and turning it back into indeterminacy.

Despite *Victim*'s speaking out, the eccentricity that I have described in the comedies does not stop in 1961. At moments, that continuation is in the unlikeliest of places. When Griffiths describes a film whose "underlying premise is to limn social and moral binarisms and the constructed, performative 'nature' of gender and sexuality from within . . . a space detached from an extra-textual outside world that was also, ironically, beginning to exhibit a similar fascination with more fluid and transgressive re-configurations of identity," he could be discussing an eccentric postwar comedy.[21] The film being described is, in fact, *Performance* (Donald Cammell and Nicolas Roeg, 1970). I shall not list the differences between the postwar comedies and the controversial *Performance* ("a film 'on the edge' of polymorphous perversity"), but perhaps the similarities—including an interest in the artifice of gender, genre, and convention—are more surprising and more helpful.[22] When seen as cousins to the notorious *Performance*, postwar comedies can begin to shake off their reputations as relics of a dull period, celluloid clichés made between the shocks of war and the bright lights of permissiveness. With their spectacles of collapsing heterocentric myths, these comedies are their own experiments of living and I am still laughing along with the child I was when I first fell in love with shameless Alastair Sim, Margaret Rutherford, Irene Handl, Joan Greenwood, and the rest of the gang in their unstructured, ex-centered, queer worlds.

Notes

Introduction

1. Tony Williams, "The Repressed Fantastic in *Passport to Pimlico*," in *Re-Viewing British Cinema, 1900–1992: Essays and Interviews*, ed. Wheeler Winston Dixon (Albany: State University of New York Press, 1994), 96.

2. Sue Harper and Vincent Porter, *British Cinema of the 1950s: The Decline of Deference* (Oxford: Oxford University Press, 2003), 183.

3. Raymond Durgnat, *A Mirror for England: British Movies from Austerity to Affluence*, 2nd ed. (London: Palgrave Macmillan, 2011), 7.

4. Durgnat, *Mirror for England*, 195.

5. Ian Christie, "English Eccentric," in *John Smith*, ed. Tanya Leighton and Kathrin Meyer (London: Sternberg, 2013), 55, 61.

6. I return to and further explain this use of *ex-center* as a verb in chapter 1. Fundamentally, *to ex-center*, as I see it, is not simply to decenter a structure by displacing an existing center and replacing it with another but, rather, to expose the contingency and limitation of all centric structures.

7. Stephen Bourne, *Brief Encounters: Lesbians and Gays in British Cinema 1930–1971* (London: Cassell, 1996), 155.

8. Estella Tincknell, "Unpiecing the *Jigsaw*: Compulsive Heterosexuality, Sex Crime, Class and Masculinity in Early 1960s British Cinema," *Journal of British Cinema and Television* 18, no. 2 (2021): 136.

9. Andy Medhurst, "In Search of Nebulous Nancies: Looking for Queers in Pre-Gay British Film," in *British Queer Cinema*, ed. Robin Griffiths (London: Routledge, 2006), 23.

10. Medhurst, "Nebulous Nancies," 23.

11. Richard Hornsey, *The Spiv and the Architect: Unruly Life in Postwar London* (Minneapolis: Minnesota University Press, 2010), 90.

12. Roland Barthes, *Mythologies*, trans. Annette Lavers (London: Cape, 1972), 143.

13. Andrew Higson, *Waving the Flag: Constructing a National Cinema in Britain* (Oxford: Oxford University Press, 1995), 23.

14. Harper and Porter, *British Cinema*, 2.

15. Harper and Porter, 2.

16. Quoted in Hugh David, *On Queer Street: A Social History of British Homosexuality 1895–1995* (London: HarperCollins, 1997), 264.

17. Raphael Samuel, "Mrs. Thatcher's Return to Victorian Values," in *Proceedings of the British Academy*, 78: *Victorian Values* (1992): 9.

18. Samuel, "Victorian Values," 18.

19. Williams, "Repressed Fantastic," 95.

20. David English, "This Is My New Crusade!," *Daily Mail*, April 29, 1988, 6.

21. English, "New Crusade!," 6.

22. English, 7.

23. Durgnat, *Mirror for England*, 15.

24. Peter Hennessy, *Never Again: Britain 1945–1951* (London: Penguin, 2006), 435.

25. Quoted in Anthony Aldgate and Jeffrey Richards, *Best of British: Cinema and Society from 1930 to the Present* (London: I. B. Tauris, 2002), 186.

26. Harper and Porter, *British Cinema*, 1.

27. Andrew Spicer, *Typical Men: The Representation of Masculinity in Popular British Cinema* (London: I. B. Tauris, 2001), 204.

28. Durgnat, *Mirror for England*, 50 and 51.

29. Melanie Bell, "'A Prize Collection of Familiar Feminine Types': The Female Group Film in 1950s British Cinema," in *British Women's Cinema*, ed. Melanie Bell and Melanie Williams (London: Routledge, 2010). 96.

30. English, "New Crusade!," 7.

31. English, "New Crusade!," 6–7.

32. Charles Barr, *Ealing Studios*, 3rd ed. (Moffat: Cameron & Hollis, 1998), 107.

33. Alan Sinfield, *Literature, Politics and Culture in Postwar Britain*, 2nd ed. (London: Continuum, 2004), 4.

34. Hornsey, *Spiv and Architect*, 46.

35. Dominic Sandbrook, *The Great British Dream Factory: The Strange History of Our National Imagination* (London: Allen Lane, 2015), 442.

36. Paul Addison, *No Turning Back: The Peacetime Revolutions of Post-War Britain* (Oxford: Oxford University Press, 2010), 129.

37. Adison, *No Turning Back*, 130.

38. Jeffrey Weeks, *Sex, Politics and Society: The Regulation of Sexuality since 1800*, 3rd ed. (London: Routledge, 2012), 306.

39. Roger Scruton, *England: An Elegy* (London: Chatto & Windus, 2000), 22.

40. Scruton, *Elegy*, 234.

41. Martin Francis, "A Flight from Commitment? Domesticity, Adventure and the Masculine Imaginary in Britain after the Second World War," *Gender & History* 19, no. 1 (April 2007): 167; Bell, "Female Group Film," 94–95; Addison, *No Turning Back*, 129.

42. Roger Rawlings, *Ripping England! Postwar British Satire from Ealing to the Goons* (Albany: State University of New York Press, 2017), 9.

43. See Keith Dockray and Alan Sutton, *Politics, Society and Homosexuality in Post-War Britain: The Sexual Offences Act of 1967 and Its Significance* (Stroud, UK: Fonthill, 2017), 43.

44. Rawlings, *Ripping England!*, 61; Aneurin Bevan, *In Place of Fear* (London: Heinemann, 1952), 93.

45. Pam Cook, *Fashioning the Nation: Costume and Identity in British Cinema* (London: BFI, 1996), 11.

46. Sue Harper, "From *Holiday Camp* to High Camp: Women in British Feature Films, 1945–1951," in *Dissolving Views: Key Writings on the British Cinema*, ed. Andrew Higson (London: Cassell, 1996), 95.

47. Nikki Sullivan, *A Critical Introduction to Queer Theory* (Edinburgh: Edinburgh University Press, 2003), 192.

48. Laura Doan, *Disturbing Practices: History, Sexuality, and Women's Experience of Modern War* (Chicago: University of Chicago Press, 2013), 16.

49. Doan, *Disturbing Practices*, 16.

50. Durgnat, *Mirror for England*, 3.

51. Bruce Babington, *Launder and Gilliat* (Manchester: Manchester University Press, 2002), 171.

52. Scruton, *Elegy*, 51.

53. Several excellent histories of this kind exist: see Kynaston (2008, 2010, and 2015) and Hennessy (2006 and 2007) for detailed general histories of the period; see Mort (2010) and Hornsey (2010) for histories of postwar sexuality; see Nead (2017) for a history of British art's engagement with political and social change.

54. Barr, *Ealing Studios*, 8.

55. Harper and Porter, *British Cinema*, 2.

56. Lynda Nead, *The Tiger in the Smoke: Art and Culture in Post-War Britain* (New Haven, CT: Yale University Press, 2017), 6.

57. Doan, *Disturbing Practices*, 6.

58. Doan, 104.

59. Christian Hite, "The Gift from (of the) 'Behind' (*Derrière*): Intro-extro-duction," in *Derrida and Queer Theory*, ed. Christian Hite (Goleta, CA: Punctum Books, 2017), 13.
60. Hite, "The Gift," 11.
61. Hite, 11.
62. Lee Edelman, *Homographesis: Essays in Gay Literary and Cultural Theory* (New York: Routledge, 1994), 191.
63. Edelman, *Homographesis*, 191.
64. Michel Foucault, *Politics, Philosophy, Culture: Interviews and Other Writings of Michel Foucault*, ed. Lawrence D. Kritzman (London: Routledge, 1988), 37.
65. Heather Love, *Feeling Backward* (Cambridge, MA: Harvard University Press, 2007), 27.
66. Love, *Feeling Backward*, 4.
67. Medhurst, "Nebulous Nancies," 33.
68. Love, *Feeling Backward*, 5.
69. Love, 162–63.
70. José Esteban Muñoz, *Cruising Utopia: The Then and There of Queer Futurity* (New York: New York University Press, 2009), 1.
71. Muñoz, *Cruising Utopia*, 4.
72. Jacques Derrida, "A Certain Impossible Possibility of Saying the Event," *Critical Inquiry* 33, no. 2 (Winter 2007): 456.
73. Eve Kosofsky Sedgwick, *Tendencies* (Durham, NC: Duke University Press, 1993), 8.
74. Friedrich Nietzsche, *Beyond Good and Evil*, trans. Walter Kaufmann (New York: Random House, 1966), 150.
75. Cook, *Fashioning the Nation*, 75.
76. Michel Foucault, *Discipline and Punish: The Birth of the Prison*, trans. Alan Sheridan (London: Penguin, 1991), 152.
77. See Judith Butler, *Gender Trouble: Feminism and the Subversion of Identity* (New York: Routledge, 2006) and Eve Kosofsky Sedgwick, *Touching Feeling: Affect, Pedagogy, Performativity* (Durham, NC: Duke University Press, 2003).
78. Hornsey, *Spiv and Architect*, 3.
79. Bertolt Brecht, *Brecht on Theatre: The Development of an Aesthetic*, ed. and trans. John Willett (London: Methuen, 1974), 136.
80. Brecht, *Brecht on Theatre*, 125.
81. Barr, *Ealing Studios*, 89.
82. John Ellis, "The Quality Film Adventure: British Critics and the Cinema 1942–1948," in *Dissolving Views: Key Writings on the British Cinema*, ed. Andrew Higson (London: Cassell, 1996), 89.

83. Sedgwick, *Tendencies*, 10–11.
84. Muñoz, *Cruising Utopia*, 65.
85. Muñoz, 65.
86. Sarah Street, *British National Cinema*, 2nd ed. (London: Routledge, 2009), 79.
87. Street, *British National Cinema*, 79.

Chapter 1

1. The UK government maintained, and in some instances increased, rationing in the years after the war ended: bread rationing began in July 1946 and continued until July 1948; clothes rationing continued until May 1949; petrol rationing continued until May 1950; sweets were rationed until April 1949, but the subsequent rush on sweetshops led to their rationing being reintroduced until 1953; sugar rationing continued until September 1953; meat and other food rationing continued until July 1954; and coal rationing continued until July 1958.

2. Barr, *Ealing Studios*, 95.
3. Quoted in Sarah Street, "Margaret Rutherford and Comic Performance," in *British Comedy Cinema*, ed. I. Q. Hunter and Larraine Porter (London: Routledge, 2012), 95.
4. Christine Geraghty, *British Cinema in the 1950s: Gender, Genre, and the "New Look"* (London: Routledge, 2000), 23.
5. Robert Murphy, *Realism and Tinsel: Cinema and Society in Britain 1939–49* (London: Routledge, 1989), 211.
6. Murphy, *Realism and Tinsel*, 216.
7. Durgnat, *Mirror for England*, 290.
8. Henry Hemming, *In Search of the English Eccentric* (London: John Murray, 2008), 5.
9. Pierre Maillaud, *The English Way* (Oxford: Oxford University Press, 1945), 40–41.
10. Maillaud, *English Way*, 41.
11. Paul Langford, *Englishness Identified: Manners and Character 1650–1850* (Oxford: Oxford University Press, 2001), 301.
12. Hemming, *English Eccentric*, 80.
13. Street, "Margaret Rutherford," 97.
14. John Stuart Mill, *On Liberty* (Cambridge: Cambridge University Press, 2012), 114.
15. Mill, *On Liberty*, 102–3.
16. Mill, 117–18.

17. Mill, 126.
18. Mill, 120–21.
19. Harold Nicolson, *The English Sense of Humour* (London: Constable, 1956), 39.
20. Jack Halberstam, *The Queer Art of Failure* (Durham, NC: Duke University Press, 2011), 3.
21. Nicolson, *English Sense of Humour*, 38.
22. This link has been observed historically. See Langford 2001, 285, for details of how eccentricity was traditionally considered to be the result of an excess of one of the four bodily humors of ancient medicine.
23. Henri Bergson, *Laughter: An Essay on the Meaning of the Comic*, trans. Cloudesley Brereton and Fred Rothwell (Cabin John, MD: Wildside, 2008), 7 and 9.
24. Bergson, *Laughter*, 11.
25. Bergson, 82.
26. W. H. Auden, *Collected Poems*, ed. Edward Mendelson (London: Faber and Faber, 1991), 890; see Stott 2014, 178–80, for details of the superiority theory of laughter.
27. Bergson, *Laughter*, 13.
28. Bergson, 13.
29. Bergson, 84 and 13.
30. Bergson, 93.
31. Bergson, 13.
32. Bergson, 22.
33. Bergson, 22.
34. Bergson, 65.
35. Street, "Margaret Rutherford," 90.
36. Bergson, *Laughter*, 25.
37. Bergson, 40.
38. Bergson, 75.
39. Bergson, 93 and 92.
40. John Caputo, ed., *Deconstruction in a Nutshell: A Conversation with Jacques Derrida* (New York: Fordham University Press, 2021), xxvi.
41. Caputo, *Deconstruction*, lvii.
42. Jacques Derrida, *Writing and Difference*, trans. Alan Bass (London: Routledge, 2001), 351–52.
43. Derrida, *Writing and Difference*, 353.
44. Derrida, 352.
45. Derrida, 356.
46. Derrida, 353.
47. Derrida, 353–54.

48. Derrida, 374.
49. Jacques Derrida, *Points . . . : Interviews, 1974–1994*, ed. Elisabeth Weber, trans. Peggy Kamuf and others (Stanford, CA: Stanford University Press, 1995), 98.
50. Derrida, *Writing and Difference*, 87.
51. Derrida, 102.
52. Derrida, 133.
53. Derrida, 31.
54. Christopher Norris, *Deconstruction: Theory and Practice* (London: Methuen, 1982), 5.
55. William Fowler and Vic Pratt, *The Bodies Beneath: The Flipside of British Film and Television* (London: Strange Attractor, 2019), 17.
56. Fowler and Pratt, *Bodies Beneath*, 291.
57. Fowler and Pratt, 289 and 291.
58. Fowler and Pratt, 292.
59. Bergson, *Laughter*, 13.
60. Some of these details *were* provided in Toye's own remake of the story as part of *Tales of the Unexpected* in 1982 in which the past crime is revealed to have been murder.
61. Derrida, *Writing and Difference*, 369.
62. Derrida, 369.
63. David Kynaston, *Austerity Britain 1945–51* (London: Bloomsbury, 2008), 20.
64. Fowler and Pratt, *Bodies Beneath*, 299.
65. Barr, *Ealing Studios*, 53.
66. Barr, 61.
67. Cook, *Fashioning the Nation*, 16.
68. Harper, "Women in British Films," 103.
69. Cook, *Fashioning the Nation*, 3.
70. Cook, 4–5.
71. Barr, *Ealing Studios*, 103 and 107.
72. Barr, 104.
73. Barr, 104.
74. Amy Sargeant, *British Cinema: A Critical History* (London: British Film Institute, 2005), 166.
75. Street, *British National Cinema*, 78.
76. Tim Pulleine, "A Song and Dance at the Local: Thoughts on Ealing," in *The British Cinema Book*, 3rd ed., ed. Robert Murphy (London: Palgrave Macmillan, 2009), 263.
77. Higson, *Waving the Flag*, 268.
78. Norris, *Deconstruction*, 51.

79. See Derrida, *Grammatology*, 375.
80. Jacques Derrida, *Of Grammatology*, 40th anniversary ed., trans. Gayatri Chakravorty Spivak (Baltimore: Johns Hopkins University Press, 2016), xxxii.
81. Derrida, *Writing and Difference*, 369.
82. Barr, *Ealing Studios*, 98.
83. Barr, 54.
84. Caputo, *Deconstruction*, lviii

Chapter 2

1. Melanie Bell-Williams, "Gender and Modernity in Post-War British Cinema: A Case Study of *Young Wives' Tale* (1951)," *Women's History Review* 16, no. 2 (2007): 227.
2. Bell-Williams, "Gender and Modernity," 229.
3. Marcia Landy, *British Genres: Cinema and Society, 1930–1960* (Princeton, NJ: Princeton University Press, 1991), 381.
4. Nead, *Tiger in the Smoke*, 261 and 269.
5. Francis, "Flight from Commitment?," 163.
6. Bell-Williams, "Gender and Modernity," 228.
7. Bell-Williams, 228 and 229.
8. Bell-Williams, 229.
9. Tincknell, "Unpiecing the *Jigsaw*," 133.
10. Geraghty, *British Cinema*, 159.
11. Francis, "Flight from Commitment?," 166.
12. Tincknell, "Unpiecing the *Jigsaw*," 134.
13. Bell-Williams, "Gender and Modernity," 229.
14. Doan, *Disturbing Practices*, 103.
15. J. Samaine Lockwood, "Queer Critical Regionalism," in *The Cambridge Companion to Queer Studies*, ed. Siobhan Somerville (Cambridge: Cambridge University Press, 2020), 238.
16. Norris, *Deconstruction*, 2,
17. Lee Edelman, *No Future: Queer Theory and the Death Drive* (Durham, NC: Duke University Press, 2004), 16.
18. Sara Ahmed, *Queer Phenomenology: Orientations, Objects, Others* (Durham, NC: Duke University Press, 2006), 4; Muñoz, *Cruising Utopia*, 73.
19. Mill, *On Liberty*, 110.
20. Mill, 110.
21. Sedgwick, *Tendencies*, 10–11.
22. Derrida, *Grammatology*, 54.
23. Michael Warner, "Introduction: Fear of a Queer Planet," *Social Text*, no. 29 (1991): 8.

24. Warner, "Fear of a Queer Planet," 6.
25. Warner, 6.
26. Lauren Berlant and Michael Warner, "Sex in Public," *Critical Inquiry* 24, no. 2 (Winter 1998): 548.
27. Berlant and Warner, "Sex in Public," 562.
28. Warner, "Fear of a Queer Planet," 6.
29. Landy, *British Genres*, 381 and 382.
30. Bell, "Female Group Film," 96.
31. Bell-Williams, "Gender and Modernity," 233.
32. Bell-Williams, 227.
33. Bell-Williams, 232 and 240.
34. Bell-Williams, 240.
35. Roland Barthes, *Roland Barthes by Roland Barthes*, trans. Richard Howard (London: Macmillan, 1977), 71.
36. Sedgwick, *Tendencies*, 10–11.
37. Judith Butler, *Gender Trouble: Feminism and the Subversion of Identity* (New York: Routledge, 2006), 187.
38. Judith Butler, "Critically Queer," in *The Routledge Queer Studies Reader*, ed. Donald E. Hall and Annamarie Jagose, with Andrea Bebell and Susan Potter (London: Routledge, 2013), 22–23.
39. Butler, "Critically Queer," 27.
40. Fenton Litwiller, "Normative Drag Culture and the Making of Precarity," *Leisure Studies* 39, no. 4 (2020): 600.
41. Bell-Williams, "Gender and Modernity," 236.
42. Bell-Williams, 238.
43. Bell-Williams, 238.
44. Bell-Williams, 237.
45. Bell-Williams, 236.
46. Bell-Williams, 233–34.
47. Durgnat, *Mirror for England*, 213.
48. Bell-Williams, "Gender and Modernity," 235 and 236.
49. Butler, "Critically Queer," 27.
50. Bell-Williams, "Gender and Modernity," 233.
51. Durgnat, *Mirror for England*, 63.
52. Geoff Brown, "Paradise Found and Lost: The Course of British Realism," in *The British Cinema Book*, 3rd ed., ed. Robert Murphy (London: Palgrave Macmillan, 2009), 32.
53. Quoted in Patrick Higgins, ed., *A Queer Reader* (London: Fourth Estate, 1993), 178.
54. Alan Burton, "'From Adolescence into Maturity': The Film Comedy of the Boulting Brothers," in *British Comedy Cinema*, ed. I. Q. Hunter and Larraine Porter (London: Routledge, 2012), 81.

55. Francis, "Flight from Commitment?," 164.
56. Francis, 175.
57. Sinfield, *Postwar Britain*, 77.
58. Sinfield, 77.
59. Francis, "Flight from Commitment?," 167–68.
60. Doan, *Disturbing Practices*, 2.
61. Barr, *Ealing Studios*, 83.
62. Durgnat, *Mirror for England*, 31.
63. Weeks, *Sex, Politics and Society*, 300.
64. Geraghty, *British Cinema*, 18; see also Charles Barr, "Broadcasting and Cinema: 2: Screens within Screens," in *All Our Yesterdays: 90 Years of British Cinema*, ed. Charles Barr (London: British Film Institute, 1986), 212–15.
65. Bourne, *Brief Encounters*, 123.
66. Landy, *British Genres*, 37.
67. Landy, 37.
68. Weeks, *Sex, Politics and Society*, 298.
69. Weeks, 296.
70. Warner, "Fear of a Queer Planet," 9.
71. Landy, *British Genres*, 326.
72. Calvin Thomas, *Straight with a Twist: Queer Theory and the Subject of Heterosexuality* (Champaign: University of Illinois Press, 2000), 33.
73. Bell-Williams, "Gender and Modernity," 238.
74. Harper and Porter, *British Cinema*, 201.
75. Brecht, *Brecht on Theatre*, 136.

Chapter 3

1. Barr, *Ealing Studios*, 117.
2. Robert Murphy, "Dark Shadows around Ealing," in *Ealing Revisited*, ed. Mark Duguid, Lee Freeman, Keith M. Jonhston, and Melanie Williams (London: Palgrave Macmillan, 2012), 83.
3. Andrew Stott, *Comedy*, 2nd ed. (London: Routledge, 2014), 1.
4. Laraine Porter and I. Q. Hunter, "British Comedy Cinema: Sex, Class and Very Naughty Boys," in *British Comedy Cinema*, ed. I. Q. Hunter and Laraine Porter (London: Routledge, 2012), 1.
5. Landy, *British Genres*, 329.
6. Noël Carroll, *Humour* (Oxford: Oxford University Press, 2014), 4.
7. Nicolson, *English Sense of Humour*, 4–5.
8. Andy Medhurst, *A National Joke: Popular Comedy and English Cultural Identity* (London: Routledge, 2007), 5.

9. John Morreall, *Taking Laughter Seriously* (Albany: State University of New York Press, 1983), 60.

10. Morreall, *Taking Laughter Seriously*, 102–3.

11. Terry Eagleton, *Humour* (New Haven, CT: Yale University Press, 2019), 88.

12. Eagleton, *Humour*, 88.

13. Eagleton, 89.

14. Steve Neale, *Genre* (London: British Film Institute, 1983), 40.

15. Quoted in Medhurst, *National Joke*, 16.

16. Mikhail Bakhtin, *Rabelais and His World*, trans. Hélène Iswolsky (Bloomington: Indiana University Press, 1984), 7.

17. Morreall, *Taking Laughter Seriously*, 118.

18. Mikhail Bakhtin, *Problems of Dostoevsky's Poetics*, ed. and trans. Caryl Emerson (Manchester: Manchester University Press, 1984), 122 and 123.

19. Adrian Stevens, "Carnival and Comedy: On Bakhtin's Misreading of Boccaccio," *Opticon 1826*, no. 3 (2007): 1.

20. Barr, *Ealing Studios*, 117.

21. Peter Stallybrass and Allon White, *The Politics and Poetics of Transgression* (London: Methuen, 1986), 56.

22. Derrida, *Points*, 98.

23. Stevens, "Carnival and Comedy," 1.

24. Terry Eagleton, *Walter Benjamin, or Towards a Revolutionary Criticism* (London: New Left Books, 1981), 50; Eagleton, *Humour*, 34.

25. Bakhtin, *Rabelais*, 84.

26. George Orwell, "Funny, but Not Vulgar," in *George Orwell: The Collected Essays, Journalism and Letters*, vol. 3, *As I Please 1943–1945*, ed. Sonia Orwell and Ian Angus (London: Seckler & Warburg, 1968), 284.

27. Alex Clayton, *Funny How? Sketch Comedy and the Art of Humor* (Albany: State University of New York Press, 2020), 58.

28. Rawlings, *Ripping England!*, 2 and 7.

29. Harper and Porter, *British Cinema*, 107.

30. Rawlings, *Ripping England!*, 8.

31. Rawlings, 31.

32. Rawlings, 31.

33. Rawlings, 71.

34. Carroll, *Humour*, 6.

35. See Stott, *Comedy*, 98.

36. Quoted in Morreall, *Taking Laughter Seriously*, 87.

37. Stott, *Comedy*, 98.

38. John Durant and Jonathan Miller, eds., *Laughing Matters: A Serious Look at Humour* (Harlow, Essex, England: Longman, 1988), 6.

39. Nicolson, *English Sense of Humour*, 9.
40. Clayton, *Funny How?*, 45.
41. Quoted in Stott, *Comedy*, 186.
42. Sigmund Freud, *Jokes and Their Relation to the Unconscious*, ed. James Strachey (London: Vintage, 2001), 149.
43. See Clayton, *Funny How?* for a critique of the three theories of laughter.
44. Theodor Adorno and Max Horkheimer, *Dialectic of Enlightenment*, trans. John Cumming (London: Continuum, 2001), 140.
45. Stott, *Comedy*, 171.
46. Eagleton, *Humour*, 3.
47. Eagleton, 27.
48. Quoted in Stott, *Comedy*, 186.
49. Harper and Porter, *British Cinema*, 203.
50. Derrida, *Writing and Difference*, 352.
51. Barr, *Ealing Studios*, 117; Landy, *British Genres*, 376; Geraghty, *British Cinema*, 69; Harper and Porter, *British Cinema*, 60; Rawlings, *Ripping England!*, 92.
52. Geraghty, *British Cinema*, 69.
53. Morreall, *Taking Laughter Seriously*, 114.
54. Eagleton, *Humour*, 9.
55. Leo Bersani, "Is the Rectum a Grave?," *October*, no. 43: "AIDS: Cultural Analysis/Cultural Activism" (Winter 1987): 217; Sullivan, *Queer Theory*, 130.
56. Eagleton, *Walter Benjamin*, 149–50.
57. Eagleton, *Humour*, 159.
58. Convictions for homosexual offenses rose from 572 in 1938 to 1,405 in 1948 and 2,513 in 1961; many involved undercover police officers soliciting the sexual attentions of suspects.
59. Hélène Cixous, "The Laugh of the Medusa," trans. Keith Cohen and Paula Cohen, *Signs* 1, no. 4 (Summer 1976): 888.
60. Cixous, "Laugh of the Medusa," 888.
61. Cixous, 887.
62. Eagleton, *Humour*, 28–29.
63. Caputo, *Deconstruction*, 108.
64. Medhurst, *National Joke*, 25.
65. James F. English, *Comic Transactions: Literature, Humor, and the Politics of Community in Twentieth-Century Britain* (Ithaca, NY: Cornell University Press, 1994), 9.
66. See Eagleton, *Humour*, 56.
67. Durgnat, *Mirror for England*, 209.
68. Rawlings, *Ripping England!*, 80.

69. Jack Halberstam, *In a Queer Time and Place: Transgender Bodies, Subcultural Lives* (New York: New York University Press, 2005), 2.
70. Eagleton, *Humour*, 6.
71. Quoted in Eagleton, *Humour*, 54.
72. Eagleton, 16.
73. Jean-Luc Nancy, "Elliptical Sense," *Research in Phenomenology* 18 (1988): 180.

Chapter 4

1. See Kynaston, *Austerity Britain*, 20.
2. Quoted in Kynaston, 124.
3. Quoted in Kynaston, 344.
4. Nead, *Tiger in the Smoke*, 55.
5. John Grindrod, *Concretopia: A Journey around the Rebuilding of Postwar Britain* (Brecon, Wales, UK: Old Street, 2013), 22.
6. Sinfield, *Postwar Britain*, xii.
7. Hornsey, *Spiv and Architect*, 201.
8. Quoted in Barr, *Ealing Studios*, 61.
9. Barr, 61.
10. Nead, *Tiger in the Smoke*, 78.
11. Lynda Nead gives an account of how psychoanalysis can present these ruins and bomb sites "in terms of the topography of the mind" (*Tiger in the Smoke*, 90–92). This reading is fascinating, but depends on an idea of putting the fragments back together in the form of a healthy, whole mind. My analysis favors the idea of fragmentation as a mark of possibilities when constraining structures fail.
12. Love, *Feeling Backward*, 21.
13. See Ben Highmore, "Playgrounds and Bombsites: Postwar Britain's Ruined Landscapes," *Cultural Politics* 9, no. 3 (2013): 323–36 and Nead, *Tiger in the Smoke* for discussion of these images.
14. Quoted in Barr, *Ealing Studios*, 59.
15. Sinfield, *Postwar Britain*, 17–18.
16. Harper, "Women in British Films," 94.
17. Cook, *Fashioning the Nation*, 18.
18. Cook, 86–87.
19. Derrida, *Points*, 355.
20. Sinfield, *Postwar Britain*, xiii.
21. The Anglocentric mythologies of empire as the inevitable and legitimate inheritance of a virile nation of intrepid masculine conquerors were unwinding throughout this period. In August 1947, British rule in

India ended; in January 1948, Burma became independent; in February 1948, Ceylon became independent; in May 1948, the British Mandate in Palestine formally ended and British soldiers were rapidly evacuated; in December 1948, a bill was passed in Parliament that saw, four months later, the declaration of the Republic of Ireland. With the Suez Crisis in 1956 (described by Roger Rawlings as "the true end of English international hegemony" [Rawlings, *Ripping England!*, 205]), Britain gave up its global dominance—while America, popularly understood through an uninterrogated family metaphor to be Britain's cousin, declined to help.

22. Barr, *Ealing Studios*, 81.

23. Nead, *Tiger in the Smoke*, 65.

24. See Benedict Morrison, *Complicating Articulation in Art Cinema* (Oxford: Oxford University Press, 2021), 31–55 for a full discussion of *Germania anno zero* and its presentation of ruined buildings and political concepts.

25. Barr, *Ealing Studios*, 95.

26. D. A. Miller, "Anal Rope," *Representations*, no. 32 (Autumn 1990): 118.

27. Derrida, *Writing and Difference*, 353.

28. Nead, *Tiger in the Smoke*, 71.

29. Grindrod, *Concretopia*, 21.

30. Derek Jarman, *At Your Own Risk: A Saint's Testament* (London: Hutchinson, 1992), 14.

31. Rose Macaulay, *Pleasure of Ruins*, rev. ed., ed. Constance Babington Smith (London: Thames & Hudson, 1964), 237.

32. Scruton, *Elegy*, 51.

33. Walter Benjamin and Asja Lacis, "Naples," in *Reflections: Essays, Aphorisms, Autobiographical Writings*, ed. Peter Demetz and trans. Edmund Jephcott (New York: Schocken Books, 1978), 171.

34. Benjamin and Lacis, "Naples," 171.

35. Benjamin and Lacis, 172.

36. Benjamin and Lacis, 168.

37. Barr, *Ealing Studios*, 94.

38. Benjamin and Lacis, "Naples," 166.

39. Benjamin and Lacis, 167.

40. Douglas Smith, "Porosity and the Transnational: Travelling Theory between Naples and Frankfurt (Walter Benjamin, Asja Lacis and Ernst Bloch)," *Forum for Modern Language Studies* 57, no. 2 (April 2021): 244.

41. Tim O'Sullivan, "That Ealing Feeling: 'Ealing Comedies' and 'Comedies Made at Ealing,'" in *Ealing Revisited*, ed. Mark Duguid, Lee Freeman, Keith M. Jonhston, and Melanie Williams (London: Palgrave Macmillan, 2012), 137; Mark Duguid and Katy McGahan, "From Tinsel to Realism and Back Again: Balcon, Ealing and Documentary," in *Ealing Revisited*, ed. Mark Duguid, Lee Freeman, Keith M. Jonhston, and Melanie Williams (London: Palgrave Macmillan, 2012), 68.

42. Andrew Moor, "Kind Hearts and Campery: The Ealing Family Perverts," in *Ealing Revisited*, ed. Mark Duguid, Lee Freeman, Keith M. Jonhston, and Melanie Williams (London: Palgrave Macmillan, 2012), 130.

43. Rawlings, *Ripping England!*, 57.

44. Derrida, *Writing and Difference*, 360.

45. Derrida, 4–5.

46. Jarman, *At Your Own Risk*, 3.

47. Nead, *Tiger in the Smoke*, 56.

48. Smith, "Porosity and the Transnational," 246.

49. Durgnat, *Mirror for England*, 50 and 51.

50. Durgnat, 50.

51. Geraghty, *British Cinema*, 164.

52. Geraghty, 164.

53. Becky Conekin, Frank Mort, and Chris Waters, "Introduction," in *Moments of Modernity: Reconstructing Britain 1945–1964*, ed. Becky Conekin, Frank Mort, and Chris Waters (London: Rivers Oram, 1999), 20; Bell-Williams, "Gender and Modernity," 239.

54. Geraghty, *British Cinema*, 163–64.

55. Andy Medhurst, "Music Hall and British Cinema," in *All Our Yesterdays: 90 Years of British Cinema*, ed. Charles Barr (London: British Film Institute, 1986), 182.

56. Bell-Williams, "Gender and Modernity," 237.

57. Bell-Williams, 230.

58. Quoted in Doan, *Disturbing Practices*, 97.

59. Quoted in Peter Hennessy, *Having It So Good: Britain in the Fifties* (London: Penguin, 2007), 123.

60. Lynne Segal, *Slow Motion: Changing Masculinities, Changing Men*, 3rd ed. (London: Palgrave Macmillan, 2007), 2.

61. Chris Waters, "Disorders of the Mind, Disorders of the Body Social: Peter Wildeblood and the Making of the Modern Homosexual," in *Moments of Modernity: Reconstructing Britain 1945–1964*, ed. Becky Conekin, Frank Mort, and Chris Waters (London: Rivers Oram, 1999), 138.

62. Douglas Warth, "Evil Men," *Sunday Pictorial*, May 25, 1952, 15.

63. Warth, "Evil Men," 6 and 15.

64. Peter Wildeblood, *Against the Law* (London: Weidenfeld & Nicolson, 2019), 7.

65. Wildeblood, *Against the Law*, 2.

66. Love, *Feeling Backward*, 30.

67. Eve Kosofksy Sedgwick, *Between Men: English Literature and Male Homosocial Desire*, 30th anniversary ed. (New York: Columbia University Press, 2015), 21.

68. Sedgwick, *Between Men*, 21.

69. Geraghty, *British Cinema*, 163.

70. See Orwell, "Funny, but Not Vulgar."
71. Quoted in Barr, *Ealing Studios*, 50.
72. Pat Thane, "Population Politics in Post-War British Culture," in *Moments of Modernity: Reconstructing Britain 1945–1964*, ed. Becky Conekin, Frank Mort, and Chris Waters (London: Rivers Oram, 1999), 133.
73. Quoted in Kynaston, *Austerity Britain*, 31.
74. Quoted in Kynaston, 33.
75. Thane, "Population Politics," 133.
76. Quoted in Higgins, *Queer Reader*, 185.
77. Quoted in David Kynaston, *Family Britain 1951–57* (London: Bloomsbury, 2010), 420.
78. Durgnat, *Mirror for England*, 290.

Chapter 5

1. Paul de Man, *Aesthetic Ideology*, ed. Andrzej Warminski (Minneapolis: University of Minnesota Press, 1996), 181.
2. Babington, *Launder and Gilliat*, 24.
3. The *Oxford English Dictionary* includes the following examples: the line "Paul, thou art beside thy selfe, much learning doeth make thee mad" from the King James translation of the Acts of the Apostles 26:24 and Queen Victoria's observation that "I felt quite beside myself for joy and gratitude."
4. Jasbir Puar, *Terrorist Assemblages: Homonationalism in Queer Times* (Durham, NC: Duke University Press, 2007), 211.
5. See Gilles Deleuze and Félix Guattari, *A Thousand Plateaus: Capitalism and Schizophrenia* (London: Bloomsbury, 2013).
6. Eve Kosofsky Sedgwick, *Touching Feeling: Affect, Pedagogy, Performativity* (Durham, NC: Duke University Press, 2003), 8.
7. Derrida, *Writing and Difference*, 353.
8. Sedgwick, *Touching Feeling*, 8.
9. Rawlings, *Ripping England!*, 218.
10. Michael Newton, *Kind Hearts and Coronets* (London: British Film Institute, 2003), 59.
11. Newton, *Kind Hearts*, 59.
12. Carolyn Dinshaw, Lee Edelman, Roderick A. Ferguson, Carla Freccero, Elizabeth Freeman, Judith Halberstam, Annamarie Jagose, Christopher S. Nealon, and Tan Hoang Nguyen, "Theorizing Queer Temporalities: A Roundtable Discussion," *GLQ: A Journal of Lesbian and Gay Studies* 13, no. 2–3 (2007): 181.
13. Dinshaw et al., "Queer Temporalities," 181.
14. Sedgwick, *Touching Feeling*, 8.

15. Newton, *Kind Hearts*, 59.
16. Andrew Roberts, "'Gird Your Armour On': The Genteel Subversion of the *St. Trinian's* Films," in *British Comedy Cinema*, ed. I. Q. Hunter and Laraine Porter (London: Routledge, 2012), 123.
17. Landy, *British Genres*, 365.
18. Landy, 364.
19. Babington, *Launder and Gilliat*, 172.
20. Babington, 173.
21. Melanie Williams, "'Twilight Women' of 1950s British Cinema," in *The British Cinema Book*, 3rd ed, ed. Robert Murphy (London: Palgrave Macmillan, 2009), 294.
22. Landy, *British Genres*, 365.
23. Butler, *Gender Trouble*, xv.
24. Sedgwick, *Touching Feeling*, 9.
25. Sedgwick, 9.
26. Sedgwick, 9.
27. Geraghty, *British Cinema*, 159.
28. Deleuze and Guattari, *Thousand Plateaus*, 16.
29. Deleuze and Guattari, 16.
30. Deleuze and Guattari, 17.
31. Deleuze and Guattari, 22.
32. Edelman, *No Future*, 3.
33. Sullivan, *Queer Theory*, 134.
34. Sedgwick, *Tendencies*, 6.
35. Medhurst, "Music Hall and British Cinema," 182.
36. Medhurst, 182.
37. Landy, *British Genre*, 361.
38. Richard Dacre, "Norman Wisdom: Rank Studios and the Rise of the Super Chump," in *British Comedy Cinema*, ed. I. Q. Hunter and Laraine Porter (London: Routledge, 2012), 136.
39. Landy, *British Genres*, 361.
40. Quoted in David Kynaston, *Modernity Britain 1957–62* (London: Bloomsbury, 2015), 266.
41. Quoted in Grindrod, *Concretopia*, 30.
42. Kynaston, *Family Britain*, 551.
43. Warth, "Evil Men," May 25, 1952, 6.

Chapter 6

1. Michèle Barrett and Mary McIntosh, *The Anti-Social Family*, 2nd ed. (London: Verso, 2015), 26–27.

2. The phrase "more-than-human" was introduced by David Abram in his book *The Spell of the Sensuous: Perception and Language in a More-than-Human World* (New York: Pantheon, 1996). This term avoids the binary logic of the phrase "nonhuman" and the implicit hierarchy in the phrase "subhuman" when discussing other animal species.

3. Mel Y. Chen, *Animacies: Biopolitics, Racial Mattering, and Queer Affect* (Durham, NC: Duke University Press, 2012), 13.

4. Nicole Shukin, "Capitalism," in *The Edinburgh Companion to Animal Studies*, ed. Lynn Turner, Undine Sellbach, and Ron Broglio (Edinburgh: Edinburgh University Press, 2018), 95.

5. Lori Gruen, *Entangled Empathy: An Alternative Ethic for Our Relationships with Animals* (New York: Lantern Books, 2015), 24.

6. Fiona Probyn-Rapsey, "Anthropocentrism," in *Critical Terms for Animal Studies*, ed. Lori Gruen (Chicago: University of Chicago Press, 2018), 48.

7. Carl Linnaeus, the eighteenth-century inventor of the system of binary nomenclature still used today, built an anthropocentric taxonomic structure that claimed to name animals in order to know and manage them.

8. Jack Halberstam, *Wild Things: The Disorder of Desire* (Durham, NC: Duke University Press, 2020), 29.

9. There is, of course, nothing new in such complex and contradictory rhetorics of animal symbolism. In wartime British cartoons, Churchill was presented as the British Bulldog, suggesting loyalty and steadfastness. Hitler, on the other hand, was regularly presented as a snake, a rat, a skunk, and a web-spinning spider whose many legs must be broken one by one; this dehumanization hijacks the bodies and meanings of other species in order to make the Nazi leader even more sinister and the need to control him even more urgent. The Churchill example suggested the perceived pristine goodness of more-than-human animals, while the Hitler examples perpetuated the misleading myth that deplorable behavior in human beings is best explained as unruly animality.

10. See Donna Haraway, *Manifestly Haraway* (Minneapolis: University of Minnesota Press, 2016).

11. Carla Freccero, "Queer Theory," in *The Edinburgh Companion to Animal Studies*, ed. Lynn Turner, Undine Sellbach, and Ron Broglio (Edinburgh: Edinburgh University Press, 2018), 431; Matthew R. Calarco, *Animal Studies: The Key Concepts* (London: Routledge, 2021), 110.

12. Warth, "Evil Men," May 25, 1952, 6; David, *Queer Street*, 264.

13. Calarco, *Animal Studies*, 19.

14. Derrida, *Points*, 280 and 281.

15. Derrida, 281.

16. Akira Mizuta Lippit, *Electric Animal: Toward a Rhetoric of Wildlife* (Minneapolis: University of Minnesota Press, 2000), 7.

17. Jacques Derrida, *The Animal That Therefore I Am*, ed. Marie-Louise Mallet and trans. David Wills (New York: Fordham University Press, 2008), 135.

18. Derrida, *Animal*, 31.

19. Derrida, 32.

20. Derrida, 47.

21. Freccero, "Queer Theory," 437.

22. Derrida, *Animal*, 9.

23. Babington, *Launder and Gilliat*, 158.

24. Derrida, *Animal*, 135.

25. See Rosi Braidotti, *The Posthuman* (Cambridge: Polity, 2013), 80 for a discussion of anthropocentrism as a conceptual cage for human beings; see John Gagnon and William Simon, *Sexual Conduct: The Social Sources of Human Sexuality* (Chicago: Aldine, 1973) for a discussion of sexual script theory, which argues that sexual identity and behavior are performed according to social scripts.

26. Halberstam, *Wild Things*, 29.

27. Catriona Mortimer-Sandilands and Bruce Erikson, *Queer Ecologies: Sex, Nature, Politics, Desire* (Bloomington: Indiana University Press, 2010), 6–7.

28. Freccero, "Queer Theory," 432.

29. Freccero, 432.

30. Derrida, *Animal*, 29.

31. Halberstam, *Wild Things*, 3.

32. André Bazin, "Theater and Cinema," in *What Is Cinema?*, vol. 1, ed. and trans. Hugh Gray (Berkeley: University of California Press, 1967), 102–3.

33. Calarco, *Animal Studies*, 16.

34. Laura Mulvey, "Rear-Projection and the Paradoxes of Hollywood Realism," in *Theorizing World Cinema*, ed. Lúcia Nagib, Chris Perriam, and Rajinder Dudrah (London: I. B. Tauris, 2012), 216.

35. Mulvey, "Rear-Projection," 216–17.

36. Anat Pick, "Vegan Cinema," in *Thinking Veganism in Literature and Culture: Towards a Vegan Theory*, ed. Emelia Quinn and Benjamin Westwood (London: Palgrave, 2018), 129.

37. Pick, "Vegan Cinema," 130.

38. Halberstam, *Wild Things*, 14.

39. Halberstam, 31.

40. Matthew Calarco, *Thinking through Animals: Identity, Difference, Indistinction* (Stanford, CA: Stanford University Press, 2015), 30.

41. Bazin, "Theater and Cinema," 102.

42. Pick, "Vegan Cinema," 127.
43. Anat Pick, "Animal Life in the Cinematic *Umwelt*," in *Animal Life and the Moving Image*, ed. Michael Lawrence and Laura McMahon (London: British Film Institute and Palgrave, 2015), 222.
44. Pick, "Vegan Cinema," 132.
45. Pick, 132.

Conclusion

1. Robin Griffiths, "Sad and Angry: Queers in 1960s British Cinema," in *British Queer Cinema*, ed. Robin Griffiths (London: Routledge, 2006), 75.
2. Street, *British National Cinema*, 75.
3. Griffiths, "Queers in 1960s British Cinema," 78.
4. Andy Medhurst, "*Victim*: Text as Context," in *Dissolving Views: Key Writings on British Cinema*, ed. Andrew Higson (London: Cassell, 1996), 127.
5. Stella Bruzzi, "Where Are Those Buggers? Aspects of Homosexuality in Mainstream British Cinema," in *The British Cinema Book*, 3rd ed., ed. Robert Murphy (London: Palgrave Macmillan, 2009), 133.
6. Medhurst, "*Victim*," 119.
7. Medhurst, 119.
8. Medhurst, 128.
9. Vito Russo, *The Celluloid Closet: Homosexuality in the Movies*, rev. ed. (New York: Harper & Row, 1987), 132.
10. Alan Burton, "*Victim* (1961): Text and Context," *AAA: Arbeiten aus Anglistik und Amerikanistik* 35, no. 1 (January 2010): 98.
11. See Burton, 98.
12. Medhurst, "*Victim*," 123.
13. Conekin, Mort, and Waters, "Introduction," 16.
14. Medhurst, "*Victim*," 119.
15. Medhurst, 131.
16. Mill, *On Liberty*, 101–2.
17. Richard Rorty, "Feminism, Ideology, and Deconstruction: A Pragmatist View," *Hypatia* 8, no. 2 (Spring 1993): 100.
18. Rorty, "Feminism, Ideology, and Deconstruction," 96.
19. Rorty, 101.
20. Rorty, 101.
21. Griffiths, "Queers in 1960s British Cinema," 72.
22. Griffiths, 75.

Filmography

DVD details are given only for those films that are analyzed in detail.

Alive and Kicking. 1959, UK, bw, 91mins. *d* Cyril Frankel *cast* Sybil Thorndike, Kathleen Harrison, Estelle Winwood. Associated British Picture Corporation/StudioCanal: Network DVD.

An Alligator Named Daisy. 1955, UK, color, 84mins. *d* J. Lee Thompson *cast* Donald Sinden, Jeannie Carson, James Robertson Justice, Margaret Rutherford. Raymond Stross Productions/ITV Studios DVD.

The Army Game. 1957–1961, UK, bw. ITV *cast* William Hartnell, Alfie Bass, Charles Hawtrey

The Belles of St. Trinian's. 1954, UK, bw, 88mins. *d* Frank Launder *cast* Alastair Sim, Joyce Grenfell, George Cole. London Films/StudioCanal: Vintage Classics DVD.

Brothers in Law. 1957, UK, bw, 94mins. *d* Roy Boulting *cast* Richard Attenborough, Ian Carmichael, Irene Handl.

Carry on Sergeant. 1958, UK, bw, 84mins. *d* Gerald Thomas *cast* William Hartnell, Bob Monkhouse, Shirley Eaton.

Duck Soup. 1933, US, bw, 68mins. *d* Leo McCarey *cast* Groucho Marx, Harpo Marx, Chico Marx, Zeppo Marx.

Follow a Star. 1959, UK, bw, 102mins. *d* Robert Asher *cast* Norman Wisdom, Jerry Desmonde, Fenella Fielding.

Genevieve. 1953, UK, color, 83mins. *d* Henry Cornelius *cast* John Gregson, Dinah Sheridan, Kenneth More, Kay Kendall. Sirius Productions/ITV Studios DVD.

Germania anno zero. 1948, Italy, bw, 78mins. *d* Roberto Rossellini *cast* Edmund Moeschke, Ernst Pittschau.

The Goose Steps Out. 1942, UK, bw, 75mins. *d* Basil Dearden *cast* Will Hay, Charles Hawtrey, Peter Ustinov.

The Green Man. 1956, UK, bw, 76mins. *d* Robert Day *cast* Alastair Sim, George Cole, Terry-Thomas. Grenadier Productions/StudioCanal: Optimum Classic DVD.

The Happiest Days of Your Life. 1950, UK, bw, 81mins. *d* Frank Launder *cast* Alastair Sim, Margaret Rutherford.

Hue and Cry. 1947, UK, bw, 79mins. *d* Charles Crichton *cast* Alastair Sim, Jack Warner, Harry Fowler, Douglas Barr. Ealing Studios/StudioCanal: Vintage Classics DVD.

Idol on Parade. 1959, UK, bw, 88mins. *d* John Gilling *cast* Anthony Newley.

It's Never Too Late. 1956, UK, color, 92mins. *d* Michael McCarthy *cast* Phyllis Calvert, Patrick Barr, Susan Stephen. Park Lane Films/StudioCanal: Network DVD.

Just My Luck. 1957, UK, bw, 86mins. *d* John Paddy Carstairs *cast* Norman Wisdom, Margaret Rutherford.

Kind Hearts and Coronets. 1949, UK, bw, 102mins. *d* Robert Hamer *cast* Dennis Price, Alec Guinness, Joan Greenwood, Valerie Hobson. Ealing Studios/Studio Canal: Vintage Classics DVD.

The Ladykillers. 1955, UK, color, 91mins. *d* Alexander Mackendrick *cast* Alec Guinness, Cecil Parker, Herbert Lom, Katie Johnson.

Laughter in Paradise. 1951, UK, bw, 92mins. *d* Mario Zampi *cast* Alastair Sim, Fay Compton, George Cole, Guy Middleton, Ernest Thesiger. Associated British Picture Corporation/StudioCanal: Optimum Classic DVD.

The Lavender Hill Mob. 1951, UK, bw, 77mins. *d* Charles Crichton *cast* Alec Guinness, Stanley Holloway. Ealing Studios/Studio Canal: Vintage Classics DVD.

Lucky Jim. 1957, UK, bw, 95mins. *d* John Boulting *cast* Ian Carmichael, Terry-Thomas, Hugh Griffith.

The Man in the White Suit. 1951, UK, bw, 85mins. *d* Alexander Mackendrick *cast* Alec Guinness, Joan Greenwood, Cecil Parker. Ealing Studios/Studio Canal: Vintage Classics DVD.

On the Beat. 1962, UK, bw, 106mins. *d* Robert Asher *cast* Norman Wisdom, Jennifer Jayne.

Passport to Pimlico. 1949, UK, bw, 81mins. *d* Henry Cornelius *cast* Stanley Holloway, Hermione Baddeley, Margaret Rutherford. Ealing Studios/Studio Canal: Vintage Classics DVD.

Performance. 1970, UK, color 105mins. *d* Donald Cammell and Nicolas Roeg *cast* James Fox, Mick Jagger.

Press for Time. 1966, UK, color, 102mins. *d* Robert Asher *cast* Norman Wisdom, Derek Bond, Derek Francis.

Private's Progress. 1956, UK, bw, 95mins. *d* John Boulting *cast* Ian Carmichael, Richard Attenborough, Dennis Price.

Room at the Top. 1959, UK, bw, 115mins. *d* Jack Clayton *cast* Laurence Harvey, Simone Signoret.

Sailor Beware!. 1956, UK, bw, 78mins. *d* Gordon Parry *cast* Peggy Mount, Esma Cannon, Gordon Jackson. Romulus Films/StudioCanal: Simply Home Entertainment DVD.

Simon and Laura. 1955, UK, color, 87mins. *d* Muriel Box *cast* Peter Finch, Kay Kendall, Ian Carmichael. Group Film Productions/ITV Studios: Network DVD.

The Square Peg. 1959, UK, bw, 86mins. *d* John Paddy Carstairs *cast* Norman Wisdom, Honor Blackman, Hattie Jacques. The Rank Organisation/ITV Studios DVD.

The Stranger Left No Card. 1952, UK, bw, 22mins. *d* Wendy Toye *cast* Alan Badel. Meteor Films/StudioCanal: Vintage Classics DVD.

Tawny Pipit. 1944, UK, bw, 81mins. *d* Bernard Miles and Charles Saunders *cast* Bernard Miles, Rosamund John.

Trouble in Store. 1953, UK, bw, 85mins. *d* John Paddy Carstairs *cast* Norman Wisdom, Margaret Rutherford.

Victim. 1961, UK, bw, 96mins. *d* Basil Dearden *cast* Dirk Bogarde, Sylvia Sims, Derren Nesbitt. Allied Film Makers/ITV Studios: Network DVD.

Young Wives' Tale. 1951, UK, bw, 76mins. *d* Henry Cass *cast* Joan Greenwood, Nigel Patrick, Athene Seyler. Associated British Picture Corporation/StudioCanal: Network DVD.

Bibliography

Addison, Paul. *No Turning Back: The Peacetime Revolutions of Post-War Britain.* Oxford: Oxford University Press, 2010.
Adorno, Theodor and Max Horkheimer. *Dialectic of Enlightenment.* Translated by John Cumming. London: Continuum, 2001.
Ahmed, Sara. *Queer Phenomenology: Orientations, Objects, Others.* Durham, NC: Duke University Press, 2006.
Aldgate, Anthony and Jeffrey Richards. *Best of British: Cinema and Society from 1930 to the Present.* London: I. B. Tauris, 2002.
Auden, W. H. *Collected Poems.* Edited by Edward Mendelson. London: Faber & Faber, 1991.
Babington, Bruce. *Launder and Gilliat.* Manchester: Manchester University Press, 2002.
Bakhtin, Mikhail. *Problems of Dostoevsky's Poetics.* Edited and translated by Caryl Emerson. Manchester: Manchester University Press, 1984.
———. *Rabelais and His World.* Translated by Hélène Iswolsky. Bloomington: Indiana University Press, 1984.
Barr, Charles. "Broadcasting and Cinema: 2: Screens within Screens." In *All Our Yesterdays: 90 Years of British Cinema,* edited by Charles Barr, 206–24. London: British Film Institute, 1986.
———. *Ealing Studios.* 3rd ed. Moffat, UK: Cameron & Hollis, 1998.
Barrett, Michèle and Mary McIntosh. *The Anti-Social Family.* 2nd ed. London: Verso, 2015.
Barthes, Roland. *Mythologies.* Translated by Annette Lavers. London: Cape, 1972.
———. *Roland Barthes by Roland Barthes.* Translated by Richard Howard. London: Macmillan, 1977.
Bazin, André. "Theater and Cinema." In *What Is Cinema?* Vol. 1. Edited and translated by Hugh Gray, 76–124. Berkeley: University of California Press, 1967.

Bell, Melanie. "'A Prize Collection of Familiar Feminine Types': The Female Group Film in 1950s British Cinema." In *British Women's Cinema*, edited by Melanie Bell and Melanie Williams, 94–110. London: Routledge, 2010.

Bell-Williams, Melanie. "Gender and Modernity in Post-War British Cinema: A Case Study of *Young Wives' Tale* (1951)." *Women's History Review* 16, no. 2 (2007): 227–43.

Benjamin, Walter and Asja Lacis. "Naples." In *Reflections: Essays, Aphorisms, Autobiographical Writings*, edited by Peter Demetz, 163–73. Translated by Edmund Jephcott. New York: Schocken Books, 1978.

Bergson, Henri. *Laughter: An Essay on the Meaning of the Comic*. Translated by Cloudesley Brereton and Fred Rothwell. Cabin John, MD: Wildside, 2008.

Berlant, Lauren and Michael Warner. "Sex in Public." *Critical Inquiry* 24, no. 2 (Winter 1998): 547–66.

Bersani, Leo. "Is the Rectum a Grave?" *October*, no. 43: "AIDS: Cultural Analysis/Cultural Activism" (Winter 1987): 197–222.

Bevan, Aneurin. *In Place of Fear*. London: Heinemann, 1952.

Bourne, Stephen. *Brief Encounters: Lesbians and Gays in British Cinema 1930–1971*. London: Cassell, 1996.

Braidotti, Rosi. *The Posthuman*. Cambridge: Polity, 2013.

Brecht, Bertolt. *Brecht on Theatre: The Development of an Aesthetic*. Edited and translated by John Willett. London: Methuen, 1974.

Brown, Geoff. "Paradise Found and Lost: The Course of British Realism." In *The British Cinema Book*, 3rd ed., edited by Robert Murphy, 28–38. London: Palgrave Macmillan, 2009.

Bruzzi, Stella. "Where Are Those Buggers? Aspects of Homosexuality in Mainstream British Cinema." In *The British Cinema Book*, 3rd ed., edited by Robert Murphy, 133–41. London: Palgrave Macmillan, 2009.

Burton, Alan. "'From Adolescence into Maturity': The Film Comedy of the Boulting Brothers." In *British Comedy Cinema*, edited by I. Q. Hunter and Larraine Porter, 77–88. London: Routledge, 2012.———. "*Victim* (1961): Text and Context." *AAA: Arbeiten aus Anglistik und Amerikanistik* 35, no. 1 (January 2010): 75–100.

Butler, Judith. "Critically Queer." In *The Routledge Queer Studies Reader*, edited by Donald E. Hall and Annamarie Jagose, with Andrea Bebell and Susan Potter, 18–31. London: Routledge, 2013.

———. *Gender Trouble: Feminism and the Subversion of Identity*. New York: Routledge, 2006.

Calarco, Matthew. *Thinking through Animals: Identity, Difference, Indistinction*. Stanford, CA: Stanford University Press, 2015.

Calarco, Matthew R. *Animal Studies: The Key Concepts*. London: Routledge, 2021.

Caputo, John, ed. *Deconstruction in a Nutshell: A Conversation with Jacques Derrida*. New York: Fordham University Press, 2021.
Carroll, Noël. *Humour*. Oxford: Oxford University Press, 2014.
Chen, Mel Y. *Animacies: Biopolitics, Racial Mattering, and Queer Affect*. Durham, NC: Duke University Press, 2012.
Christie, Ian. "English Eccentric." In *John Smith*, edited by Tanya Leighton and Kathrin Meyer, 47–70. London: Sternberg, 2013.
Cixous, Hélène. "The Laugh of the Medusa." Translated by Keith Cohen and Paula Cohen. *Signs* 1, no. 4 (Summer, 1976): 875–93.
Clayton, Alex. *Funny How?: Sketch Comedy and the Art of Humor*. Albany: State University of New York Press, 2020.
Conekin, Becky, Frank Mort, and Chris Waters. "Introduction." In *Moments of Modernity: Reconstructing Britain 1945–1964*, edited by Becky Conekin, Frank Mort, and Chris Waters, 1–21. London: Rivers Oram, 1999.
Cook, Pam. *Fashioning the Nation: Costume and Identity in British Cinema*. London: BFI, 1996.
Dacre, Richard. "Norman Wisdom: Rank Studios and the Rise of the Super Chump." In *British Comedy Cinema*, edited by I. Q. Hunter and Laraine Porter, 128–40. London: Routledge, 2012.
David, Hugh. *On Queer Street: A Social History of British Homosexuality 1895–1995*. London: HarperCollins, 1997.
Deleuze, Gilles and Félix Guattari. *A Thousand Plateaus: Capitalism and Schizophrenia*. London: Bloomsbury, 2013.
de Man, Paul. *Aesthetic Ideology*. Edited by Andrzej Warminski. Minneapolis: University of Minnesota Press, 1996.
Derrida, Jacques. *The Animal That Therefore I Am*. Edited by Marie-Louise Mallet and translated by David Wills. New York: Fordham University Press, 2008.
———. "A Certain Impossible Possibility of Saying the Event." *Critical Inquiry* 33, no. 2 (Winter 2007): 441–61.
———, *Of Grammatology*. Fortieth anniversary ed. Translated by Gayatri Chakravorty Spivak. Baltimore: Johns Hopkins University Press, 2016.
———. *Points . . . : Interviews, 1974–1994*. Edited by Elisabeth Weber and translated by Peggy Kamuf and others. Stanford, CA: Stanford University Press, 1995.
———. *Writing and Difference*. Translated by Alan Bass. London: Routledge, 2001.
Dinshaw, Carolyn, Lee Edelman, Roderick A. Ferguson, Carla Freccero, Elizabeth Freeman, Judith Halberstam, Annamarie Jagose, Christopher S. Nealon, and Tan Hoang Nguyen. "Theorizing Queer Temporalities: A Roundtable Discussion." *GLQ: A Journal of Lesbian and Gay Studies* 13, no. 2–3 (2007): 177–95.

Doan, Laura. *Disturbing Practices: History, Sexuality, and Women's Experience of Modern War*. Chicago: University of Chicago Press, 2013.

Dockray, Keith and Alan Sutton. *Politics, Society and Homosexuality in Post-War Britain: The Sexual Offences Act of 1967 and Its Significance*. Stroud, Gloucestershire, England: Fonthill, 2017.

Duguid, Mark and Katy McGahan. "From Tinsel to Realism and Back Again: Balcon, Ealing and Documentary." In *Ealing Revisited*, edited by Mark Duguid, Lee Freeman, Keith M. Jonhston, and Melanie Williams, 58–70. London: Palgrave Macmillan, 2012.

Durant, John and Jonathan Miller, eds. *Laughing Matters: A Serious Look at Humour*. Harlow, Essex, England: Longman, 1988.

Durgnat, Raymond. *A Mirror for England: British Movies from Austerity to Affluence*. 2nd ed. London: Palgrave Macmillan, 2011.

Eagleton, Terry. *Humour*. New Haven, CT: Yale University Press, 2019.

———. *Walter Benjamin, or Towards a Revolutionary Criticism*. London: New Left Books, 1981.

Edelman, Lee. *Homographesis: Essays in Gay Literary and Cultural Theory*. New York: Routledge, 1994.

———. *No Future: Queer Theory and the Death Drive*. Durham, NC: Duke University Press, 2004.

Ellis, John. "The Quality Film Adventure: British Critics and the Cinema 1942–1948." In *Dissolving Views: Key Writings on the British Cinema*, edited by Andrew Higson, 66–93. London: Cassell, 1996.

English, David. "This Is My New Crusade!" *Daily Mail*, April 29, 1988.

English, James F. *Comic Transactions: Literature, Humor, and the Politics of Community in Twentieth-Century Britain*. Ithaca, NY: Cornell University Press, 1994.

Foucault, Michel. *Discipline and Punish: The Birth of the Prison*. Translated by Alan Sheridan. London: Penguin, 1991.

———. *Politics, Philosophy, Culture: Interviews and Other Writings of Michel Foucault*. Edited by Lawrence D. Kritzman. London: Routledge, 1988.

Fowler, William and Vic Pratt. *The Bodies Beneath: The Flipside of British Film and Television*. London: Strange Attractor, 2019.

Francis, Martin. "A Flight from Commitment? Domesticity, Adventure and the Masculine Imaginary in Britain after the Second World War." *Gender & History* 19, no. 1 (April 2007): 163–85.

Freccero, Carla. "Queer Theory." In *The Edinburgh Companion to Animal Studies*, edited by Lynn Turner, Undine Sellbach, and Ron Broglio, 430–43. Edinburgh: Edinburgh University Press, 2018.

Freud, Sigmund. *Jokes and Their Relation to the Unconscious*. Edited by James Strachey. London: Vintage, 2001.

Gagnon, John and William Simon. *Sexual Conduct: The Social Sources of Human Sexuality*. Chicago: Aldine, 1973.

Geraghty, Christine. *British Cinema in the 1950s: Gender, Genre, and the "New Look."* London: Routledge, 2000.

Griffiths, Robin. "Sad and Angry: Queers in 1960s British Cinema." In *British Queer Cinema*, edited by Robin Griffiths, 71–90. London: Routledge, 2006.

Grindrod, John. *Concretopia: A Journey around the Rebuilding of Postwar Britain*. Brecon, Wales, UK: Old Street, 2013.

Gruen, Lori. *Entangled Empathy: An Alternative Ethic for Our Relationships with Animals*. New York: Lantern Books, 2015.

Halberstam, Jack. *The Queer Art of Failure*. Durham, NC: Duke University Press, 2011.

———. *Wild Things: The Disorder of Desire*. Durham, NC: Duke University Press, 2020.

Haraway, Donna. *Manifestly Haraway*. Minneapolis: University of Minnesota Press, 2016.

Harper, Sue. "From *Holiday Camp* to High Camp: Women in British Feature Films, 1945–1951." In *Dissolving Views: Key Writings on the British Cinema*, edited by Andrew Higson, 94–116. London: Cassell, 1996.

Harper, Sue and Vincent Porter. *British Cinema of the 1950s: The Decline of Deference*. Oxford: Oxford University Press, 2003.

Hemming, Henry. *In Search of the English Eccentric*. London: John Murray, 2008.

Hennessy, Peter. *Having It So Good: Britain in the Fifties*. London: Penguin, 2007.

———. *Never Again: Britain 1945–1951*. London: Penguin, 2006.

Higgins, Patrick, ed. *A Queer Reader*. London: Fourth Estate, 1993.

Highmore, Ben. "Playgrounds and Bombsites: Postwar Britain's Ruined Landscapes." *Cultural Politics* 9, no. 3 (2013): 323–36.

Higson, Andrew. *Waving the Flag: Constructing a National Cinema in Britain*. Oxford: Oxford University Press, 1995.

Hite, Christian. "The Gift from (of the) 'Behind' (*Derrière*): Intro-extro-duction." In *Derrida and Queer Theory*, edited by Christian Hite, 10–23. Goleta, CA: Punctum Books, 2017.

Hornsey, Richard. *The Spiv and the Architect: Unruly Life in Postwar London*. Minneapolis: University of Minnesota Press, 2010.

Jarman, Derek. *At Your Own Risk: A Saint's Testament*. London: Hutchinson, 1992.

Kynaston, David. *Austerity Britain 1945–51*. London: Bloomsbury, 2008.

———. *Family Britain 1951–57*. London: Bloomsbury, 2010.

———. *Modernity Britain 1957–62*. London: Bloomsbury, 2015.

Landy, Marcia. *British Genres: Cinema and Society, 1930–1960*. Princeton, NJ: Princeton University Press, 1991.
Langford, Paul. *Englishness Identified: Manners and Character 1650–1850*. Oxford: Oxford University Press, 2001.
Lippit, Akira Mizuta. *Electric Animal: Toward a Rhetoric of Wildlife*. Minneapolis: University of Minnesota Press, 2000.
Litwiller, Fenton. "Normative Drag Culture and the Making of Precarity." *Leisure Studies* 39, no. 4 (2020): 600–612.
Lockwood, J. Samaine. "Queer Critical Regionalism." In *The Cambridge Companion to Queer Studies*, edited by Siobhan Somerville, 228–40. Cambridge: Cambridge University Press, 2020.
Love, Heather. *Feeling Backward*. Cambridge, MA: Harvard University Press, 2007.
Macaulay, Rose. *Pleasure of Ruins*. Rev. ed. Edited by Constance Babington Smith. London: Thames & Hudson, 1964.
Maillaud, Pierre. *The English Way*. Oxford: Oxford University Press, 1945.
Medhurst, Andy. "In Search of Nebulous Nancies: Looking for Queers in Pre-Gay British Film." In *British Queer Cinema*, edited by Robin Griffiths, 21–34. London: Routledge, 2006.
———. "Music Hall and British Cinema." In *All Our Yesterdays: 90 Years of British Cinema*, edited by Charles Barr, 168–88. London: British Film Institute, 1986.
———. *A National Joke: Popular Comedy and English Cultural Identity*. London: Routledge, 2007.
———. "*Victim*: Text as Context." In *Dissolving Views: Key Writings on British Cinema*, edited by Andrew Higson, 117–32. London: Cassell, 1996.
Mill, John Stuart. *On Liberty*. Cambridge: Cambridge University Press, 2012.
Miller, D. A. "Anal Rope." *Representations*, no. 32 (Autumn 1990): 114–33.
Moor, Andrew. "Kind Hearts and Campery: The Ealing Family Perverts." In *Ealing Revisited*, edited by Mark Duguid, Lee Freeman, Keith M. Jonhston, and Melanie Williams, 125–34. London: Palgrave Macmillan, 2012.
Morreall, John. *Taking Laughter Seriously*. Albany: State University of New York Press, 1983.
Morrison, Benedict. *Complicating Articulation in Art Cinema*. Oxford: Oxford University Press, 2021.
Mort, Frank. *Capital Affairs: London and the Making of the Permissive Society*. New Haven, CT: Yale University Press, 2010.
Mortimer-Sandilands, Catriona and Bruce Erikson. *Queer Ecologies: Sex, Nature, Politics, Desire*. Bloomington: Indiana University Press, 2010.
Mulvey, Laura. "Rear-Projection and the Paradoxes of Hollywood Realism." In *Theorizing World Cinema*, edited by Lúcia Nagib, Chris Perriam, and Rajinder Dudrah, 207–20. London: I. B. Tauris, 2012.

Muñoz, José Esteban. *Cruising Utopia: The Then and There of Queer Futurity*. New York: New York University Press, 2009.
Murphy, Robert. "Dark Shadows around Ealing." In *Ealing Revisited*, edited by Mark Duguid, Lee Freeman, Keith M. Jonhston, and Melanie Williams, 81–90. London: Palgrave Macmillan, 2012.
———. *Realism and Tinsel: Cinema and Society in Britain 1939–49*. London: Routledge, 1989.
Nancy, Jean-Luc. "Elliptical Sense." *Research in Phenomenology*, no. 18 (1988): 175–90.
Nead, Lynda. *The Tiger in the Smoke: Art and Culture in Post-War Britain*. New Haven, CT: Yale University Press, 2017.
Neale, Steve. *Genre*. London: British Film Institute, 1983.
Newton, Michael. *Kind Hearts and Coronets*. London: British Film Institute, 2003.
Nicolson, Harold. *The English Sense of Humour*. London: Constable, 1956.
Nietzsche, Friedrich. *Beyond Good and Evil*. Translated by Walter Kaufmann. New York: Random House, 1966.
Norris, Christopher. *Deconstruction: Theory and Practice*. London: Methuen, 1982.
Orwell, George. "Funny, but Not Vulgar." In *George Orwell: The Collected Essays, Journalism and Letters*. Vol. 3, *As I Please 1943–1945*, edited by Sonia Orwell and Ian Angus, 283–87. London: Seckler & Warburg, 1968.
O'Sullivan, Tim. "That Ealing Feeling: 'Ealing Comedies' and 'Comedies Made at Ealing.'" In *Ealing Revisited*, edited by Mark Duguid, Lee Freeman, Keith M. Jonhston, and Melanie Williams, 135–44. London: Palgrave Macmillan, 2012.
Pick, Anat. "Animal Life in the Cinematic *Umwelt*." In *Animal Life and the Moving Image*, edited by Michael Lawrence and Laura McMahon, 221–37. London: British Film Institute and Palgrave, 2015.
———. "Vegan Cinema." In *Thinking Veganism in Literature and Culture: Towards a Vegan Theory*, edited by Emelia Quinn and Benjamin Westwood, 125–46. London: Palgrave, 2018.
Porter, Laraine and I. Q. Hunter. "British Comedy Cinema: Sex, Class and Very Naughty Boys." In *British Comedy Cinema*, edited by I. Q. Hunter and Laraine Porter, 1–17. London: Routledge, 2012.
Probyn-Rapsey, Fiona. "Anthropocentrism." In *Critical Terms for Animal Studies*, edited by Lori Gruen, 47–63. Chicago: University of Chicago Press, 2018.
Puar, Jasbir. *Terrorist Assemblages: Homonationalism in Queer Times*. Durham, NC: Duke University Press, 2007.
Pulleine, Tim. "A Song and Dance at the Local: Thoughts on Ealing." In *The British Cinema Book*. 3rd ed., edited by Robert Murphy, 259–66. London: Palgrave Macmillan, 2009.

Rawlings, Roger. *Ripping England! Postwar British Satire from Ealing to the Goons*. Albany: State University of New York Press, 2017.

Roberts, Andrew. "'Gird Your Armour On': The Genteel Subversion of the St. Trinian's Films." In *British Comedy Cinema*, edited by I. Q. Hunter and Laraine Porter, 116–27. London: Routledge, 2012.

Rorty, Richard. "Feminism, Ideology, and Deconstruction: A Pragmatist View." *Hypatia* 8, no. 2 (Spring 1993): 96–103.

Russo, Vito. *The Celluloid Closet: Homosexuality in the Movies*. Rev. ed. New York: Harper & Row, 1987.

Samuel, Raphael. "Mrs. Thatcher's Return to Victorian Values." *Proceedings of the British Academy*, no. 78: *Victorian Values* (1992): 9–29.

Sandbrook, Dominic. *The Great British Dream Factory: The Strange History of Our National Imagination*. London: Allen Lane, 2015.

Sargeant, Amy. *British Cinema: A Critical History*. London: British Film Institute, 2005.

Scruton, Roger. *England: An Elegy*. London: Chatto & Windus, 2000.

Sedgwick, Eve Kosofsky. *Between Men: English Literature and Male Homosocial Desire*. Thirtieth anniversary ed. New York: Columbia University Press, 2015.

———. *Tendencies*. Durham, NC: Duke University Press, 1993.

———. *Touching Feeling: Affect, Pedagogy, Performativity*. Durham, NC: Duke University Press, 2003.

Segal, Lynne. *Slow Motion: Changing Masculinities, Changing Men*. 3rd ed. London: Palgrave Macmillan, 2007.

Shukin, Nicole. "Capitalism." In *The Edinburgh Companion to Animal Studies*, edited by Lynn Turner, Undine Sellbach, and Ron Broglio, 94–115. Edinburgh: Edinburgh University Press, 2018.

Sinfield, Alan. *Literature, Politics and Culture in Postwar Britain*. 2nd ed. London: Continuum, 2004.

Sissons, Michael and Philip French. *Age of Austerity: 1945–1951*. London: Penguin, 1964.

Smith, Douglas. "Porosity and the Transnational: Travelling Theory between Naples and Frankfurt (Walter Benjamin, Asja Lacis and Ernst Bloch)." *Forum for Modern Language Studies* 57, no. 2 (April 2021): 240–59.

Spicer, Andrew. *Typical Men: The Representation of Masculinity in Popular British Cinema*. London: I. B. Tauris, 2001.

Stallybrass, Peter and Allon White. *The Politics and Poetics of Transgression*. London: Methuen, 1986.

Stead, Naomi. "The Value of Ruins: Allegories of Destruction in Benjamin and Speer." *Form/Work: An Interdisciplinary Journal of the Built Environment*, no. 6 (October 2003): 51–64.

Stevens, Adrian. "Carnival and Comedy: On Bakhtin's Misreading of Boccaccio." *Opticon 1826*, no. 3 (2007): 1–5.
Stott, Andrew. *Comedy*. 2nd ed. London: Routledge, 2014.
Street, Sarah. *British National Cinema*. 2nd ed. London: Routledge, 2009.
———. "Margaret Rutherford and Comic Performance." In *British Comedy Cinema*, edited by I. Q. Hunter and Larraine Porter, 89–99. London: Routledge, 2012.
Sullivan. Nikki. *A Critical Introduction to Queer Theory*. Edinburgh: Edinburgh University Press, 2003.
Thane, Pat. "Population Politics in Post-War British Culture." In *Moments of Modernity: Reconstructing Britain 1945–1964*, edited by Becky Conekin, Frank Mort, and Chris Waters, 114–33. London: Rivers Oram, 1999.
Thomas, Calvin. *Straight with a Twist: Queer Theory and the Subject of Heterosexuality*. Champaign: University of Illinois Press, 2000.
Tincknell, Estella. "Unpiecing the *Jigsaw*: Compulsive Heterosexuality, Sex Crime, Class and Masculinity in Early 1960s British Cinema." *Journal of British Cinema and Television* 18, no. 2 (2021): 131–51.
Warner, Michael. "Introduction: Fear of a Queer Planet." *Social Text*, no. 29 (1991): 3–17.
Warth, Douglas. "Evil Men." *Sunday Pictorial*, May 25, 1952.
———. "Evil Men." *Sunday Pictorial*, June 1, 1952.
Waters, Chris. "Disorders of the Mind, Disorders of the Body Social: Peter Wildeblood and the Making of the Modern Homosexual." In *Moments of Modernity: Reconstructing Britain 1945–1964*, edited by Becky Conekin, Frank Mort, and Chris Waters, 134–51. London: Rivers Oram, 1999.
Weeks, Jeffrey. *Sex, Politics and Society: The Regulation of Sexuality since 1800*. 3rd ed. London: Routledge, 2012.
West, D. J. *Homosexuality*. London: Duckworth, 1955.
Wildeblood, Peter. *Against the Law*. London: Weidenfeld & Nicolson, 2019.
Williams, Melanie. "'Twilight Women' of 1950s British Cinema." In *The British Cinema Book*, 3rd ed., edited by Robert Murphy, 286–95. London: Palgrave Macmillan, 2009.
Williams, Tony. "The Repressed Fantastic in *Passport to Pimlico*." In *Re-Viewing British Cinema, 1900–1992: Essays and Interviews*, edited by Wheeler Winston Dixon, 95–106. Albany: State University of New York Press, 1994.

Index

Adams, Jill, 166
Addison, Joseph, 115
Addison, Paul, 15
Adorno, Theodor and Max Horkheimer, 117–18
Ahmed, Sara, 75
Alec-Tweedie, Ethel, 159
Alexander, Terence, 171
Alfvén, Hugo, 53, 57
Alive and Kicking (Cyril Frankel), 33, 220–29
Alligator Named Daisy, An (J. Lee Thompson), 33, 203–18, 219
Anderson, Lindsay, 12, 13
Angers, Avril, 166
animacies, 202–3
animal, the (as cultural concept), 33, 112, 201–18, 256n2, 256n9
animot, the, 212
anthropocentrism: as anti-queer, 209, 212, 214, 217, 218; as arrogance, 216; contrasted to the wild, 219–20, 228; and expressionism, 224; links to sexism, racism, and ableism, 207, 214, 218; outline of the term, 205–6; and rear projection, 222–23. *See also* expressionism; wild, the

Army Game, The, 193
Asher, Robert, 191, 192
assemblages, 180–82, 183, 187, 212. *See also* multiroling
Atlee, Clement, 15, 64
Attenborough, Richard, 115
Attfield, Judy, 72
Auden, W. H., 43

Babington, Bruce, 20, 179, 185, 214
Badel, Alan, 52, 53
Bakhtin, Mikhail, 111–14. *See also* carnivalesque, the
Balcon, Michael, 21, 60, 143
Barr, Charles, 21, 29, 30, 59–60, 99, 143; on *Hue and Cry*, 38, 144, 145, 146, 151, 155; on *The Lavender Hill Mob*, 106, 112–13, 122, 124; on *Passport to Pimlico*, 13, 38, 59, 63, 65–66, 68, 69
Barr, Cleeve, 197
Barr, Douglas, 151
Barr, Patrick, 125, 131
Barrett, Michèle, 201
Barthes, Roland, 6, 80. *See also* myth
Bass, Alfie, 119
Bataille, Georges, 116
Baudelaire, Charles, 115

Bazin, André, 219–20, 224, 225
Bell, Melanie, 12, 79
Belles of St. Trinian's, The (Frank Launder), 1, 20, 28–29, 33, 175–90, 192, 200, 202
Bell-Williams, Melanie, 71, 72, 73, 79–80, 82–83, 85–86, 87, 104, 158
Benjamin, Walter, 33, 136, 150, 152–53; and the Angel of History, 156. *See also* porosity
Bergson, Henri: philosophy of laughter, 32, 43–46, 47, 53, 55, 61, 68, 88, 128. *See also* humor, theories of
Berlant, Lauren, 77. *See also* heteronormativity
*beside*ness, 33, 179–200, 201, 208, 216, 222, 225, 235, 236, 237; as opposed to *beneath*ness, 181–84, 188, 190, 199. *See also* multiroling
Bevan, Aneurin, 17–18
Beveridge report, the, 73, 159
bewilderment, 56, 80, 225. *See also* wild, the
Blackman, Honor, 193, 196, 197
blitz, the, 37, 40, 68, 146, 147, 162, 168. *See also* ruins
Bogarde, Dirk, 231, 232, 235
bomb sites. *See* ruins
Borch-Jacobsen, Mikkel, 118
Boulting brothers, 114, 187
Bourne, Stephen, 4, 100
Box, Muriel, 32, 98, 100–101
Boyd, Stephen, 204
Brecht, Bertolt, 28; and gest, 28, 104
Brothers in Law (Roy Boulting), 114–15
Brown, Geoff, 91
Bruzzi, Stella, 231
Burton, Alan, 233

Butler, Judith, 81, 186–87. *See also* drag; performativity

Calarco, Matthew, 206–7, 220, 225
Calvert, Phyllis, 125, 131
Cammell, Donald, 238
Campbell, Beatrice, 134
Cannon, Esma, 9, 89, 91–92
Caputo, John, 47–48, 69, 127–28
Carmichael, Ian, 98, 115
carnivalesque, the, 111–13, 114, 122, 135, 143, 196; outline of the term, 111
Carrol, Noël, 108
Carry On films, 199
Carry on Sergeant (Gerald Thomas), 193
Carson, Jeannie, 203, 216, 218
Carstairs, John Paddy, 33, 191, 192, 193
Cass, Henry, 32, 78
Chandos, John, 166
Chen, Mel Y., 202–3
Cherry, Helen, 78
Christie, Ian, 3
Churchill, Winston, 15, 64, 256n9
Cixous, Hélène, 123–24
Clayton, Alex, 114, 116
Clayton, Jack, 3
Cocteau, Jean, 52
Cole, George, 1, 132, 166
comedies of marriage. *See* domestic comedies
comedy: difficulties in defining the term, 108–9; as eccentric, 3, 7, 19, 21, 22, 32, 109–19, 136–37, 161, 233, 236; as a genre, 108, 131; in postwar Britain, 9, 20, 23, 26, 107, 181–82, 218; types of, 108. *See also* carnivalesque, the; domestic comedies; humor, theories of; satire

companionate marriage, 16, 71, 73–74, 98, 110, 132, 136, 157–58, 160, 164, 188
Compton, Fay, 132, 133
Conekin, Becky, 158
connotation (in queer theory), 18, 26, 147, 148
consensus cinema, 18, 30, 31, 69, 122, 144–45
consensus politics, 10, 14, 15–16, 18, 39, 65, 144, 184, 197; as myth, 16, 31, 141, 145
conviction rates for homosexuals in postwar Britain, 250n58
Cook, Pam, 18, 26, 64, 144
Cornelius, Henry, 13, 20, 21, 37, 157
Crichton, Charles, 5, 33, 106, 120, 142

Dacre, Richard, 193
Daily Mail, 11, 13
Day, Robert, 20, 165
Dearden, Basil, 4, 193, 231
deconstruction, 47–48, 50, 63, 75, 113, 128, 143, 148, 237
decriminalization of homosexuality in the UK, 4, 10, 17, 160–61, 232
Deleuze, Gilles and Félix Guattari, 181, 188–89
de Man, Paul, 179
Denham, Maurice, 102
Derrida, Jacques: on the "animal," 210–12; on binary structures, 112; on bricolage, 155; on carnophallogocentrism, 209, 225; on consensus as threat, 145; on ex-centric structure, 32, 47–52, 58, 66, 68, 75, 145, 181, 236; on lability, 155, 225; on limitrophy, 219; on preposterousness, 22; on promises, 25; on solicitation, 51, 76; on *sous rature*, 67; on spectrality, 69
Descartes, René, 205
Desmonde, Jerry, 191
Dixon, Jill, 192
Doan, Laura, 19, 22, 75, 97. *See also* queer history
domestic comedies, 32, 71–74, 77, 78–104, 131, 161, 216. *See also* domestic drag
domestic drag, 32, 81–104, 107, 113, 125, 126, 129, 141, 151, 153, 158, 181, 201, 202, 203, 208, 222, 226; definitions of, 32, 81–82
Dors, Diana, 203
drag, 80–81, 84, 108, 175, 186–87, 198–200; as a filmic phenomenon, 187. *See also* domestic drag
Drake, Fabia, 79
Duck Soup (Leo McCarey), 195, 197
Duguid, Mark, 153
Dupuis, Paul, 65
Durgnat, Raymond: on conservative elements of British cinema, 11, 12, 20, 99; on eccentricity in postwar British cinema, 2–3; on *Genevieve*, 158; on Joan Greenwood, 83; on *Laughter in Paradise*, 133; on Launder and Gilliat, 172; on Margaret Rutherford, 39; on *Sailor Beware!*, 90

Eagleton, Terry, 110, 113, 118, 122–23, 134, 136
Ealing Studios, 2, 8–9, 31, 60, 64, 106, 143
Eaton, Shirley, 89
eccentricity: and the carnivalesque, 111–12, 113; and deconstructionist theory, 3–4, 14,

eccentricity *(continued)*
19, 25, 27, 32, 38–40, 47–52, 55, 59, 63–64, 75, 88, 107, 118, 145, 155, 180, 232, 236–37; as English national characteristic, 40–41; in film form, 29–30, 104, 116, 120–21, 132; outline of the term in film criticism, 2–4, 14, 38; and queerness, 1, 4–5, 8, 22, 30, 47, 73, 75–76, 86, 110, 132, 147, 161, 197, 202, 204, 218; and theories of social control, 32, 43–47, 61, 68, 88; and theories of social progress, 32, 40–43, 46–47, 236. *See also* Bergson, Henri; comedy; deconstruction; Derrida, Jacques; gesture; Mill, John Stuart; porosity; wild, the
Edelman, Lee, 22, 25, 75, 183, 189
Eden, Anthony, 15
Ellis, John, 29
empire, 11, 15, 15, 17, 49, 145, 251–52n21
English, David, 11
English, James, 128
expressionism, 153, 223–24, 226, 228. *See also* anthropocentrism

family comedies. *See* domestic comedies
family planning, 167–68, 169. *See also* planning in postwar Britain
Farr, Derek, 78
Fielding, Fenella, 191
Finch, Peter, 98, 152
Follow a Star (Robert Asher), 191
Foucault, Michel, 23, 27
Fowler, Harry, 142
Fowler, William, 52–53, 54
Fox, Gerald, 149
Francis, Martin, 72, 73, 96, 97
Frankel, Cyril, 33, 220
Freccero, Carla, 206, 212, 218

Freud, Sigmund, 64, 117
Frye, Northrop, 115

Genevieve (Henry Cornelius), 20, 33, 157–65, 202, 219
Geraghty, Christine, 39, 73, 99, 122, 124, 158, 162, 187–88, 189
Germania anno zero (Roberto Rossellini), 146–47
gesture: as eccentric, 28, 31, 50, 52, 54, 60, 61, 63, 66, 67–68, 96, 104, 145, 152, 220, 236; kissing as gesture, 84–5, 86, 102–3, 104; laughter as gesture, 44, 115, 118, 119, 124–25, 127, 130–31; outline of the term, 27–31; as queer, 30–31, 45, 86, 96, 104, 200, 232. *See also* performativity
Giddens, Anthony, 39
Gilliat, Sidney, 172, 179
Gilling, John, 193
Girard, René, 161
Goldfinger, Ernö, 168
Goose Steps Out, The (Basil Dearden), 193
Gordon, Colin, 166
Gregson, John, 157
Green Man, The (Robert Day), 20, 33, 165–73, 175
Greenwood, Joan, 6, 9, 78, 82–84, 152, 238
Grenfell, Joyce, 9, 15, 132
Griffith, Hugh, 132
Griffiths, Robin, 231, 238
Grindrod, John, 142, 148
Gruen, Lori, 205
Guinness, Alec, 5, 9, 32, 33, 106, 124, 153, 182–84, 190, 200

Halberstam, Jack, 43, 134, 206, 219, 225. *See also* bewilderment; wild, the
Hall, Cameron, 55

Hamer, Robert, 33, 39, 182
Hammond, Peter, 127
Handl, Irene, 9, 15, 21, 32, 115, 127–31, 153, 238
Happiest Days of Your Life, The (Frank Launder), 179
Haraway, Donna, 206
Harper, Sue, 9, 12, 18, 21, 61–63, 104, 120, 122, 144
Harrison, Kathleen, 220, 221, 224, 225, 227
Hawtrey, Charles, 9, 65
Hay, Will, 193
Heap, Anthony, 194
Hemming, Henry, 40, 41
Hepburn, Audrey, 84, 121
heterocentrism: as myth, 32, 47, 51, 77, 78, 80, 88, 104, 108, 109, 110, 136, 148, 236, 238; outline of the term, 4–8. *See also* myth; queer
heteronormativity: outline of the term, 76–77. *See also* queer
Higson, Andrew, 8, 66
Hill, Benny, 199
Hite, Christian, 22, 23. *See also* preposterousness
Hitler, Adolf, 146, 160, 200, 256n9
Hobbes, Thomas, 43, 46, 117
Holloway, Stanley, 9, 32, 106, 153, 213, 221
homoeroticism, 19, 92–98, 162
homosocial triangles, 161–65
homosociality in postwar Britain, 17, 33, 72, 73, 95–96, 97, 98, 124, 125, 173
Hornsey, Richard, 5, 15, 28, 142, 241n53
Hue and Cry (Charles Crichton), 33, 38, 142–57, 157, 190, 202
humor, theories of: the incongruity theory, 24, 63, 65, 116–17, 128, 155, 211; the release theory, 116–17, 128; the superiority theory, 43–44, 116–17, 128
Hunter, I. Q., 108
Huntley, Raymond, 166
Hylton, Jane, 65

Idol on Parade (John Gilling), 193
inheritance: alternatives to conventions of, 235, 237; and empire, 251n21; in *Laughter in Paradise*, 133–37; and linear time, 183, 188–89, 192; as part of heterocentrism, 5, 15, 30, 49, 64, 74, 81, 104, 133–37, 148, 202, 218, 232; and postwar social shifts, 26
Italian neorealism, 146–47
It's Never Too Late (Michael McCarthy), 27, 32, 125–32, 133, 136, 153, 202, 219

Jackson, Gordon, 89, 129
Jacques, Hattie, 194
James, Sid, 119
Jarman, Derek, 7, 148, 155–56
Justice, James Robertson, 204
Just My Luck (John Paddy Carstairs), 192, 194

Kant, Immanuel, 117
Keen, Geoffrey, 90
Kendall, Kay, 98, 152, 157
Keynes, John Maynard, 15
Kierkegaard, Søren, 131
Kind Hearts and Coronets (Robert Hamer), 33, 39, 182–84, 192, 200
King Lear, 63, 126
Kinsey, Alfred, 161
kissing. *See* gesture
Kynaston, David, 199, 241n53

Labour Government (1945–1951), 15, 60, 143

Lacis, Asja, 150, 152–53. *See also* porosity
Ladykillers, The (Alexander Mackendrick), 39
Lambert, Jack, 147
Landy, Marcia: on *The Belles of St. Trinian's* 184–85, 186; on *The Lavender Hill Mob*, 122; on Muriel Box, 100–101; on Norman Wisdom, 191; on types of film comedy, 71, 108; on *Young Wives' Tale*, 79, 80, 85
Langford, Paul, 41
laughing forward: and domestic drag, 78; and eccentric laughter, 116; exemplified in the films, 31, 33, 58, 64, 66, 69, 87–88, 98, 102, 124–25, 132, 136, 156, 164, 173, 185, 189–90, 197, 199–200, 218, 226, 228; outline of the term, 24–27, 51–52, 234, 236
laughter: as ambiguous, 115, 117–19, 123–25; as carnivalesque, 113–14; as censored, 126–27; as communal, 43, 122–23, 131; as eccentric, 49, 63, 105–7, 115–16, 129–32, 136–37, 161; as excluding and controlling of eccentricity, 32, 43–46, 68, 88, 117, 127–31; as fatal, 134; as queering, 13, 18, 24, 32, 74, 78, 113; as transcendental, 137. *See also* comedy; gesture; humor, theories of; *laughing forward*
Laughter in Paradise (Mario Zampi), 32, 132–37, 152, 190
Launder, Frank, 1, 172, 175, 179
Lavender Hill Mob, The (Charles Crichton), 5, 32, 105–7, 112–13, 115–25, 128, 133, 135, 136, 137, 166, 169, 180
Lawrence, Delphi, 125

Lawson, Sarah, 125
Lawson, Wilfred, 203
Leech, Richard, 125
Lessing, Doris, 141, 142
Lewis, Ronald, 89
Linnaeus, Carl, 256n7
Lippit, Akira Mizuta, 210
Love, Heather, 24, 144, 161
Lucky Jim (John Boulting), 114
Lumière brothers, the, 228

Macaulay, Rose, 148–49
Mackendrick, Alexander, 5, 39
Macmillan, Harold, 233
Maillaud, Pierre, 40–41, 47
Malleson, Miles, 9, 15
Man in the White Suit, The (Alexander Mackendrick), 5, 14, 19, 25, 27, 33
Martin, Edie, 9
Martin, Vivienne, 175
Matthews, A. E., 133
McCarey, Leo, 195
McCarthy, Michael, 27, 125
McGahan, Katy, 153
McIntosh, Mary, 201
Medhurst, Andy, 4, 24, 109, 128, 158, 191, 231, 232, 233, 234–35
Middleton, Guy, 79, 132
Miles, Bernard, 16
Mill, John Stuart, 32, 41–43, 44, 46, 47, 75–76, 236
Miller, D. A., 147. *See also* connotation
Moeschke, Edmund, 146
Moor, Andrew, 153
Moore, Eileen, 166
More, Kenneth, 157
Morreall, John, 109, 110, 111, 122
Mort, Frank, 158, 241n53
Mount, Peggy, 88, 92, 93
multiroling, 33, 175–200, 202

Mulvey, Laura, 222. *See also* rear projection
Muñoz, José Esteban, 25, 26, 30, 75
Murphy, Robert, 106
Murray, Barbara, 65
myth: outline of the term, 5–7; underpinning national identity, 10–11, 49, 145. *See also* eccentricity; heterocentrism; natural, the (as myth)

Nairn, Ian, 171–72
Nancy, Jean-Luc, 137
natural, the (as myth), 4, 6–7, 22, 29, 32, 33, 202, 205–8, 210, 212, 213, 216–18, 219, 226; and film form, 208–9, 222–23; and heterocentrism, 74, 76, 80, 81, 85, 99, 104, 160, 201–2, 216. *See also* wild, the
Nazism, 147, 193, 194, 196–200
Nead, Lynda, 72, 156, 241n53
Neale, Steve, 110
Nesbit, Derren, 235
New Jerusalem, 15, 124, 143, 147
Newton, Michael, 182–84
New Wave, the, 3, 4, 12, 99, 231
Nicolson, Harold, 42–43, 46, 47, 108
Nietzsche, Friedrich, 26, 68
Norris, Christopher, 52, 66, 75
nostalgia for the 1950s, 10–11, 14, 16, 24; in *Passport to Pimlico*, 65, 66, 68
nuclear family, the, 5, 98–99, 100, 127

On the Beat (Robert Asher), 192
Orwell, George, 114, 165
O'Sullivan, Tim, 153

Parker, Cecil, 6

Parritt, Clive, 101
Parry, Gordon, 32, 89
Passport to Pimlico (Henry Cornelius), 13, 18, 19, 21, 31, 32, 37–40, 41, 42, 45–47, 52, 59–69, 84, 113, 114, 129, 142, 146, 152, 166, 180, 208
Patrick, Nigel, 78
Pavlow, Muriel, 100
Performance (Donald Cammell and Nicolas Roeg), 238
performativity, 28, 32, 39, 41, 61, 75, 81, 198, 238; outline of the term, 186–87. *See also* gesture
Pick, Anat, 224, 225–26, 228
planning in postwar Britain, 15, 58–59, 69, 124, 137, 156, 167–68, 219; as bureaucracy, 197–200; housebuilding program, 15, 28, 33, 141–42, 146, 148, 168–69, 171–72; as opposed to play, 167, 236
Plato, 115
polyamory, 7, 69, 77, 88, 103, 110, 164–65, 221, 223, 233, 235
porosity, 7, 33, 128, 131, 132, 137, 149–57, 159, 160, 164–65, 166, 173, 210, 212, 225, 237; generic and stylistic porosity, 153–55; outline of the term, 149–152. *See also* ruins
Porter, Laraine, 108
Porter, Vincent, 9, 12, 21, 104, 120, 122
Pratt, Vic, 52, 54
preposterousness, 24, 26, 33, 51; outline of the term, 22–23. *See also laughing forward*; queer history
Press for Time (Robert Asher), 192
Priestley, J. B., 167, 168. *See also* planning in postwar Britain

Private's Progress (John Boulting), 114
Probyn-Rapsey, Fiona, 205
Puar, Jasbir, 180–81. *See also* assemblages
Pulleine, Tim, 66

queer: and connotation, 147; as disruption of identity, 4–5, 7, 9, 19, 49, 51, 74, 80–81, 96–97, 99, 103–4; outline of the term, 7, 26, 74–75, 228–29; as eccentric, 75, 104; as futurity, 25
queer history, 21–23, 144. *See also* preposterousness

Radford, Basil, 64
rationing, 15, 16, 37, 60, 65, 66, 141, 243n1
Rawlings, Roger, 114–15, 122, 133
realism: and fantasy, 104, 120; and porosity, 153–55; and queerness, 153; and the wild, 220, 224
rear projection, 29, 120, 222–23, 226, 227, 228
rebuilding in the postwar period. *See* planning in postwar Britain
Redmond, Liam, 223
reprosexuality, 101. *See also* Warner, Michael
rhizome, 189–90
Rhodes, Marjorie, 192
Richards, Jeffrey, 12
Richardson, Tony, 13
Reisz, Karel, 13
Roeg, Nicolas, 238
Rolfe, Guy, 125
Room at the Top (Jack Clayton), 3
Rorty, Richard, 236–37
Rossellini, Roberto, 146
ruins: as ambiguous, 147–48, 155; as eccentrically queer, 74, 144,
147–48, 152, 181; of gender and sexual convention, 159–73; and psychoanalysis, 251n11; of tradition and custom, 143–44, 145, 149, 158, 237; of urban spaces, 21, 32–33, 37, 65, 68, 141–57, 168, 175, 219. *See also* porosity
Rumbold, Richard, 171
Russo, Vito, 232
Rutherford, Margaret, 9, 15, 21, 29, 37–40, 41, 45–46, 60–63, 84, 129, 152, 179, 191, 192, 204, 208–9, 210, 211–12, 214, 238

Sailor Beware! (Gordon Parry), 32, 88–98, 99, 100, 101, 102, 129, 180, 202
Salew, John, 221
Samuel, Raphael, 10–11
Sanger, Margaret, 168
Sargeant, Amy, 66
satire, 99, 114–16, 137, 185, 200
Saunders, Charles, 16
Schopenhauer, 117
Scruton, Roger, 16, 20, 149, 150
Section 28 of the Local Government Act (1988), 10, 32, 207. *See also* Thatcher, Margaret
Sedgwick, Eve Kosofsky: on *beside*ness, 181–83, 186–87; on defining queer, 26; on heteronormativity, 30, 190; on homosociality, 161. See also *beside*ness
service comedies, 95–96
Sexual Offences Act (1967). *See* decriminalization of homosexuality in the UK
Seyler, Athene, 79, 86
Sheridan, Dinah, 157

Sim, Alastair, 1, 9, 15, 21, 28, 33, 132, 133, 143, 151–53, 165, 167, 172, 175–79, 181, 183–90, 200, 238
Simon and Laura (Muriel Box), 32, 98–104
Sinden, Donald, 203
Sinfield, Alan, 14, 96, 142, 144
Slater, John, 65
Smith, Cyril, 89
Smith, Douglas, 153, 156
sous rature, 67, 226
Spicer, Andrew, 12
Spivak, Gayatri, 67
split-screen effects, 175, 176, 190
Square Peg, The (John Paddy Carstairs), 33, 192–200
Stainton, Philip, 63
Stephen, Susan, 125
Stevens, Adrian, 111
Stott, Andrew, 108
Stranger Left No Card, The (Wendy Toye), 32, 52–59
Street, Sarah, 30–31, 41, 46, 66
suburbia, 21, 33, 166, 168–73. *See also* planning in postwar Britain
Suez Crisis, the, 15, 251–52n21. *See also* empire
Sullivan, Nikki, 19
Summerfield, Eleanor, 133
Sunday Express, 17
Sunday Pictorial, 160, 173, 200. *See also* Warth, Douglas

Tales of the Unexpected, 245n60
Tawny Pipit (Bernard Miles and Charles Saunders), 16
Taylor Smith, Jean, 125
Thane, Pat, 168, 169
Thatcher, Margaret, 10–13, 19, 32, 207, 234, 235, 237

Thesiger, Ernest, 132
Thomas, Calvin, 103
Thomas, Gerald, 193
Thomas, Terry-, 9
Thompson, J. Lee, 33, 203
Thorndike, Sybil, 220, 221, 224, 225
Tincknell, Estella, 73
totalitarianism, 42, 51, 196, 200. *See also* Nazism
Toye, Wendy, 32, 52, 245n60
Trouble in Store (John Paddy Carstairs), 191
Trubshawe, Michael, 122

uniforms: in drag, 198–200; as erotic, 92–93, 97, 98

vegan cinema, 225–26
Victim (Basil Dearden), 4, 13, 33, 77, 231–38

Ward, Michael, 24
Warner, Jack, 143
Warner, Michael, 77, 101
Warren, Betty, 65
Warth, Douglas, 160, 161, 200, 207
Waters, Chris, 158, 159–60
Wattis, Richard, 98, 102
Wayne, Naunton, 64
Webster, Joy, 97
Weeks, Jeffrey, 16, 99
Weil, Simone, 224, 228
Weldon, Fay, 141, 142
West, D. J., 160
Wheatley, Alan, 100
White, Allon, 111
White, Valerie, 147
wild, the, 33, 201, 202, 220–29, 237; outline of the term, 219–20; *sous rature*, 226. *See also* natural, the (as myth)

Wildeblood, Peter, 160–61, 237
Williams, Melanie, 186
Winwood, Estelle, 220, 221, 224
Wisdom, Norman, 33, 191–200
Wolfenden Report, the, 17, 160–61. *See also* decriminalization of homosexuality in the UK

women's liberation, 73

Young Wives' Tale (Henry Cass), 32, 78–88, 99, 100, 101, 102, 103, 104, 152, 202

Zampi, Mario, 32, 132, 133

www.ingramcontent.com/pod-product-compliance
Lightning Source LLC
Chambersburg PA
CBHW062021020325
22763CB00004B/136